# AN EXEGETICAL SUMMARY OF
# TITUS and PHILEMON

# AN EXEGETICAL SUMMARY OF TITUS and PHILEMON

**Second Edition**

**J. Harold Greenlee**

**SIL International**

Second Edition
© 1989, 2008 by SIL International

Library of Congress Catalog Card Number: 2008923518
ISBN: 978-155671-192-3

Printed in the United States of America

All Rights Reserved
No part of this publication may be reproduced, stored in a retrieval system, or transmitted in any form or by any means without the express permission of SIL International. However, brief excerpts, generally understood to be within the limits of fair use, may be quoted without written permission.

Copies of this and other publications
of SIL International may be obtained from

International Academic Bookstore
SIL International
7500 West Camp Wisdom Road
Dallas, TX 75236-5699, USA

Voice: 972-708-7404
Fax: 972-708-7363
academic_books@sil.org
www.ethnologue.com

# PREFACE

Exegesis is concerned with the interpretation of a text. Exegesis of the New Testament involves determining the meaning of the Greek text. Translators must be especially careful and thorough in their exegesis of the New Testament in order to accurately communicate its message in the vocabulary, grammar, and literary devices of another language. Questions occurring to translators as they study the Greek text are answered by summarizing how scholars have interpreted the text. This is information that should be considered by translators as they make their own exegetical decisions regarding the message they will communicate in their translations.

**The Semi-Literal Translation**

As a basis for discussion, a semi-literal translation of the Greek text is given so that the reasons for different interpretations can best be seen. When one Greek word is translated into English by several words, these words are joined by hyphens. There are a few times when clarity requires that a string of words joined by hyphens have a separate word, such as 'not' (μή), inserted in their midst. In this case, the separate word is surrounded by spaces between the hyphens. When alternate translations of a Greek word are given, these are separated by slashes.

**The Text**

Variations in the Greek text are noted under the heading TEXT. The base text for the summary is the text of the fourth revised edition of *The Greek New Testament,* published by the United Bible Societies, which has the same text as the twenty-sixth edition of the *Novum Testamentum Graece* (Nestle-Aland). The versions that follow different variations are listed without evaluating their choices.

**The Lexicon**

The meaning of a key word in context is the first question to be answered. Words marked with a raised letter in the semi-literal translation are treated separately under the heading LEXICON. First, the lexicon form of the Greek word is given. Within the parentheses following the Greek word is the location number where, in the author's judgment, this word is defined in the *Greek-English Lexicon of the New Testament Based on Semantic Domains* (Louw and Nida 1988). When a semantic domain includes a translation of the particular verse being treated, **LN** in bold type indicates that specific translation. If the specific reference for the verse is listed in *A Greek-English Lexicon of the New Testament and Other Early Christian Literature* (Bauer, Arndt, Gingrich, and Danker 1979), the outline location and page number is given. Then English equivalents of the Greek word are given to show how it is translated by commentators who offer their own translations of the whole text and, after a semicolon, all the versions in the list of abbreviations for translations. When reference is made to "all versions," it refers to only the versions in the list of translations. Sometimes further comments are made about the meaning of the word or the significance of a verb's tense, voice, or mood.

**The Questions**

Under the heading QUESTION, a question is asked that comes from examining the Greek text under consideration. Typical questions concern the identity of an implied actor or object of an event word, the antecedent of a pronominal reference, the connection indicated by a relational word, the meaning of a genitive construction, the meaning of figurative language, the function of a rhetorical question, the identification of an ambiguity, and the presence of implied information that is needed to understand the passage correctly. Background information is also considered for a proper understanding of a passage. Although not all implied information and background information is made explicit in a translation, it is important to consider it so that the translation will not be stated in such a way that prevents a reader from arriving at the proper interpretation. The question is answered with a summary of what commentators have said. If there are contrasting differences of opinion, the different interpretations are numbered and the commentaries that support each are listed. Differences that are not treated by many of the commentaries often are not numbered, but are introduced with a contrastive 'Or' at the beginning of the sentence. No attempt has been made to select which interpretation is best.

In listing support for various statements of interpretation, the author is often faced with the difficult task of matching the different terminologies used in commentaries with the terminology he has adopted. Sometimes he can only infer the position of a commentary from incidental remarks. This book, then, includes the author's interpretation of the views taken in the various commentaries. General statements are followed by specific statements, which indicate the author's understanding of the pertinent relationships, actors, events, and objects implied by that interpretation.

**The Use of This Book**

This book does not replace the commentaries that it summarizes. Commentaries contain much more information about the meaning of words and passages. They often contain arguments for the interpretations that are taken and they may have important discussions about the discourse features of the text. In addition, they have information about the historical, geographical, and cultural setting. Translators will want to refer to at least four commentaries as they exegete a passage. However, since no one commentary contains all the answers translators need, this book will be a valuable supplement. It makes more sources of exegetical help available than most translators have access to. Even if they had all the books available, few would have the time to search through all of them for the answers.

When many commentaries are studied, it soon becomes apparent that they frequently disagree in their interpretations. That is the reason why so many answers in this book are divided into two or more interpretations. The reader's initial reaction may be that all of these different interpretations complicate exegesis rather than help it. However, before translating a passage, a translator needs to know exactly where there is a problem of interpretation and what the exegetical options are.

# ABBREVIATIONS FOR TITUS AND PHILEMON

## COMMENTARIES AND REFERENCE BOOKS

Alf     Alford, Henry. 1856. *The Greek Testament,* vol. 3. London: Rivingtons.

BAGD     Bauer, Walter. 1979. *A Greek-English Lexicon of the New Testament and Other Early Christian Literature*, translated and adapted from the 5th ed., 1958 by William F. Arndt and F. Wilbur Gingrich, 2d English ed. revised and augmented by F. Wilbur Gingrich and Frederick W. Danker. Chicago: University of Chicago Press.

Bg     Bengel, John Albert. 1877. *Gnomon of the New Testament,* vol. 4. 7th ed. Edinburgh: Clark.

Blm     Bloomfield, S. T. 1839. *The Greek Testament, with English Notes,* vol. 2. 3d ed. London: Longman, Orme, Brown, Green, and Longmans.

Brt     Burton, Edward. 1835. *The Greek Testament with English Notes,* vol. 2. Oxford: University Press.

CBC     Hanson, Anthony Tyrell. 1966. *The Pastoral Letters.* The Cambridge Bible Commentary. Cambridge: University Press.

       Thompson, G. H. P. 1967. *The Letters of Paul to the Ephesians, to the Colossians, and to Philemon.* The Cambridge Bible Commentary. Cambridge: University Press.

CGTC     Moule, C. F. D. 1968. *The Epistles of Paul the Apostle to the Colossians and to Philemon.* Cambridge Greek Testament Commentary. Cambridge: University Press.

EBC     Hiebert, D. Edmond. 1978. "Titus," in *The Expositor's Bible Commentary,* vol. 11. Grand Rapids: Zondervan.

       Rupprecht, Arthur A. 1978. "Philemon," in *The Expositor's Bible Commentary*, vol. 11. Grand Rapids: Zondervan.

EGT     White, Newport J. D. n.d. "The Epistle to Titus," in *The Expositor's Greek Testament,* vol. 4. New York: Doran.

       Oesterley, W. E. n.d. "The Epistle to Philemon," in *The Expositor's Greek Testament*, vol. 4. New York: Doran.

El     Ellicott, Charles J. 1864. *The Pastoral Epistles of St. Paul.* London: Longman, Green, Longmans, Roberts and Green.

       Ellicott, C. J. 1861. *A Critical and Grammatical Commentary on St. Paul's Epistles to the Philippians, Colossians, and to Philemon.* 2d ed. London: Parker, Son, and Bourn.

EPC     Moulton, Harold K. 1963. *Colossians, Philemon and Ephesians.* Epworth Preacher's Commentaries. London: Epworth Press.

GNC     Fee, Gordon D. 1984. *1 and 2 Timothy, Titus.* A Good News Commentary. San Francisco: Harper and Row.

Herm     Dibelius, Martin, and Hans Conzelmann. 1966. *The Pastoral Epistles,* translated by Philip Buttolph and Adela Yarbro, 1972. Hermeneia. Philadelphia: Fortress Press.

|      | Lohse, Eduard. 1968. *Colossians and Ephesians*, translated by William R. Poehlmann and Robert J. Karris, 1971. Hermeneia. Philadelphia: Fortress Press. |
|------|---|
| Hn   | Hendriksen, William. 1957. *Exposition of the Pastoral Epistles.* Grand Rapids, Michigan: Baker. |
|      | Hendriksen, William. 1964. *A Commentary on Colossians and Philemon.* London: Banner of Truth Trust. |
| HNTC | Kelly, J. N. D. 1963. *A Commentary on the Pastoral Epistles.* Harper's New Testament Commentaries. London: Adam & Charles Black. |
| IB   | Gealy, Fred D., and Morgan P. Noyes. 1955. "The First and Second Epistles to Timothy and The Epistle to Titus," in *The Interpreter's Bible,* vol. 11. New York and Nashville: Abingdon. |
|      | Knox, John, and George A. Buttrick. 1955. "The Epistle to Philemon," in *The Interpreter's Bible*, vol. 11. New York and Nashville: Abingdon. |
| ICC  | Lock, Walter. 1924. *A Critical and Exegetical Commentary on The Pastoral Epistles.* The International Critical Commentary. Edinburgh: Clark. |
|      | Vincent, Marvin R. 1897. *A Critical and Exegetical Commentary on the Epistles to the Philippians and to Philemon.* The International Critical Commentary. Edinburgh: Clark. |
| Lg   | Van Oosterzee, J. J. n.d. "The Epistle of Paul to Titus," translated, with additions, by George E. Day, 1868, the additions indicated by the abbreviation *Lg(D)*, in *Lange's Commentary on the Holy Scriptures*, vol. 11. Reprinted 1960. Grand Rapids: Zondervan. |
|      | Lange, John Peter. n.d. "The Epistle of Paul to Philemon," translated, with additions, by Horatio B. Hackett, 1868, the additions indicated by the abbreviation *Lg(H)*, in *Lange's Commentary on the Holy Scriptures*, vol. 11. Reprint 1960. Grand Rapids: Zondervan. |
| LN   | Louw, Johannes P. and Eugene A. Nida. 1988. *Greek-English Lexicon of the New Testament Based on Semantic Domains.* New York: United Bible Societies. |
| Lns  | Lenski, R. C. H. 1946. *The Interpretation of St. Paul's Epistles to the Colossians, to the Thessalonians, to Timothy, to Titus and to Philemon.* Minneapolis, Minnesota: Augsburg. |
| Lt   | Lightfoot, J. B. 1886. *Saint Paul's Epistles to the Colossians and to Philemon.* 8th ed. London: Macmillan. |
| MNTC | Scott, E. F. 1936. *The Pastoral Epistles.* The Moffatt New Testament Commentary. London: Hodder and Stoughton. |
|      | Scott, E. F. 1930. *The Epistles of Paul to the Colossians, to Philemon and to the Ephesians.* The Moffatt New Testament Commentary. New York and London: Harper. |

| | |
|---|---|
| My | Huther, Joh. Ed. 1890. *Critical and Exegetical Handbook to the Epistles to Timothy and Titus.* 4th ed. Translated by David Hunter, with supplementary notes by Timothy Dwight, the notes indicated by the abbreviation *My(D)*. (This commentary is a continuation of the series formerly ed. by H. A. W. Meyer.) New York and London: Funk and Wagnalls. |
| | Meyer, Heinrich August Wilhelm. 1880. *Critical and Exegetical Handbook to the Epistles to the Philippians and Colossians, and to Philemon.* Translated, revised, and edited by William P. Dickson. New York: Funk and Wagnalls. |
| NCB | Barrett, C. K. 1963. *The Pastoral Epistles.* The New Clarendon Bible. Oxford: Clarendon Press. |
| NCBC | Hanson, A. T. 1982. *The Pastoral Epistles.* New Century Bible Commentary. Grand Rapids: Eerdmans. |
| | Martin, Ralph P. 1974. *Colossians and Philemon.* New Century Bible Commentary. Grand Rapids: Eerdmans. |
| NIC | Bruce, F. F. 1984. *The Epistles to the Colossians, to Philemon, and to the Ephesians.* The New International Commentary on the New Testament. Grand Rapids, Eerdmans. |
| Rb | Robertson, Archibald Thomas. 1931. *Word Pictures in the New Testament,* vol. 4. Nashville: Broadman. |
| SSA | Banker, John. 1987. *Semantic Structure Analysis of Titus.* Dallas: Summer Institute of Linguistics. |
| TC | Bernard, J. H. 1899. *The Pastoral Epistles.* Thornapple Commentaries. Grand Rapids: Baker. |
| TG | Bratcher, Robert G. 1983. *A Translator's Guide to Paul's Letters to Timothy and to Titus.* London, New York, Stuttgart: United Bible Societies. |
| TH | Bratcher, Robert G., and Eugene A. Nida. 1977. *A Translator's Handbook on Paul's Letters to the Colossians and to Philemon.* Stuttgart: United Bible Societies. |
| TNTC | Guthrie, Donald. 1957. *The Pastoral Epistles.* The Tyndale New Testament Commentaries. Grand Rapids: Eerdmans. |
| | Carson, Herbert M. 1960. *The Epistles to the Colossians and Philemon.* The Tyndale New Testament Commentaries. Grand Rapids: Eerdmans. |
| WBC | O'Brien, Peter T. 1982. "Colossians, Philemon," in *Word Biblical Commentary,* vol. 44. Waco: Word. |
| WC | Brown, Ernest Faulkner. 1917. *The Pastoral Epistles.* Westminster Commentaries. London: Methuen. |
| WPC | Houlden, J. L. 1970. *Paul's Letters from Prison—Philippians, Colossians, Philemon, and Ephesians.* Westminster Pelican Commentaries. Philadelphia: Westminster Press. |

## GREEK TEXT AND TRANSLATIONS

GNT    Aland, Kurt, Matthew Black, Carlos Martini, Bruce Metzger, and Allen Wikgren. 1983. *The Greek New Testament.* 3d ed. (corrected). London, New York: United Bible Societies.

KJV    *The Holy Bible.* Authorized (or King James) Version. 1611.

NAB    *The New American Bible.* 1971. Camden, New Jersey: Thomas Nelson.

NASB    *The New American Standard Bible.* 1977. Nashville, Tennessee: Holman.

NEB    *The New English Bible.* 1970. 2d ed. (corrected) 1972. New York: Oxford University Press.

NIV    *The Holy Bible: New International Version.* 1978. Grand Rapids: Zondervan.

NJB    *The New Jerusalem Bible.* 1985. Garden City, New York: Doubleday.

RSV    *The Bible: Revised Standard Version.* 2d ed. 1971. New York: American Bible Society.

TEV    *Holy Bible: Today's English Version.* 1976. New York: American Bible Society.

TNT    *The Translator's New Testament.* 1973. London: British and Foreign Bible Society.

## GRAMMATICAL TERMS

| | | | |
|---|---|---|---|
| act. | active | mid. | middle |
| fut. | future | opt. | optative |
| impera. | imperative | pass. | passive |
| imperf. | imperfect | perf. | perfect |
| indic. | indicative | pres. | present |
| infin. | infinitive | subj. | subjunctive |

# EXEGETICAL SUMMARY OF TITUS

**DISCOURSE UNIT: 1:1–4** [Alf, CBC, EBC, EGT, GNC, GNT, Herm, Hn, HNTC, IB, ICC, Lg, Lns, MNTC, NCB, NCBC, SSA, TC, TG, TNTC, WC]. The topic is salutation [EBC, EGT, GNT, Hn, IB, ICC, MNTC, NCB, TC, TNTC, WC], greetings [Herm, HNTC, Lns, NCBC], salutations and greetings [Alf, Hn], introduction [TG].

**1:1** **Paul slave[a] of-God, and apostle of-Jesus Christ**

TEXT—Instead of Ἰησοῦ Χριστοῦ 'Jesus Christ' some manuscripts read Χριστοῦ Ἰησοῦ 'Christ Jesus'. GNT does not deal with this variant, and only Alf and CBC read 'Christ Jesus'.

LEXICON—a. δοῦλος (LN **87.76**): 'slave' [BAGD, LN, Lns, WC], 'servant' [Herm, Hn, HNTC; all versions except NASB], 'bond-servant' [NASB].

QUESTION—How are the two nouns related in the genitive construction δοῦλος θεοῦ 'slave of God'?

1. Paul means that he is in God's service, carrying out a work for him [EBC, HNTC, IB, SSA]: Paul, who is engaged in God's service. Although the word δοῦλος 'slave' emphasizes complete dependence upon a master, as it is used here it carries the sense of honor; both as servant and as apostle Paul has authority [HNTC, IB, SSA]. Many commentators note that this is the only place in which Paul refers to himself as a slave of God rather than a slave of Christ [Alf, CBC, EBC, El, HNTC, IB, ICC, NCBC, TC, TNTC].
2. Paul means that he is owned by God and is dependent upon him [Lns]: Paul, a bond-servant owned by God. A slave's will is entirely subject to his owner [Lns].

QUESTION—What relationship is indicated by δέ 'and'?

1. It indicates a more specific designation of Paul's office [Alf, EGT, El, HNTC, Lg, Lns, My, SSA, TC]: God's slave, specifically, an apostle.
2. It adds something different [EBC, Lns, SSA]: God's slave and also an apostle. Some commentators refer to this difference as a contrast between the two relationships [EGT, SSA].

QUESTION—How are the two persons related in the genitive construction ἀπόστολος Ἰησοῦ Χριστοῦ 'apostle of Jesus Christ'?

Paul, the apostle, has been commissioned and sent forth as Jesus Christ's official messenger [EBC, Hn, IB, SSA, TNTC]: an official messenger of Jesus Christ, an apostle who represents Jesus Christ. This indicates his official rank [EBC]. This phrase is added because the situation addressed, like that of many of his letters, requires his authority as an apostle [GNC, SSA, TC]. It is an appropriate term in an official letter [TC].

**according-to[a] (the) faith[b] of-(the)-chosen-ones[c] of-God**

LEXICON—a. κατά with accusative object (LN **89.8**): 'according to' [Herm; KJV], 'in accord with' [Lns], 'concerned with' [HNTC], 'with a view to'

[WC], 'in the interest of' [Hn], 'for the sake of' [NAB], 'for' [NASB, NIV], 'to further' [RSV], 'chosen and sent to help' [RSV], 'sent to build up' [TNT], 'to bring to' [NJB], 'marked as such by' [NEB].
    b. πίστις (LN 31.85; 31.102): 'faith' [BAGD, Herm, Hn, HNTC, LN, Lns, WC; all versions].
    c. ἐκλεκτός (LN 30.93): 'elect' [Hn, HNTC, Lns; KJV, NIV, RSV], 'chosen' [BAGD, Herm, LN; NASB, NJB], 'chosen ones' [WC], 'chosen people' [NEB, TEV, TNT], 'those whom God has chosen' [NAB].

QUESTION—What relationship is indicated by κατά 'according to'?
1. This indicates the purpose of Paul's work as an apostle [Blm, EGT, El, GNC, IB, Lg, SSA, WC; NASB, NIV, NJB, RSV, TEV, TNT]: Paul, an apostle for the purpose of helping God's elect people to believe.
2. This indicates that Paul's work as an apostle is in connection with the faith of God's elect people [Alf, CBC, HNTC, NCB]: Paul, an apostle in reference to the faith of God's elect people. This general relationship is variously explained. His relationship to their faith is to bring it about and strengthen it [Alf]. It defines the sphere in which Paul exercises his apostleship, that is, he aims to increase their faith [CBC, HNTC].
3. This indicates that Paul's apostleship is in accordance with the faith held by God's people [EBC, ICC, Lns, MNTC]: Paul, an apostle in harmony with the Christian faith. This means that although Paul's apostleship is not governed by their faith, it is in harmony with it [EBC]. It may indicate that what Paul taught agreed with what Christians believe [Lns].

QUESTION—How are the two nouns related in the genitive construction πίστιν ἐκλεκτῶν 'faith of (the) chosen ones'?
1. The subjective act of faith is exercised by God's chosen ones [EGT, GNC, Hn, HNTC, IB, Lg, SSA, TG]: to help God's chosen people to believe as they should. Some commentators refer this faith to the initial act of believing the gospel [GNC, IB, Lg, Lns]. Others refer it to the faith of Christians which needs to be developed and strengthened [EGT] and corrected [SSA]. Some refer it to both coming to believe and to growing in one's faith [HNTC].
2. The objective content of what Christians believe is accepted by God's chosen ones [Herm, Lns, MNTC, My]: according to the Christian doctrine, which God's people believe. The true Christian faith is being contrasted with the false faith of the heretics [My]. One commentator refers it to the Christian faith in contrast with Old Testament faith [MNTC].

QUESTION—How are the two nouns related in the genitive construction ἐκλεκτῶν θεοῦ 'chosen ones of God'?
The people are chosen by God [Alf, Blm, EGT, Hn, IB, Lns, TNTC]: those whom God has chosen. They are the people who have responded to God's call [EBC, EGT, My]; the phrase is never used in the NT to refer to people who have not yet responded to God's call [My]. This phrase strikes a balance between God's action and man's response [EBC]. Paul here uses OT

language to refer to Christian believers [GNC, ICC]. The body of Christians has replaced Israel as God's chosen race [Blm, HNTC]. The chosen ones include both Jews and Gentiles [Bg] and means all Christians [NCBC].

**and knowledge[a] of-truth the according-to[b] piety[c]**
LEXICON—a. ἐπίγνωσις (LN 28.2): 'knowledge' [BAGD, HNTC, LN; NAB, NASB, NEB, NIV, NJB, RSV], 'the acknowledging' [KJV], 'acknowledgment' [Hn], 'recognition' [BAGD, Herm, WC], 'realization' [Lns]. The phrase κατά…ἐπίγνωσιν ἀληθείας τῆς κατ᾽ εὐσέβειαν 'according to…knowledge of truth according to piety' is translated 'to lead (them) to the truth taught by our religion' [TEV], 'to teach (them) the truth of our religion' [TNT].
  b. κατά with accusative object (LN 89.8): 'after' [KJV], 'according to' [WC; NASB], 'in accord with' [Lns], 'as it corresponds to' [Herm]. The phrase τῆς κατ᾽ εὐσέβειαν 'which is according to piety' is translated 'which accords with godliness' [Hn; RSV], 'which goes with godliness' [HNTC], 'that leads to godliness' [NIV], 'that leads to true religion' [NJB], 'as our religion embodies it' [NAB], 'as our religion has it' [NEB].
  c. εὐσέβεια (LN 53.5; 53.1): 'piety' [BAGD, LN, WC], 'godliness' [BAGD, Hn, HNTC, LN, Lns; KJV, NASB, NIV, RSV], 'religion' [BAGD, Herm; NAB, NEB, TEV, TNT], 'true religion' [NJB].
QUESTION—How is this phrase related to the preceding context?
  It is the second object of the preposition κατά 'according to' [Alf, Blm, GNC, Herm, HNTC, ICC, Lg, Lns, NCB, SSA, TC]: according to faith…and (according to) knowledge.
QUESTION—How are the two nouns related in the genitive construction ἐπίγνωσιν ἀληθείας 'knowledge of truth'?
  'Truth' is the content of what they are to know [Alf, EBC, El, Herm, Hn, HNTC, IB, Lg, Lns, MNTC, My, SSA, TC]: that they may know the truth. It means to know the truth as it is revealed in the Christian faith [Blm, EBC, El, GNC, Herm, Hn, HNTC, IB, Lg, Lns, MNTC, SSA, TC]. It refers to the acknowledgment by Christians of the message of redemption [Hn]. It is knowledge which comes from faith [Lg].
QUESTION—What relationship is indicated by κατά 'according to'?
  1. It indicates that the truth referred to is that truth which pertains to piety [Alf, El, SSA]. This general relationship is variously explained. The truth belongs to and is coincident with piety [Alf]. The truth is designed to produce piety [El]. The truth teaches them how to live in a godly manner [SSA].
  2. It indicates that the truth is in accord with piety [EBC, GNC, Lns, MNTC; RSV, TEV]. It defines the truth as that which is in accord with piety [GNC].
  3. It indicates that this truth has the purpose of producing piety [Blm, Hn, ICC, Lg; NIV, NJB]. Truth is in the interest of piety; that is, it promotes it [Hn]. It makes piety its goal [Lg].

**1:2** on-the-basis-of[a] hope[b] of-life eternal,
LEXICON—a. ἐπί with dative object (LN 89.13; 89.27; 89.60): 'on the basis of' [BAGD, Herm, Lns], 'based on' [Hn], 'which is based on' [TEV], 'in' [KJV, NAB, NASB, RSV], 'by' [NEB], 'resting on' [WC; NIV], 'for the sake of' [HNTC], 'which looks to' [TNT], not explicit [NJB].
  b. ἐλπίς (LN 25.59): 'hope' [BAGD, Herm, Hn, HNTC, LN, Lns, WC; all versions].
QUESTION—What is ἐπί 'on the basis of' connected with and what relationship is indicated?
  1. It is connected with Paul's ministry.
    1.1 It indicates a third aspect of his service [Herm, HNTC, MNTC, NCB]: an apostle in regard to faith and knowledge of the truth and for the sake of the hope of eternal life.
    1.2 It indicates a third purpose for his service [NJB]: an apostle in order to bring God's elect people to faith and knowledge and to give them hope of eternal life.
    1.3 It indicates a reason why he serves [Lg]: I am an apostle because I hope for eternal life.
  2. It is connected with 'faith' and 'knowledge of the truth'.
    2.1 It indicates the reason or grounds for Christians' faith and knowledge [EGT, El; NIV]: their faith and knowledge of the truth are caused by or based on their hope of eternal life.
    2.2 It indicates the result of their faith and knowledge [GNC, SSA]: so that they will have faith and knowledge of the truth, and, as a result, they will hope for eternal life.
    2.3 It indicates an accompanying circumstance [Alf]: so that they may have faith and knowledge of the truth as they hope for eternal life.
  3. It is connected with truth [TG]: knowledge of the truth, and that truth is based on our hope for eternal life.
  4. It is connected with and gives a reason for all that precedes [EBC, Hn]. Paul's service and life were based on his hope of eternal life.
QUESTION—How are the two nouns related in the genitive construction ἐλπίδι ζωῆς αἰωνίου 'hope of eternal life'?
  The object of hope is to obtain eternal life [Blm, EBC, Hn, HNTC, Lg, Lns, SSA, TG]: on the basis of their/my hope that they/I will obtain eternal life. The hope is based on God's promise mentioned in the following clause [Bg, GNC, WC].

**which promised[a] the not-lying[b] God before[c] times[d] eternal[e]**
LEXICON—a. aorist mid. (deponent = act.) indic. of ἐπαγγέλλω (LN 33.286): 'to promise' [BAGD, Herm, Hn, HNTC, LN, Lns, WC; all versions].
  b. ἀψευδής (LN 88.40): 'never-lying' [Hn], 'unlying' [WC], 'truthful' [BAGD, LN]. This adjective is also translated as a verb phrase: 'that cannot lie' [KJV], 'who cannot lie' [Herm; NAB, NASB, NEB], 'who

TITUS 1:2

does not lie' [HNTC, Lns; NIV, TEV], 'who never lies' [RSV], 'He does not lie' [NJB], 'he keeps his word' [TNT].
  c. πρό with genitive object (LN 67.17): 'before' [Hn, LN, Lns, WC; KJV, NIV, TEV, TNT].
  d. χρόνος (LN 67.78): 'time' [BAGD, Hn, LN, Lns, WC; NIV, TEV, TNT], 'age' [NAB, NASB, NEB, RSV].
  e. αἰώνιος (LN 67.96): 'eternal' [BAGD, LN, WC], 'everlasting' [Hn], 'age long' [Lns]. The phrase πρὸ χρόνων αἰωνίων 'before times eternal' is translated 'before the world began' [KJV], 'before time began' [Herm], 'before the beginning of time' [NIV, TEV], 'from all eternity' [HNTC], 'in endless ages past' [NAB], 'ages ago' [RSV], 'long ages ago' [NASB, NEB], 'so long ago' [NJB].
QUESTION—To what does ἥν 'which' refer?
  It refers to 'life eternal' [Alf, Bg, GNC, Lg, My, SSA, TC]: eternal life which God promised.
QUESTION—What is the significance of the adjective ἀψευδής 'not lying'?
  It states the basis of our confidence in God's promise [Bg, EBC, GNC, HNTC, TNTC, WC]: we are confident of God's promise because he does not lie. It states the character of God [Lg].
QUESTION—What is meant by πρὸ χρόνων αἰωνίων 'before times eternal'?
  1. It means that the promise was based on God's purpose, which was from eternity [Alf, Bg, EBC, El, GNC, Herm, Hn, HNTC, My, NCBC, SSA, TC, TNTC, WC]: which God promised, based on his purpose which existed from eternity. It does not mean merely 'from ancient times' [Alf].
  2. It refers to a promise God made in the Old Testament [Blm, Brt, IB, ICC, Lg, Lns, MNTC, Rb]: which God promised in ancient times. It refers to the promise first given to Adam and Eve in Gen. 3:15 [Blm, Brt] and other Old Testament patriarchs [IB, Lns].

**1:3** and/but manifested[a] at-times[b] one's-own[c] the word[d] of-him
LEXICON—a. aorist act. indic. of φανερόω (LN 28.36): 'to manifest' [WC; KJV, NAB, NASB, RSV], 'to make manifest' [HNTC], 'to declare openly' [NEB], 'to bring to light' [NIV], 'to make known' [BAGD, LN; NJB], 'to reveal' [BAGD, Herm, Hn; TEV], 'to disclose' [LN], 'to make plain' [TNT], 'to make public' [Lns].
  b. καιρός (LN 67.1): 'time' [BAGD, Herm, HNTC, LN; KJV, NAB, NASB, NEB, NJB, RSV, TEV, TNT], 'season' [Hn; NIV], 'seasons' [WC], 'periods' [Lns].
  c. ἴδιος (LN 57.4): 'due' [Hn; KJV, NJB], 'the proper' [BAGD; NASB, RSV], 'the right' [TEV], 'their own' [Lns], 'its own' [WC], 'one's own' [LN], 'his own' [Herm; TNT], 'his own good' [HNTC; NAB, NEB], 'his appointed' [NIV].
  d. λόγος (LN 33.98): 'word' [Herm, Hn, HNTC, LN, Lns, WC; KJV, NAB, NASB, NIV, RSV], 'message' [LN; NJB, TNT]; not explicit [NEB, TEV].

QUESTION—What relationship is indicated by δέ 'and/but'?
1. It indicates the sequence or progression of events [SSA; NEB, NIV, NJB, RSV, TEV]: God promised eternal life and then he manifested his word.
2. It indicates a contrast with the time of the promise (1:2) [Alf, El, Herm, Hn, Lg, Lns, My; KJV, NASB]: God promised eternal life before eternal times, but he manifested his word at the proper time.

QUESTION—What is meant by καιροῖς ἰδίοις 'at one's own times'?
Most refer ἰδίοις 'one's own' to God [EBC, EGT, El, Herm, HNTC, ICC, Lg, Rb; NAB, NEB, NIV, TNT]: God manifested *his* word at his own time. Others refer it to the word's own time [Alf, Lns, TC, WC]: God manifested his word at *its* own time. Its own time is the appropriate time that was determined by God [Alf, Lns]. Others merely refer to the appropriate, due, proper, or right time [Hn; KJV, NAB, NASB, NJB, RSV, TEV]: God manifested his word at *the appropriate* time. The plural ἰδίοις 'times' is used in the sense of the singular [TNTC and presumably those who translate in the singular: Hn, HNTC; all versions except KJV], or the plural form indicates that the manifestation occurred at various times in the earthly life of Jesus and in the apostles' preaching [ICC].

QUESTION—What does τὸν λόγον αὐτοῦ 'his word' refer to?
1. It refers to the gospel or the Christian message [Alf, Brt, EBC, El, GNC, Hn, HNTC, My, NCB, NCBC, TC, TNTC]: God made known his promise of eternal life in the gospel. Paul expresses himself more precisely by using the phrase 'manifested his word' instead of 'manifested eternal life', since, strictly speaking, eternal life was still in the future [El].
2. It refers to Jesus Christ [IB] (this interpretation adds the preposition 'in' with no Greek support): he made the message known in his Word (Jesus).

**in[a] (the) preaching[b] with-which I have-been-entrusted[c]**
LEXICON: a. ἐν with dative object (LN 90.10; 89.76): 'in' [Herm, HNTC, Lns, WC; NAB, NASB, NEB, TEV], 'through' [KJV, NIV, RSV], 'by' [Hn; NJB]; not explicit [TNT].
b. κήρυγμα (LN 33.258): 'preaching' [BAGD, HNTC, LN; KJV, NAB, NIV, RSV], 'proclamation' [BAGD, Herm, Hn, WC; NASB, NEB, NJB, TNT], 'herald proclamation' [Lns], 'message' [TEV].
c. aorist pass. indic. of πιστεύω (LN 35.50): 'to be committed' [KJV], 'to be entrusted' [BAGD, Herm, Hn, HNTC, LN, Lns, WC; all versions except KJV].

QUESTION—What relationship is indicated by ἐν 'in'?
1. It indicates the element in which the manifestation took place [Alf, GNC, HNTC, TC]: God made his word known in the form of a message which is preached. The manifestation has occurred in Paul's proclamation of the message [GNC].
2. It expresses the means by which the message was made known [Hn, HNTC, My, SSA, TG]: God made his word known by the message which is preached.

QUESTION—What is the meaning of κηρύγματι 'preaching'?

This refers to a message that is preached [EBC, EGT, HNTC, LN, Lns, Rb, TC]. Some commentators describe this as a preaching in general by whoever proclaims it [HNTC, Lns, SSA, TC]: God revealed his word in the form of preaching, a preaching with which I (along with others) have been entrusted. Most commentators do not address this aspect and apparently focus on Paul's preaching: God revealed his word in the preaching with which I have been entrusted.

QUESTION—What is indicated by the explicit pronoun ἐγώ 'I'?

'I' is emphatic [EBC, HNTC, Lns, WC], emphasizing the personal experience involved [EBC], or hinting that the false teachers do not have such authority as Paul does [HNTC]: the message with which I personally have been entrusted. His preaching is not on his own initiative; it has been entrusted to him by God [GNC, TC].

**according-to[a] (the) commandment[b] of-the Savior of-us God,**

LEXICON: a. κατά with accusative object (LN 89.8): 'according to' [BAGD, Herm, WC; KJV, NASB], 'in accord with' [BAGD, Lns], 'in virtue of' [HNTC], 'by' [Hn; NAB, NEB, NIV, NJB, RSV, TEV]; not explicit [TNT].

b. ἐπιταγή (LN 33.326): 'commandment' [KJV, NASB], 'command' [BAGD, LN, WC; NAB, NIV, NJB, RSV], 'commission' [Herm, HNTC], 'ordinance' [NEB], 'order' [BAGD, Hn, LN, Lns; TEV]; not explicit [TNT].

QUESTION—What relationship is indicated by κατά 'according to'?

It indicates agreement between the act of entrusting the message to Paul and the command that he preach it [Herm, Lns, WC; KJV, NASB]: God entrusted the preaching of the message to me, this commission being in accordance with what God commanded me to do; that is, God entrusted the message to me and commanded me to preach it. This points out that his message was not merely a matter of his own pleasure [My]. The phrase implies the authority involved [EBC]. It expresses his apostleship in different words [EGT].

QUESTION—What is implied by the phrase τοῦ σωτῆρος ἡμῶν θεοῦ 'our Savior God'?

The word 'God' identifies who is meant by 'our Savior' [EBC, EGT]: God, the source of our salvation (through Christ). The phrase points to the fact that God the Father is the final source of salvation [EBC, El, MNTC, WC]. God is Savior of all Christians [EBC], but some think that here there is a particular reference to God as the Savior of Paul and Titus [ICC, Lns].

**1:4 to-Titus genuine[a] child[b] according-to[c] (our) common[d] faith;[e]**

LEXICON—a. γνήσιος (LN 73.1): 'genuine' [LN, Lns], 'my genuine' [Hn, WC], 'mine own' [KJV], 'real' [LN], 'true' [BAGD, Herm, HNTC; all versions except KJV, NEB], 'my true-born' [NEB].

b. τέκνον (LN 9.46; 36.40): 'son' [KJV, NEB, NIV, TEV, TNT], 'child' [BAGD, Herm, Hn, HNTC, LN, Lns, WC; NAB, NASB, NJB, RSV], 'disciple' [LN].
  c. κατά with accusative object (LN 89.4; 89.8): 'according to' [WC], 'in accord with' [Lns], 'after' [KJV], 'in' [Herm, HNTC; all versions except KJV], 'in terms of' [Hn].
  d. κοινός (LN 57.9): 'common' [BAGD], 'our common' [NAB, NIV], 'the common' [Herm, Hn, Lns; KJV], 'a common' [WC; NASB, RSV], 'that we have in common' [LN; TEV], 'that we share' [HNTC; NEB, NJB, TNT].
  e. πίστις (LN 31.104): 'faith' [BAGD, Herm, Hn, HNTC, LN, Lns, WC; all versions].

QUESTION—What is meant by γνησίῳ τέκνῳ '(my) genuine child'?

Titus is called Paul's child because he was converted by Paul [Brt, EBC, El, Hn, HNTC, MNTC, NCBC, SSA, TC, WC], and so Paul was a means God used in giving Timothy spiritual life [Hn]. The term also expresses Paul's affection for Timothy [Hn, Lns]. He is called 'genuine' because he is not just a nominal believer, but is loyal to the common faith [EBC, Hn, IB, Lns, SSA], and because Paul could depend on his service [WC].

QUESTION—What relationship is indicated by κατά 'according to'?

The preposition κατά indicates in what respect Timothy can be called a genuine child of Paul [El, Hn, Lg, My, NCB, SSA]: my genuine child in respect to our common faith.

QUESTION—What is meant by κοινὴν πίστιν 'a common faith'?

  1. It is the faith shared by Paul, Titus, and all of God's people [Alf, Blm, CBC, EBC, EGT, ICC, Lns, Rb, TG, TNTC, WC]: according to the faith which all Christians share. It refers to the faith shared by Jewish and Gentile believers [CBC, ICC, Rb].
  2. It is the faith shared by Paul and Titus [El, GNC, Hn, HNTC, Lg, My]: according to the faith which you and I share. They share because Paul has nurtured Titus in the faith [HNTC]. The phrase does not here refer to the faith in which all Christians share; the context implies a more intimate sense [El, HNTC]. Some commentators take it to refer to the faith of Paul as a Jew and of Titus as a Gentile [GNC, Lg], but another does not think that Paul is focusing on this difference [My].

QUESTION—What is the meaning of πίστιν 'faith' here?

It has the subjective sense of true knowledge of God and his word, and full confidence in him and in his love [Hn]. It means that they believe the same Christian doctrine [SSA].

**grace[a] and peace[b] from God (the) Father and Christ Jesus the Savior[c] of-us.**

TEXT—Some manuscripts have ἔλεος 'mercy' instead of the first καί 'and'. GNT does not mention this variant; only Blm and KJV read 'mercy'.

LEXICON—a. χάρις (LN 88.66): 'grace' [BAGD, Herm, Hn, HNTC, LN, Lns, WC; all versions], 'kindness' [LN].
  b. εἰρήνη (LN 22.42): 'peace' [Herm, Hn, HNTC, LN, Lns, WC; all versions].
  c. σωτήρ (LN 21.31): 'Savior' [Herm, Hn, HNTC, LN, Lns, WC; all versions].

QUESTION—What is meant by χάρις 'grace'?
  It is God's unmerited favor working in the Christian's life [EBC, Hn, SSA]: may God act favorably toward you. Grace characterizes God's favorable dealings with men [SSA].

QUESTION—What is meant by εἰρήνη 'peace'?
  It is the harmony and well-being that results from God's grace at work in the Christian's life [EBC, SSA]: may God give you inner well-being. It results from the realization of reconciliation to God through Christ [Hn]. It is a state of well-being for the whole person [SSA].

QUESTION—What is implied by combining 'God' and 'Christ Jesus' as objects of the one preposition ἀπό 'from'?
  It implies that God the Father and Jesus are one united source of the blessings mentioned [EBC, Hn]: from God and Christ (as one source). 'Savior' has its full redemptive meaning here [Hn].

QUESTION—How is the phrase 'Christ Jesus our Savior' related to 'God our Savior' in 1:3?
  God the Father is the ultimate source of our salvation, and it is accomplished through Jesus [EBC, EGT, GNC, MNTC]. The Father and the Son together are Saviors [EGT, Lg, Lns]. Father and Son are in agreement in their desire for the salvation of mankind [WC]. Christ and the Father are placed on the same level in regard to salvation [ICC].

**DISCOURSE UNIT: 1:5–16** [EBC, GNT, ICC, Lg, NCB; NAB, NASB, NIV, TEV]. The topic is Paul's charge to Titus [NAB], the qualifications required for elders [NASB], Titus's responsibilities [NIV, TEV], matters concerning elders and concerning false teachers [EBC], a charge to Titus concerning the ministry [GNT, ICC], how the work is to be developed [NCB], directions concerning the selection of church officials [Lg].

**DISCOURSE UNIT: 1:5–9** [Alf, EBC, EGT, GNC, Herm, Hn, HNTC, ICC, MNTC, NCBC, TNTC, WC; NJB]. The topic is the appointment of elders [EBC, GNC, Herm, MNTC; NJB], the reason Titus was left in Crete [Alf, WC], directions concerning church officials [HNTC], instructions concerning elders and bishops [Herm], qualities which church officials must have [NCBC, TNTC].

**DISCOURSE UNIT: 1:5–8** [IB]. The topic is matters concerning elders and bishops.

**DISCOURSE UNIT: 1:5** [TC]. The topic is the responsibilities of Titus in appointing elders.

**1:5** **for-the-cause-of**[a] **this I-left**[b] **you in Crete,**
LEXICON—a. χάριν with genitive object preceding (LN 89.60): 'for the sake of' [BAGD, LN, WC], 'for the purpose of' [LN]. The prepositional phrase τούτου χάριν is translated 'for this cause' [KJV], 'for this reason' [Hn, Lns; NASB], 'my purpose was' [NAB], 'my intention was' [NEB], 'the reason was' [NIV, NJB], 'the reason why was' [HNTC], 'this is why' [RSV]. This phrase is also combined with the following ἵνα 'that': 'so that' [Herm; TEV], 'that' [TNT].
  b. aorist act. indic. of ἀπολείπω (LN **85.65**):'to leave' [Herm, HNTC, LN, Lns; KJV, NAB, NASB, NEB, NIV, RSV, TEV], 'to leave behind' [BAGD, Hn, WC; NJB, TNT].
QUESTION—What is the significance of this clause?
  It reinforces Titus's authority with Paul's [IB]: I reiterate my instructions for you to carry out: I left you in Crete for this reason. It does not necessarily imply that Titus had written to ask Paul why he had been left in Crete [Lns], but it may add to his previous instructions and also reply to a letter from Titus [Rb].
QUESTION—What relationship is indicated by the phrase τούτου χάριν 'for this cause'?
  It indicates the purpose for Paul's leaving Titus in Crete, which is specified in the following ἵνα 'that' clause [Hn, HNTC, Lg, Lns, TC, TG]: I left you in Crete for this purpose—that you set in order the things that are lacking and appoint elders.
QUESTION—What is implied by the phrase ἀπέλιπόν σε 'I left you'?
  It implies that Paul and Titus had been together in Crete, and when Paul departed, he left Titus behind in order to carry out some specific responsibilities [EBC, GNC, Hn, HNTC, ICC, Lg, Lns, MNTC, TNTC]: I left you behind to fulfill some assignments. The ἀπο- compound of the verb implies that Titus was left in Crete temporarily [Alf, EGT, Rb]; or it simply adds the idea of leaving behind [HNTC, Lns]; or it brings in the idea of purpose [ICC].

**that**[a] **the lacking-things**[b] **you-might-set-in-order**[c]
LEXICON—a. ἵνα (LN 89.59): 'that' [Hn, HNTC, Lns; all versions except NJB, TEV], 'in order that' [WC], 'for' [NJB].
  b. pres. act. participle of λείπω (LN 57.43): 'to want' [KJV], 'to be left undone' [NAB], 'to be left unfinished' [NIV], 'to be left over' [NEB], 'to remain' [Herm; NASB], 'to remain to be done' [Hn; TNT], 'to be lacking' [BAGD, LN, WC], 'to be still lacking' [Lns], 'to have still to be done' [NJB], 'to need still to be doing' [TEV], 'to be defective' [BAGD, HNTC; RSV].
  c. aorist mid. subj. of ἐπιδιορθόω (LN **62.4**): 'to set in order' [KJV, NASB, NEB], 'to further set in order' [WC], 'to set right' [BAGD, Herm], 'to put in order' [LN, Lns; TEV, TNT], 'to put right' [HNTC], 'to straighten out'

TITUS 1:5 23

[Hn; NIV], 'to amend' [RSV], 'to organize' [NJB], 'to accomplish' [NAB].

QUESTION—What meant by τὰ λείποντα ἐπιδιορθώσῃ 'to set right the lacking things'?
1. This means that Titus was to correct matters that were defective and needed to be changed [Alf, EBC, EGT, HNTC, IB, SSA, TC]: that you correct the things that are wrong. Paul had possibly begun this task [EGT]. Some of the matters that needed correcting were the teaching of false doctrine [EBC, SSA] and lack of organization [EBC, IB].
2. This means that Titus was to complete matters that had not yet been finished [GNC, ICC, Lns, MNTC, My, NCB, NCBC, TNTC]: that you finish what yet remains to be done. Paul had not had time to complete these matters [My]. The phrase τὰ λείποντα 'the lacking things' has a neutral sense [ICC].
3. This means that Titus was to do whatever remained to be done, both correcting wrong situations and completing what was still undone [Rb].

**and appoint[a] elders[b] according-to[c] city,[d]**

LEXICON—a. aorist act. subj. of καθίστημι (LN 37.104): 'to ordain' [KJV], 'to appoint' [BAGD, Hn, HNTC, LN; NASB, NIV, NJB, RSV, TEV, TNT], 'to institute' [NEB], 'to install' [Herm], 'to place into office' [Lns], 'to set up' [WC]. This verb is also translated as a noun: 'the appointment' [NAB].
  b. πρεσβύτερος (LN 53.77): 'elder' [BAGD, Hn, HNTC, LN, Lns; all versions except NAB, TEV], 'church elder' [TEV], 'presbyter' [Herm, WC; NAB].
  c. κατά with accusative object (LN 89.90): 'in every' [BAGD, HNTC; all versions except NEB], 'in each' [Herm, Hn; NEB]. The phrase κατὰ πόλιν 'according to city' is translated 'city by city' [Lns, WC].
  d. πόλις (LN 1.88): 'city' [Herm, Hn, LN, Lns, WC; KJV, NASB], 'town' [LN; all versions except KJV, NASB], 'place' [HNTC].

QUESTION—What relationship is indicated by καί 'and'?
1. It introduces one of several matters that are to be set right [Alf, EBC, EGT, Lg, Lns, NCB, SSA]: that you set in order the things that lack, including, among other things, that you appoint elders. This is the most important of these matters [EGT, Lg, Lns]: that you set in order the things that lack, especially that you appoint elders.
2. It introduces the one specific matter that was lacking [GNC, Hn, Lg, My]: that you set in order the things that lack, specifically, that you appoint elders.
3. It indicates another purpose [SSA]: I left you in Crete for these purposes: that you set in order the things that lack, and that you appoint elders.

QUESTION—What is implied by the verb καταστήσῃς 'appoint'?
1. It does not specify the method, and does not mean 'ordain' in a formal ecclesiastical sense [EBC, MNTC, NCB]: that you should put elders in

charge. Perhaps the elders were chosen by the congregation with Titus' encouragement, who then officially appointed them [EBC]. Paul does not exclude the participation of the congregation in the selection [Hn, ICC, Rb]. They were to be elected by the respective congregations [Lns].
2. The verb shows that Titus had the full episcopal authority to appoint these elders [Blm, My, NCBC]: that you (personally) should appoint elders. Titus evidently had the full responsibility for selecting the elders [HNTC, My].

QUESTION—What is meant by κατὰ πόλιν 'according to city'?

It means each city or town in which there was a Christian congregation [Blm, EBC]: in each town (in which there is a Christian congregation). It does not mean that there was a Christian congregation in every city of Crete [Blm, IB, TG]. It implies that there were congregations all over the island [MNTC]. It is not indicated whether there was to be one elder in each city or more than one elder in any one city [EGT, GNC]. Some think that more than one elder was intended [EBC, ICC, Lns, My, TC].

## as[a] I directed[b] you,

LEXICON—a. ὡς (LN 64.12): 'as' [BAGD, HNTC, Lns, WC; KJV, NAB, NASB, NIV, RSV], 'in such a manner as' [Hn], 'in the way that' [NJB]. This clause is translated 'observe the tests I prescribed' [NEB], 'remember my instructions' [TEV], 'my instructions to you were' [TNT], 'according to my directions to you' [Herm].

b. aorist mid. indic. of διατάσσω (LN 33.325): 'to direct' [BAGD, HNTC, Lns, WC; NASB, NIV, RSV], 'to appoint' [KJV], 'to instruct' [LN; NAB], 'to prescribe' [NEB], 'to order' [LN], 'to tell' [NJB]. This verb is also translated as a noun: 'instructions' [TEV, TNT], 'directions' [Herm, Hn].

QUESTION—What relationship is indicated by ὡς 'as'?

1. It reminds Titus that Paul had previously instructed him to appoint elders [Bg, Blm, EBC, GNC, Lns, NCBC; TNT]: appoint elders; remember that I instructed you to do so. Paul evidently had not had time to instruct Titus in the details of appointing the elders [Blm]. Paul here states briefly in writing what he had previously told Titus orally [EBC, GNC].
2. It indicates the manner in which Titus is to appoint elders [El, Hn, SSA, TC; NJB]: appoint elders in the manner in which I instructed you. This refers to their qualifications [Hn]: appoint elders selecting the kind of men I directed you to choose.
3. It includes both of the preceding [Alf, My]: appoint elders, as (which, and in the manner in which) I instructed you.

QUESTION—What is this clause connected with?

1. It is connected with what precedes [Herm, Hn, HNTC, Lns, SSA, WC; KJV, NASB, NIV, RSV, TNT]: appoint elders, as I directed you. Paul is repeating instructions he had previously given to Titus [HNTC]. This clause again implies Paul's apostolic authority [IB].

TITUS 1:5

2. It is connected with what follows [NAB, NEB, TEV]: As I instructed you, appoint men if they are unblameable, etc.

QUESTION—What is implied by the emphatic ἐγώ 'I'?

The emphatic 'I' implies that Paul's apostolic authority is involved [Lns, MNTC, TNTC], and that those who are appointed must have the qualities of which Paul approves [EBC, HNTC]. It may imply a contrast with the wishes of some opponents to Paul [ICC]. One commentator thinks that it does not imply such a contrast [MNTC].

QUESTION—What is implied by the middle voice of the verb διεταξάμην 'I directed'?

The middle voice implies that Titus's actions should fulfill Paul's desires [EBC, ICC]: as I directed you (for myself).

**DISCOURSE UNIT: 1:6–9** [TC]. The topic is the qualifications required for an elder.

**1:6** if[a] someone[b] is unblameable,[c]

LEXICON—a. εἰ (LN 89.65): 'if' [Hn, Lns, WC; KJV, NASB, RSV]. The phrase εἴ τίς ἐστιν 'if someone is' is translated 'men who are' [HNTC], 'such a man should be' [Herm], 'a presbyter must be' [NAB], 'an elder must be' [NIV, TEV], 'each of them must be' [NJB], 'these were to be' [TNT], 'is he…?' [NEB].

b. τίς (LN 92.12): 'any' [KJV], 'any one' [WC], 'any man' [NASB, RSV], 'one' [Lns], 'a person' [Hn], 'a man' [Herm]. The singular form is also translated as a plural form: 'men' [HNTC].

c. ἀνέγκλητος (LN 33.433): 'blameless' [Hn, WC; KJV, NIV, RSV], 'without fault' [TEV], 'without accusation' [LN], 'unaccused' [Lns], 'irreproachable' [BAGD; NAB], 'above reproach' [HNTC; NASB], 'without reproach' [Herm], 'a man of irreproachable character' [NJB], 'a man of unimpeachable character' [NEB], 'men of blameless character' [TNT].

QUESTION—What relationship is indicated by εἰ 'if'?

It indicates a condition of an implied clause [Hn]: he can be appointed, if he is someone who is unblameable. This indicates the qualifications for an elder, and many treat it as a positive statement without a surface conditional statement [Blm, El, Herm, HNTC, ICC, Lg, MNTC, My, SSA, TG; NAB, NEB, NIV, NJB, TEV, TNT]: such a man must be one who is unblameable. It does not indicate doubt about the availability of such a person, rather it assumes that there are such people to appoint [Alf, EBC, El, Lg, My, TC].

**husband**[a] **of-one**[b] **wife,**[c]

LEXICON—a. ἀνήρ (LN 10.53): 'husband' [Herm, Hn, LN, Lns, WC; KJV, NASB, NIV, NJB, RSV], 'husbands' [HNTC]. The phrase μιᾶς γυναικὸς ἀνήρ 'of one wife a husband' is translated 'married only once' [NAB], 'faithful to his one wife' [NEB], 'he must have only one wife' [TEV], 'they were to have one wife only' [TNT].

b. εἷς (LN 60.10): 'one' [Herm, Hn, HNTC, LN, Lns; KJV, NASB, NEB, NJB, RSV], 'but one' [NIV], 'only one' [WC; TEV, TNT].

c. γυνή (LN 10.54): 'wife' [Herm, Hn, HNTC, LN, Lns, WC; all versions except NAB].

QUESTION—How is this phrase connected to the preceding clause?

It and the following clauses are specifics of the preceding generic qualification [EBC, GNC, SSA]: an elder must be blameless—that is, he must be the husband of one wife, etc.

QUESTION—How is the requirement of being a husband to 'one wife' to be understood?

None of the commentators state that this requires a candidate to be married; some state that a bachelor is eligible for the office of an elder [EBC, EGT, Hn]. That a candidate will normally be a married man is assumed [Hn, Lns, MNTC].

1. This requirement concerns adultery: an elder is to be faithful to his wife [GNC, Hn, ICC, Lns, MNTC, My, NCB; NEB]: he is to be a faithful husband to one woman only, his wife. Church leaders should live morally exemplary lives [MNTC, My]; polygamy, concubinage, and remarriage after divorce are prohibited, but not a second marriage of a widower [GNC, Hn]. Only this interpretation is parallel to the corresponding requirement for widows to be "wife of one husband" (1 Tim. 5:9) [Lns, My; and see Greenlee, *Notes on Translation* 108, pp. 17–18].

2. This requirement concerns remarriage after a wife's death: an elder must not have been married a second time [Alf, EGT, El, HNTC, Lg]: he must be husband to one wife only, and never be married again. If he is a widower or divorced, he must not have married again [EGT, El, HNTC].

3. This requirement concerns remarriage after divorce: an elder must not be a divorced man who has married a second woman [CBC]: he must be husband to one wife only, and never be married again if divorced from that wife.

4. This requirement concerns polygamy: an elder must not be married to more than one wife at the same time [Brt, EBC]: he must be husband to only one wife, not to two or more at the same time.

**having[a] believing/faithful[b] children, not in accusation[c] of profligacy[d] or insubordination.[e]**

LEXICON—a. pres. act. participle of ἔχω (LN 57.1): 'to have' [Herm, Hn, LN, Lns, WC; KJV, NASB], 'the father of' [NAB, NEB]. The phrase τέκνα ἔχων πιστά 'having believing children' is translated 'a man whose children believe' [NIV], 'and his children are believers' [RSV], 'with children who are believers' [HNTC], 'and his children must be believers' [NJB, TEV], 'their children were to be believers' [TNT].

b. πιστός (LN 31.86; 31.87): 'faithful' [KJV], 'trusting' [LN], 'faithful' [LN], 'believing' [BAGD, Hn, Lns], 'believers' [Herm, HNTC; NJB,

RSV, TEV, TNT], 'who are believers' [HNTC; NAB, NEB, NJB, RSV, TEV, TNT], 'who are firm believers' [WC], 'who believe' [NASB, NIV].
c. κατηγορία (LN 33.428): 'accusation' [BAGD, LN, Lns, WC], 'charge' [LN]. The phrase μὴ ἐν κατηγορίᾳ 'not in accusation' is translated 'not accused of' [KJV, NASB], 'who cannot be accused of' [Herm], 'not open to the charge of' [Hn], 'not open to the charge of being' [NIV, RSV], 'not chargeable with' [HNTC], 'not liable to be charged with' [NJB], 'who are under no imputation of' [NEB], 'and are known not to be' [NAB], 'and (must) not have the reputation of being' [TEV]. The phrase μὴ ἐν κατηγορίᾳ ἀσωτίας ἢ ἀνυπότακτα 'not in accusation of profligacy or insubordination' is translated 'above suspicion in matters of morals, and well behaved' [TNT].
d. ἀσωτία (LN 88.96): 'riot' [KJV], 'dissipation' [BAGD; NASB], 'dissolute behavior' [Hn], 'dissoluteness' [Lns, WC], 'loose living' [Herm, HNTC; NEB], 'disorderly conduct' [NJB], 'profligate' [BAGD; RSV], 'recklessness' [LN], 'wild' [NAB, NIV, TEV], 'senseless deeds' [LN].
e. ἀνυπότακτος (LN **36.26**): 'unruly' [KJV], 'refractory' [Lns], 'insubordinate' [HNTC, WC; NAB, RSV], 'unsubmissive' [Hn], 'out of control' [NEB], 'disobedient' [BAGD; NIV, TEV], 'disobedience' [Herm], 'insubordination' [NJB], 'rebellion' [NASB], 'being rebellious' [BAGD, LN].

QUESTION—What is implied by the phrase τέκνα ἔχων πιστά 'having believing/faithful children'?

It does not mean that an elder must have children [TC, TNTC, WC]. Candidates would generally be married men [CBC, Hn], and it is assumed that most would have children [EBC, Lns, MNTC]: if he has children, they must be believers/faithful.

QUESTION—What is meant by πιστά 'believing/faithful'?
1. It means that their children are to be Christian believers [Alf, Bg, EBC, EGT, El, Herm, Hn, HNTC, IB, Lg, Lns, MNTC, My, Rb, TC, TG, TNTC, WC; all versions except KJV]: having children who are Christian believers.
2. It means that their children are to be faithful [Blm, SSA; KJV] and trustworthy [ICC]: having children who are faithful to their parents and trustworthy. It is assumed that the children would be believers [Blm].

QUESTION—To whom does the phrase 'not in accusation of profligacy or insubordination' refer?

It refers to the children [Alf, EBC, EGT, El, GNC, Herm, Hn, HNTC, Lns, MNTC, My, NCB, SSA, TC, TG, TNTC; all versions (NASB is indeterminate)]: children who are not able to be accused. This is made clear by ἀνυπότακτα 'insubordinate', which is neuter plural, agreeing with τέκνα 'children' and not with τίς 'someone' (but the commentators do not point this out). The reference to accusations seems to imply that the children are adults [MNTC].

QUESTION—How are the two nouns related in the genitive construction κατηγορίᾳ ἀσωτίας 'accusation of profligacy'?

'Profligacy' is the content of the accusation [EBC, SSA]: not being liable to the accusation that they are profligate.

QUESTION—What is meant by ἀσωτία 'profligate'?

It means self-indulgent and wasteful [EBC]. It refers to debauchery [GNC, SSA] and sensuality [My], to various kinds of wild living [TC], disorderly behavior [TG], excessive indulgence in sensual pleasures [Blm].

QUESTION—What is the phrase ἢ ἀνυπότακτα 'or insubordinate' connected with?

It is dependent directly upon μή 'not'; it is not parallel to ἀσωτίας 'profligacy' [EBC, El, Hn, HNTC, Lns, NCB, SSA, WC; KJV, NEB, TNT] since it is neuter plural (accusative), not feminine singular (genitive) [SSA]: not subject to being accused of being profligate, and not being insubordinate. Some translations make 'insubordinate' parallel to 'profligacy' [Herm; NAB, NASB, NIV, NJB, RSV, TEV], but this is probably merely to make a smoother translation: not subject to being accused of being profligate or insubordinate.

QUESTION—What is meant by ἀνυπότακτος 'insubordinate'?

It means to refuse to accept parents' authority [EBC, El, ICC, Lg, Lns, SSA, TG], to be disorderly in public [Rb], and also to be disobedient to civil officials [ICC, Lg].

**1:7** For[a] it-is-necessary[b] (for) the overseer[c] to-be blameless[d] as[e] a-steward[f] of-God,

LEXICON—a. γάρ (LN 89.23): 'for' [Herm, Hn, HNTC, Lns, WC; KJV, NASB, NEB, RSV, TEV]; not explicit [NAB, NIV, NJB, TNT].

  b. pres. act. indic. of the impersonal verb δεῖ (LN 71.21): 'it is necessary' [Lns, WC]. The phrase δεῖ εἶναι 'it is necessary to be' is translated '(he) must be' [Hn; all versions except NJB, TEV], '(he) has to be' [NJB], '(he) should be' [Herm; TEV], '(he) ought to be' [HNTC].

  c. ἐπίσκοπος (LN **53.71**)): 'bishop' [Herm; KJV, NAB, NEB, RSV, TNT], 'curate' [WC], 'overseer' [BAGD, Hn, HNTC, Lns; NASB, NIV], 'president' [NJB], 'church leader' [LN; TEV].

  d. ἀνέγκλητος (LN 33.433)): 'blameless' [BAGD, Hn, WC; KJV, NAB, NIV, RSV], 'unaccused' [Lns], 'irreproachable' [BAGD; NJB], 'above reproach' [HNTC; NASB], 'without reproach' [Herm], 'without accusation' [LN], 'a man of unimpeachable character' [NEB], 'a man of blameless character' [TNT], 'without fault' [TEV].

  e. ὡς (LN 89.37): 'as' [BAGD, Herm, Hn, Lns; KJV, NAB, NASB, NEB, RSV], 'as being' [WC], 'since' [NIV, NJB, TEV], not explicit [TNT].

  f. οἰκονόμος (LN 37.39): 'steward' [BAGD, Hn, HNTC, Lns, WC; KJV, NAB, NEB, RSV], 'administrator, manager' [LN], 'householder' [Herm], 'representative' [NJB]. The phrase θεοῦ οἰκονόμον 'steward of God' is translated 'entrusted with God's work' [NIV], 'one who is in charge'

[LN], 'in charge of God's work' [TEV], 'responsible for the household of God' [TNT].

QUESTION—What relationship is indicated by γάρ 'for'?
1. It indicates the grounds or reason for the general requirement in 1:6 [GNC, HNTC, IB, MNTC, My, NCB]: a man is qualified to be an elder if he is blameless, because it is necessary that an overseer be blameless. He must be blameless in the matter of directing his own household (1:6) since his work will be to direct God's household [GNC].
2. It indicates continuation, here as a restatement of the general requirement in order to amplify it [SSA]: a man is qualified to be an elder if he is blameless. It is necessary that an overseer be blameless since he is God's steward.

QUESTION—How is τὸν ἐπίσκοπον 'the overseer' related to πρεσβυτέρους 'elders' in 1:5?
1. The two terms refer to the same people [Alf, EBC, EGT, El, IB, Lg, Lns, MNTC, My, SSA, TG]. 'Overseer' refers to the man's function [EBC, EGT, El, Hn, IB, MNTC, My, NCB, Rb, SSA], while 'elder' refers to his maturity [EBC, Hn] and office [IB, NCB, Rb, SSA]. The change from plural 'elders' to the singular 'the overseer' is explained as a change to the use of a generic term for the class to be described [EBC, Hn, NCB]: the elders should have certain qualities, since a man who oversees must have the following characteristics.
2. The term 'overseer' refers to only part of the elders. Overseers were probably executive officers chosen from among the elders; that is, the overseer is an elder, but not all elders are overseers [GNC, HNTC]. This is a generic use of the singular form [GNC, HNTC].

QUESTION—How are the two nouns related in the genitive construction θεοῦ οἰκονόμον 'of God an overseer'?

The overseer is a steward in God's household, the church [Alf, EGT, GNC, IB, Lg, Lns, MNTC, My, TC]. He is appointed by God [EGT, My, TG], under God's authority and accountable to him [EBC, TC], and administers the church as God's representative [HNTC, IB]. Since 'of God' precedes 'an overseer', the emphasis is on 'of God' [EGT, El, HNTC, SSA]; because he represents God, his life must be without basis for blame [EGT, El, HNTC, My]. He is God's steward, not the church's steward [GNC, TC, WC].

QUESTION—What relationship is indicated by ὡς 'as'?
1. It indicates the grounds or reason for the preceding clause [EBC, El, Hn, My, SSA, TNTC; NIV, NJB, TEV]: it is necessary that an overseer be blameless since/because he is God's overseer.
2. It indicates circumstance, his characteristic quality [MNTC, WC]: it is necessary that an overseer be blameless as being God's overseer.

**not self-willed,**[a] **not quick-tempered,**[b] **not addicted-to-wine,**[c] **not a-brawler,**[d] **not greedy-for-money,**[e]

LEXICON—a. αὐθάδης (LN **88.206**): 'self-willed' [BAGD, HNTC, WC; KJV, NAB, NASB], 'self-opinionated' [TNT], 'self-pleasing' [Hn, Lns], 'overbearing' [NEB, NIV], 'arrogant' [BAGD, Herm, LN; NJB, RSV, TEV].

  b. ὀργίλος (LN **88.175**)): 'soon angry' [KJV], 'arrogant' [NAB], 'irascible' [Herm, WC], 'quick-tempered' [BAGD, HNTC, LN, Lns; NASB, NIV, RSV, TEV, TNT], 'short-tempered' [NEB], 'hot-tempered' [Hn; NJB].

  c. πάροινος (LN **88.288**): 'given to wine' [Herm; KJV], 'addicted to wine' [BAGD; NASB], 'too fond of wine' [TNT], 'one who lingers beside his wine' [Hn], 'sitting long beside wine' [Lns], 'quarrelsome over wine' [WC], 'given to drunkenness' [NIV], 'drunkard' [LN; NAB, RSV, TEV], 'drinker' [NEB], 'heavy drinker' [HNTC; NJB].

  d. πλήκτης (LN 88.137): 'striker' [Lns, WC; KJV], 'pugnacious' [NASB], 'brawler' [NEB], 'bully' [LN], 'violent person' [LN], 'given to brawling' [Herm], 'given to blows' [Hn], 'aggressive' [TNT], 'violent' [HNTC; NAB, NIV, NJB, RSV, TEV].

  e. αἰσχροκερδής (LN 25.26): 'given to filthy lucre' [KJV], 'fond of sordid gain' [NASB], 'eager for base gain' [WC], 'fond of dishonest gain' [Herm], 'pursuing dishonest gain' [NIV], 'greedy for gain' [HNTC; RSV], 'greedy of shameful gain' [Hn], 'out for shameful gain' [Lns], 'greedy for money' [TEV], 'greedy' [NAB], 'shamefully greedy' [LN], 'money-grubber' [NEB], 'involved in any shady finance' [TNT], 'avaricious' [NJB].

QUESTION—How are these qualifications connected with the preceding clause?

These are specifics of the general qualification [MNTC, SSA]: an overseer must be blameless: specifically, he must not be self-willed, etc. This is a representative list and not exhaustive [GNC]. These are temptations to which their work would expose them [HNTC, IB, NCBC]: he must avoid these things, to which he may at times be tempted.

QUESTION—What is meant by αὐθάδης 'self-willed'?

It means one who disregards others in his self-will [Bg, EBC, Lns], who is arrogant [EGT, HNTC, ICC, Lns, My, TC, TNTC], self-assertive [EGT], harsh and inflexible [Bg], and who is obstinate in his opinion [HNTC, ICC, My, NCB, WC]. It is derived from the Greek words 'oneself' and 'to please' [El, Lg, My, Rb].

QUESTION—What is meant by πάροινος 'addicted to wine'?

Most commentators take the word in its literal sense of drinking too much [EBC, Hn, HNTC, IB, LN, Lns, WC]. It means addicted to wine [Hn], or an alcoholic [WC]. It may be used in an extended sense: blustering or being abusive (like a drunkard) [ICC].

QUESTION—What is meant by πλήκτης 'a brawler'?

It means a violent person who is ready to fight someone physically [EBC, IB, Lns, MNTC], or with words [EBC], or either [Hn, ICC].

QUESTION—What is meant by αἰσχροκερδής 'greedy for money'?

1. This word refers to a desire to obtain riches in a wrong way [CBC, EBC, EGT, GNC, Herm, Hn, HNTC, IB, ICC, Lns, My, NCB, NCBC; NIV, TNT]. The wrong way includes using the office of overseer as a means for obtaining riches [EBC, EGT, GNC, ICC, Lg(D), Lns, My, NCB], engaging in work that dishonors the office [CBC, ICC], engaging in work that causes him to neglect his responsibilities [IB], acquiring money dishonestly [EBC, EGT, Hn, HNTC, IB, ICC, Lns, NCBC] such as by petty theft from church funds [EGT, NCBC].
2. This word refers to the attitude of greed in general [Bg, MNTC; NJB, RSV, TEV].

**1:8 but**

LEXICON—ἀλλά (LN 89.125): 'but' [Herm, Hn, HNTC, WC; KJV, NASB, NEB, NJB, RSV, TNT], 'on the contrary' [Lns; NAB], 'rather' [NIV], not explicit [TEV].

QUESTION—What relationship is indicated by this word?

It introduces the positive contrast to the five negative qualities of 1:7 [EBC, GNC, HNTC, Lg, My, TC]. The qualities listed do not include any rare or special characteristics; the official must simply have the common ethical and moral qualities [MNTC, TNTC].

**hospitable,[a] a-lover-of-good,[b] sober,[c] righteous,[d] holy,[e] self-controlled,[f]**

LEXICON—a. φιλόξενος (LN 34.58): 'hospitable' [BAGD, Hn, HNTC, LN, WC; all versions except KJV], 'lover of hospitality' [KJV], 'devoted to hospitality' [Herm, Lns].

b. φιλάγαθος (LN **25.105**)): 'lover of goodness' [NAB, NJB, RSV], 'lover of all good' [TNT], 'loving what is good' [BAGD; NASB], 'loving the good' [Hn, WC], 'one who loves what is good' [LN; NIV], '(he must) love what is good' [TEV], 'devoted to what is good' [Herm], 'devoted to what is beneficial' [Lns], 'right-minded' [HNTC; NEB], 'lover of good men' [KJV].

c. σώφρων (LN 88.94): 'sober' [KJV], 'sober-minded' [Lns], 'steady' [NAB], 'prudent' [BAGD, Herm], 'discreet' [WC], 'temperate' [HNTC; NEB], 'moderate' [LN], 'self-restrained' [TNT], 'self-controlled' [BAGD; NIV, TEV], 'sensible' [LN; NASB, NJB], 'self-controlled (or sensible)' [Hn], 'master of himself' [RSV].

d. δίκαιος (LN 88.12): 'just' [BAGD, Herm, HNTC, LN, Lns; KJV, NAB, NASB, NEB, TNT], 'upright' [BAGD; NIV, NJB, RSV, TEV], 'fair' [Hn], 'righteous' [BAGD, LN, WC].

e. ὅσιος (LN 88.24): 'holy' [BAGD, LN; KJV, NAB, NIV, RSV, TEV], 'holy in relation to God' [WC], 'devout' [BAGD, HNTC; NASB, NEB,

NJB, TNT], 'pious' [BAGD, Herm, Hn], 'pure' [LN], 'true to moral obligation' [Lns].
f. ἐγκρατής (LN **88.84**): 'temperate' [KJV], 'self-controlled' [BAGD, Herm, HNTC, LN, Lns, WC; NAB, NASB, NEB, NJB, RSV], 'disciplined' [BAGD; NIV, TEV, TNT], 'master of himself' [Hn].

QUESTION—What is meant by φιλάγαθος 'lover of good'?

It means a lover of what is good [Alf], right-minded, a person who is devoted to what is best [EBC, Hn, HNTC], one who both is good and does good [IB, SSA], one who loves what is good in persons, actions, or qualities [EBC, Lg], one who has a helpful spirit [Lns]. It may mean either a lover of good men or a lover of goodness [Blm, My], but according to one commentator, the meaning 'lover of good men' is not likely, since it follows so closely after hospitable [Alf].

QUESTION—What is meant by σώφρων 'sober'?

It means to be calm and self-controlled so as to be able to act properly and appropriately [EBC, Lg(D), Lns], to be of sound mind [GNC, Hn], to be moderate in participation in legitimate activities [TC]. It refers to desires of the mind [EGT].

QUESTION—What is meant by δίκαιος 'just'?

1. This refers to a person's relationship with his fellowmen [Blm, GNC, Hn, HNTC, ICC, Lg, My, TC, WC]. It means to be right with regard to human laws [Blm], to have right relations with people [HNTC], to follow right standards of conduct toward other people [EBC, GNC, Hn, My, WC], to act honestly and equitably [El].
2. This refers to a person's relationship with God [Lns]. It means conduct approved by God.

QUESTION—What is meant by ὅσιος 'holy'?

'Holy' relates to God's laws and means to be pure from sin, pious [Blm, My], to be rightly related to God [HNTC, WC], to seek to fulfill one's duty toward God [GNC, Hn], to have an attitude of seeking to be pleasing to God and to conform to proper religious customs [EBC, SSA], to have a holy purity [El].

QUESTION—What is meant by ἐγκρατής 'self-controlled'?

'Self-controlled' refers to exercising proper restraint in regard to indulgence in general, not merely to sexual indulgence [Alf], the ability to abstain from what is improper [TC], having the inner resources to control one's bodily desires [EBC, EGT, Hn, ICC, Lg, My, TNTC] and focusing the will on God's will [ICC]. It means to have strength to resist doing anything unjust or contrary to God's ordinances [Lns].

**DISCOURSE UNIT: 1:9–16** [IB]. The topic is the overseer's responsibility to maintain correct teaching.

**1:9** holding-firmly[a] the according-to[b] the teaching[c] faithful[d] word,[e]
LEXICON—a. pres. mid. participle of ἀντέχομαι (LN **31.49**): 'to hold' [WC], 'to hold fast' [BAGD, HNTC; KJV, NAB, NASB], 'to hold firmly' [LN;

NIV, TEV], 'to hold firm' [RSV], 'to hold on' [Hn], 'to have a firm grasp' [NJB, TNT], 'to adhere' [NEB], 'to cling' [BAGD, Lns], 'to be concerned with' [Herm].
  b. κατά with accusative object (LN 89.8): according to [WC], 'in accordance with' [NASB], 'in accord with' [Lns], '(which) accords with' [HNTC; TNT], '(which) agrees with' [TEV], 'in line with' [Hn], 'with respect to' [Herm], 'as' [KJV, NIV, RSV], 'in' [NAB].
  c. διδαχή (LN 33.224; 33.236): 'teaching' [BAGD, Herm, HNTC, LN; NASB], 'doctrine' [Hn, LN, Lns, WC; TEV, TNT], 'teaching' [LN], 'tradition' [NJB]. The phrase κατὰ τὴν διδαχὴν 'according to the teaching' is translated 'as it has been taught' [NIV], 'as he has been taught' [KJV], 'as taught' [RSV], 'in his teaching' [NAB]. The whole phrase is also conflated: 'he must adhere to the true doctrine' [NEB], 'he must have a firm grasp of the unchanging message of the tradition' [NJB].
  d. πιστός (LN 31.87; 71.17): 'faithful' [BAGD, LN, Lns, WC; KJV, NASB], 'trustworthy' [BAGD, Hn, HNTC, LN; NIV], 'which can be trusted' [TEV, TNT], 'reliable' [Herm], 'sure' [LN; RSV], 'true' [NEB], 'authentic' [NAB], 'unchanging' [NJB].
  e. λόγος (LN 33.98; 33.260; 33.99): 'word' [Hn, HNTC, LN, Lns; KJV, NASB, RSV, TNT], 'message' [LN; NAB, NIV, NJB, TEV], 'what is preached' [LN], 'doctrine' [WC; NEB], 'preaching' [Herm].

QUESTION—What relationship is indicated by the participial form ἀντεχόμενον 'holding firmly'?
  It is attributive, further describing the requirements for an overseer [Bg, EBC, HNTC]: (he must be) one who holds fast to the word.

QUESTION—What is meant by 'holding firmly to the word'?
  It means to defend and to urge acceptance of the word [Bg], to hold it firmly [My] against anyone who would take it away or oppose it [Blm, EBC, EGT, TNTC], to be devoted to it [El, GNC, Hn], to be convinced of the truth of the message [HNTC, SSA].

QUESTION—How is the prepositional phrase κατὰ τὴν διδαχήν 'according to the teaching' related to its context?
  1. The prepositional phrase modifies the noun λόγου 'word' [Alf, Bg, Blm, EBC, EGT, El, Hn, HNTC, ICC, Lg, Lns, My, NCB, SSA, TC, TG, WC; NASB, TEV, TNT]: he must hold firmly to the trustworthy word, which is in harmony with the teaching.
  2. The prepositional phrase modifies the adjective πιστοῦ 'faithful' [Herm, ICC]: he must hold firmly to the word that is faithful in regards to the teaching. Here 'word' is taken to mean the overseer's preaching [Herm, ICC].

QUESTION—What relationship is indicated by κατά 'according to'?
  It indicates the measure or standard for the word [Alf, Hn, SSA, TC]: the word which is in harmony with the teaching.

QUESTION—What is the meaning of διδαχή 'teaching'?

It refers to the body of teaching which he has received, not the action of teaching which he is to do [Alf, Blm, EBC, EGT, El, My, SSA, TC]: the word that is in harmony with the teaching he has received.

### in-order-that[a] he-may-be able[b]

LEXICON—a. ἵνα (LN 89.59, 89.49): 'in order that' [Hn, WC], 'so that' [HNTC, Lns; NAB, NIV, NJB, RSV], 'that' [KJV, NASB], 'so' [TNT], 'in this way' [TEV].

b. δυνατός (LN **74.2**; **74.4**): 'able' [BAGD, Herm, Hn, HNTC, LN, Lns, WC; KJV, NAB, NASB, RSV, TEV, TNT], 'well able' [NEB], 'specially competent' [LN]. The phrase δυνατὸς ᾖ 'he may be able' is translated 'he can' [NIV], 'he can be counted on' [NJB].

QUESTION—What relationship is indicated by ἵνα 'in order that'?

It indicates the purpose for which the overseer should hold fast to the word [EBC, GNC, Hn, Lns, My, NCB, TC]: holding fast to the word in order that he, by teaching, may be able to exhort and refute.

### both to-exhort[a] by/in[b] the healthy[c] teaching[d]

LEXICON—a. pres. act. infin. of παρακαλέω (LN 25.150): 'to exhort' [BAGD, HNTC, Lns, WC; KJV, NASB], 'to encourage' [BAGD, Hn, LN; NAB, NIV, TEV], 'to offer encouragement' [TNT], 'to give encouragement' [NJB], 'to give instruction' [RSV], 'to move' [NEB], 'to give instructions' [Herm].

b. ἐν with dative object (LN 89.76; 89.84; 89.141): 'by' [KJV, NIV, TNT], 'by means of' [Hn], 'in' [Herm, Lns; NASB, NJB, RSV], 'with' [WC; NEB, TEV], 'on the basis of' [HNTC]. The phrase παρακαλεῖν ἐν τῇ διδασκαλίᾳ τῇ ὑγιαινούσῃ 'to exhort by/in the healthy teaching' is translated 'to encourage men to follow sound doctrine' [NAB].

c. pres. act. participle of ὑγιαίνω (LN 23.129): 'sound' [BAGD, Herm, Hn, HNTC; all versions except NEB, TEV], 'wholesome' [NEB], 'true' [TEV], 'to be healthy' [BAGD, LN], 'healthful' [Lns], 'morally healthful' [WC].

d. διδασκαλία (LN 33.224; 33.236): 'teaching' [BAGD, Hn, LN, Lns, WC; NEB, TEV, TNT], 'doctrine' [HNTC, LN; KJV, NAB, NASB, NIV, NJB, RSV].

QUESTION—What relationship is indicated by καί...καί 'both...and'?

It indicates prominence for both 'exhort' and 'refute' [EBC, El, My, NCB]: both to exhort and to refute.

QUESTION—What relationship is indicated by ἐν 'by/in'?

1. It indicates the means by which the exhortation is made [Blm, EBC, El, Hn, Lg(D), My]: to exhort by the healthy teaching.
2. It indicates the element within which the exhortation takes place [Alf, Lns, SSA, TC, TNTC, WC]: to exhort in the aspect of healthy teaching.
3. It indicates the basis of the exhortation [HNTC]: to exhort on the basis of sound doctrine.

QUESTION—What is meant by a 'healthy' teaching?
It means that the teaching is true [SSA; TEV], or spiritually beneficial [Alf, EBC, NCB], free from error and anything that would hinder its operation [Lg, NCB]. It is teaching that promotes spiritual health [EBC].

**and the-(ones) opposing[a] to refute.[b]**
LEXICON—a. pres. act. participle of ἀντιλέγω (LN 33.455): 'to contradict' [BAGD, Hn; NAB, NASB, RSV], 'to oppose' [LN; NIV], 'to be opposed to' [TEV], 'to argue against' [NJB], 'to speak against' [BAGD, Lns], 'to gainsay' [WC]. Some render the participle as a substantive: 'gainsayers' [KJV], 'objectors' [HNTC; NEB], 'opponents' [Herm; TNT].
b. pres. act. infin. of ἐλέγχω (LN 33.417): 'to refute' [Hn, HNTC; NAB, NASB, NIV, NJB], 'to rebuke' [LN], 'to convict' [BAGD, Herm, Lns], 'to confute' [NEB, RSV], 'to defeat' [TNT], 'to show the error' [TEV], 'to convince' [BAGD; KJV], 'to carry conviction to' [WC].
QUESTION—What is the meaning of ἐλέγχειν 'to refute'?
It means to show that they are wrong [EBC, NCB], to correct and reprove them [My], to convict them of their error [EBC, Lns, NCB], to enable them, if possible, to see their error and repent [Hn, WC].

**DISCOURSE UNIT: 1:10–16** [Alf, EBC, EGT, GNC, Herm, Hn, HNTC, MNTC, NCBC, TC, TNTC, WC; NJB]. The topic is the false teachers [Alf, HNTC, TNTC, WC], the false teachers and what they taught [ICC, MNTC], the false teachers and what Titus should do concerning them [TC], refuting those who teach false doctrine [EBC; NJB], exhortation against false teachers in Crete [Herm], condemnation of false teachers and a quotation from a Cretan writer [NCBC], description of the character of the false teachers and of the Cretans generally [WC], warnings concerning heretical teachings [GNC].

**1:10** For
LEXICON—γάρ (LN 89.23): 'for' [Herm, Hn, HNTC, Lns, WC; KJV, NASB, NIV, RSV, TEV], 'and in fact' [NJB]; not explicit [NAB, NEB, TNT].
QUESTION—What relationship is indicated by this word?
1. It introduces the reason for appointing church officials who have the qualities mentioned in 1:7–9 [EBC, GNC, Hn, HNTC, IB, ICC, Lg, My(D), NCB]: appoint men with blameless character and the ability to teach and refute, because there are many people who are insubordinate, etc.
2. It introduces the reason for referring to τοὺς ἀντιλέγοντας 'the opposers' in 1:9 [Alf, El, TC]: I spoke of refuting the opposers, because there are many who are insubordinate.
3. It gives the reason for urging Titus to refute those who oppose (1:9) [EGT].

**there-are many and insubordinate,[a] empty-talkers[b] and mind-deceivers,[c]**
TEXT—Some manuscripts omit καί 'even/and'. GNT includes this word in brackets, with a C rating, indicating a considerable degree of doubt. Two

commentators include καί [Alf, El], but most omit it [Blm, Brt, EBC, EGT, GNC, Herm, Hn, HNTC, Lg, Lns, MNTC, TC, WC; NAB, NASB, NIV, NJB, RSV, TEV, TNT] (the text of others is unclear).

LEXICON—a. ἀνυπότακτος 'undisciplined' [BAGD; TNT], 'disobedient' [LN]. This adjective is also translated as a verb: 'to rebel' [TEV]. This word refers to persons who were disobedient both in doctrine and in behavior [Blm, TG], who refuse to submit to authority [Lg, Lns, SSA]; who refuse to submit to the gospel and oppose it [Hn, My].

b. ματαιολόγος (LN) 'empty talker' [LN, WC; NAB, NASB, RSV], 'vain talker' [KJV], 'idle talker' [BAGD, Lns], 'futile talker' [Hn, HNTC], 'foolish talker' [Herm], 'mere talker' [NIV]. This substantive is also translated as a verb: 'to talk wildly' [NEB], 'to talk nonsense' [NJB]. They are men who engage in foolish questions, genealogies, etc. [Lg(D)]. They teach fictitious stories about the patriarchs, which serves no useful purpose [Hn].

c. φρεναπάτης (LN 31.13): 'mind-deceiver' [Hn, Lns], 'deceiver of men's minds' [WC], 'deceiver' [BAGD, Herm, HNTC, LN; KJV, NAB, NASB, NIV, RSV]. This substantive is also translated as a verb: 'to lead men's minds astray' [NEB], 'to try to make others believe nonsense' [NJB].

QUESTION—What relationship is indicated by καί 'and' ?

Καί often joins πολύς 'much/many' when there is a following adjective [Alf, El, My], that is, it joins a quantitative adjective with a qualitative adjective [SSA]: there are many (and) insubordinate people. The inclusion or omission of καί makes no significant difference in meaning [SSA].

QUESTION—What is the relationship between the three words 'insubordinate', 'empty talkers', and 'mind-deceivers'?

1. The word 'insubordinate' is described by the two following substantives [Bg, El, GNC]: they are insubordinate; that is, they are empty talkers and deceivers.
2. In addition to being insubordinate these people are empty talkers, and as a result they are deceivers of men's minds [HNTC]: they are insubordinate and empty talkers with the result that they are deceivers.
3. These people are described here by three coordinate terms [EBC, Hn, MNTC, My, SSA, TNTC]: they are insubordinate, empty talkers, and deceivers.

**especially[a] the-ones of[b] the circumcision,[c]**

LEXICON—a. μάλιστα (LN 78.7): 'especially' [BAGD, Herm, Hn, HNTC, LN, Lns, WC; all versions except KJV, NJB], 'specially' [KJV], 'particularly' [LN; NJB].

b. ἐκ with genitive object (LN 63.20): 'of' [Herm, Hn, HNTC; KJV, NASB, NIV, NJB], 'from' [BAGD, WC], 'from among' [NAB]. The phrase ἐκ τῆς περιτομῆς 'of the circumcision' is translated 'among Jewish converts' [NEB], 'among the Jewish converts' [TNT], 'the converts from Judaism' [TEV], 'the circumcision party' [RSV], 'the circumcised' [Lns].

c. περιτομή (LN 11.51): 'circumcision' [BAGD, Herm, HNTC, WC; KJV, NASB, NJB], 'those who insisted on circumcision' [LN], 'circumcision party' [Hn], 'circumcision group' [NIV], 'Jewish convert' [NAB].

QUESTION—What is the meaning of μάλιστα 'especially'?

It means that these people were mostly of this group, but some (not many, however [EGT]) were from other groups as well [Alf, Blm, EBC, HNTC, ICC, Lg, MNTC, My, TC, WC]. One commentator says that this word carries no implication about other groups, but rather that it functions as an explanation in the sense of 'I mean' [GNC].

QUESTION—Who are 'the ones of the circumcision'?

They are Jewish Christians [Alf, EBC, EGT, El, GNC, Hn, HNTC, ICC, Lg, MNTC, My, NCB, NCBC, Rb, TC, TG, WC] with Gnostic tendencies [Rb], not unconverted Jews [Alf]. They were Cretans, but their teachings had a Jewish character [HNTC]. One commentator, on the other hand, identifies them as Gentile Christians of the second century who were attracted to Jewish practices [IB].

**1:11** whom it-is-necessary to-stop-the-mouth,[a]

LEXICON—a. pres. act. infin. of ἐπιστομίζω (LN **33.124**): 'to stop the mouth' [BAGD, Hn, HNTC, WC; KJV], 'to gag' [Lns], 'to silence' [Herm, LN; NAB, NASB, NIV, NJB, RSV, TNT], 'to curb' [NEB], 'to stop their talk' [TEV].

QUESTION—How was Titus to stop the mouths of the false teachers?

He was to refute their teachings [Blm, EGT] by properly presenting the true teachings [EBC, TNTC], by admonishing them lovingly and telling them to stop their teachings [Hn], and, if necessary, by using his episcopal authority to prevent them from teaching in the churches [Blm, EBC, Hn]. Or, he was to have the elders prevent them from teaching in the churches [IB, Lns], perhaps by excommunication [Hn, NCBC].

**who are-upsetting[a] whole[b] households[c]**

LEXICON—a. pres. act. indic. of ἀνατρέπω (LN **31.72**): 'to subvert' [KJV], 'to upset' [Hn, HNTC, LN; NAB, NASB, NJB, RSV, TEV, TNT], 'to turn upside down' [Lns], 'overturn' [BAGD, WC], 'to ruin' [Herm; NEB, NIV].

b. ὅλος (LN 63.1): 'whole' [BAGD, HNTC, LN, Lns, WC; all versions], 'entire' [BAGD, Herm, Hn, LN].

c. οἶκος (LN 10.8): 'household' [BAGD, HNTC, LN; NIV], 'family' [BAGD, Herm, Hn, LN; all versions except KJV, NIV], 'house' [KJV].

QUESTION—How is the pronoun οἵτινες 'who' related to the preceding clause?

It introduces the reason why the false teachers should be silenced [Alf, EBC, El, GNC, Hn, Lg, Lns, My, SSA, TC]: it is necessary to silence them because they are upsetting whole households.

QUESTION: How were the false teachers upsetting whole households?
1. They were turning entire families aside from the true faith [Blm, EBC, El, GNC, Hn, IB, Lg, My, SSA, TG, WC]; it is not that families are being upset by one or two of their members being led astray [GNC]: they are causing entire families to turn aside from the true faith.
2. They were upsetting whole families if they turned even one member of the family from the true faith [EGT, MNTC, TNTC]: they are upsetting whole families by turning aside some members of the families. It might be by setting family members at odds with one another [NCBC].

**teaching (things) which not it-is-necessary[a] for-the-sake-of[b] sordid[c] gain.[d]**
LEXICON—a. pres. act. indic. of δεῖ (LN 71.21): 'to be necessary' [BAGD], 'ought' [LN; KJV, NIV, NJB], 'must' [BAGD, Lns], 'should' [HNTC, LN, WC; NASB, NEB, TEV], 'to have a right' [NAB, RSV], 'to be becoming' [Herm], 'to be proper' [Hn]. The phrase διδάσκοντες ἃ μὴ δεῖ αἰσχροῦ κέρδους χάριν 'teaching things which it is not necessary for the sake of sordid gain' is translated 'shamelessly teaching error for the sake of money' [TNT].
  b. χάριν (LN 89.60; 89.29): 'for the sake of' [BAGD, Herm, Hn, HNTC, LN, Lns, WC; NASB, NIV, NJB, TNT], 'for' [NAB, NEB, RSV], 'for the purpose of' [LN; TEV], 'because of' [LN].
  c. αἰσχρός (LN 88.150): 'filthy' [KJV], 'sordid' [HNTC; NAB, NASB, NEB, NJB], 'shameful' [BAGD, Hn, LN, Lns], 'disgraceful' [LN], 'base' [BAGD, WC; RSV], 'dishonest' [Herm; NIV]. The phrase αἰσχροῦ κέρδους χάριν 'for the sake of sordid gain' is translated 'and all for the shameful purpose of making money' [TEV].
  d. κέρδος (LN **57.192**): 'gain' [BAGD, Herm, LN, WC; NAB, NASB, NEB, NIV, NJB, RSV], 'profit' [Hn, HNTC, Lns], 'lucre' [KJV].
QUESTION—What is meant by μὴ δεῖ 'it is not necessary'?
  It is a litotes [Blm], meaning things which ought not be taught [EBC, Lns, My, NCB, Rb, SSA, TC, TNTC]: things which must not be taught.
QUESTION—What is the significance of the use of μή rather than οὐ for 'not'?
  Μή is used instead of οὐ because the statement is one of subjective judgment rather than objective fact [EGT, El]: things which from the point of view of orthodox Christianity ought not be taught.
QUESTION—What is meant by αἰσχροῦ κέρδους 'sordid gain'?
  It refers to the false teachers' appeal for financial support [EGT, MNTC, NCBC, SSA]: they are teaching in order to get money from their hearers. Their motivation was not to promote their teachings but simply selfish gain [El, GNC, ICC, Lg, My, NCB, SSA, TC, TG, TNTC], even when this meant the spiritual ruin of others [Hn]. The gain is sordid because of the sordid means by which it was acquired [My]. Perhaps they charged fees for their teaching or expected gifts from their followers [MNTC].

**1:12** Said someone of<sup>a</sup> them, a-prophet<sup>b</sup> their-own of-them:
LEXICON—a. ἐκ with genitive object (LN 63.20): 'of' [Herm, Hn, HNTC, Lns; all versions except NAB, TEV], 'from among' [WC]. The phrase τις ἐξ αὐτῶν 'someone of them' is translated 'a man of Crete' [NAB], 'a Cretan himself' [TEV].

b. προφήτης (LN 53.79): 'prophet' [BAGD, Herm, Hn, HNTC, LN, Lns, WC; all versions].

QUESTION—What relationship is indicated by the preposition ἐξ 'of (them)'?
The preposition ἐκ is partitive here [Lns] and means that the prophet referred to was a Cretan [Alf, Bg, El, ICC, MNTC, My, NCBC, SSA, TG, TNTC]: someone who was one of the Cretans. This does not mean that the prophet was a member of the congregation [Alf]. Because he was one of them, he ought to know whether his characterization of Cretans was true [Lns].

QUESTION—What is implied by the phrase ἴδιος αὐτῶν 'their own of them'?
It implies that he was one of them; 'their own' emphasizes that he was not from another country [El]. This, with the preceding 'someone of them' gives a further emphasis to the fact that it was a Cretan describing his own people [My]. One commentator, however, states that the addition of αὐτῶν 'of them' merely shows that the meaning of ἴδιος 'their own' had weakened and required the pronoun to give the full sense [Herm].

QUESTION—What is meant by προφήτης 'prophet'?
It means that he did have, or was believed to have, prophetic power [Alf, Bg, Blm, Brt, CBC, EBC, EGT, El, GNC, Herm, Hn, HNTC, ICC, NCBC, SSA, WC], or that he was a prophet in a popular but incorrect sense [Hn, Lg], or that he was a prophet because he correctly described the Cretan character as it was in Paul's time [ICC, My]. This does not necessarily imply that Paul considered him a true prophet of God [Hn, WC]. Most identify the prophet as Epimenides who lived about 500 B.C. [Bg, Blm, Brt, CBC, EBC, EGT, GNC, Herm, Hn, HNTC, ICC, Lg, Lns, MNTC, NCB, Rb, TC, TNTC, WC].

**Cretans (are) always liars<sup>a</sup>, evil<sup>b</sup> beasts<sup>c</sup>, idle<sup>d</sup> bellies.<sup>e</sup>**
LEXICON—a. ψεύστης (LN 33.255): 'liar' [BAGD, Herm, HNTC, LN, Lns, WC; all versions], 'deceiver' [Hn].

b. κακός (LN 88.106): 'evil' [BAGD, Hn, LN, WC; KJV, NASB, NIV, RSV], 'wicked' [TEV, TNT], 'vicious' [NEB], 'base' [Lns], 'pernicious' [BAGD, HNTC], 'harmful' [LN], 'dangerous' [BAGD; NJB]; not explicit [Herm; NAB].

c. θηρίον (LN **88.119**): 'beast' [BAGD, HNTC, LN, Lns, WC; KJV, NAB, NASB, RSV, TEV, TNT], 'brute' [Herm, Hn; NEB, NIV], 'animal' [NJB].

d. ἀργός (LN **88.248**): 'slow' [KJV], 'lazy' [BAGD, HNTC, LN, Lns, WC; NAB, NASB, NEB, NIV, RSV, TEV], 'loitering' [Herm], 'idle' [BAGD], 'inactive' [Hn]. The phrase γαστέρες ἀργαί 'idle bellies' is translated 'all greed and laziness' [NJB], 'gluttonous idlers' [TNT].

e. γαστήρ (LN **23.192**): 'belly' [BAGD, Hn, HNTC, Lns, WC; KJV], 'glutton' [BAGD, Herm, LN; NAB, NASB, NEB, NIV, RSV, TEV].

QUESTION—What is meant by κακὰ θηρία 'evil beasts'?

It refers to the people's boorishness [HNTC], their brutish and untamed character [Blm, EBC, El, Herm, Hn, Lg, MNTC, My, TNTC]: they are wild and brutish in their character.

QUESTION—What is meant by γαστέρες ἀργαί 'idle bellies'?

It means that they were lazy [Lns, TG, WC] and also gluttonous [Alf, Blm, EBC, El, Hn, Lg, MNTC, My, WC]. They were greedy [HNTC, TG, TNTC], they loved pleasure [Herm]. One commentator states that it refers to the protruding stomach of such persons [EGT].

**1:13** This testimony[a] is true.[b]

LEXICON—a. μαρτυρία (LN 33.264): 'testimony' [BAGD, Herm, Hn, HNTC, LN, Lns, WC; NASB, NIV, RSV], 'witness' [LN; KJV], 'statement' [NJB]. This noun is also translated as a verb: 'to tell' [NEB], 'to speak' [TEV].

b. ἀληθής (LN 72.1): 'true' [BAGD, Herm, Hn, LN, Lns, WC; KJV, NASB, NIV, RSV, TNT], 'correct' [HNTC]. This adjective is also translated as a noun: 'the truth' [NEB, TEV], 'the simple truth' [NAB].

QUESTION—What does this statement imply?

It implies that Paul's experience (or possibly the common opinion) confirmed the statement he had just quoted [EBC, El, Hn, IB, MNTC, Rb, TNTC]: I have found out that that quotation is true. The false teachers themselves were evidence that the quotation was still true [GNC, Lns]. He does not imply that the description applies to all church members [Lns].

**On-account-of[a] which cause[b] reprove[c] them sharply,[d]**

LEXICON—a. διά with accusative object (LN 89.26): 'for' [Lns, WC; NASB, TEV]. The phrase δι' ἥν 'on account of which cause' is translated 'wherefore' [KJV], 'all the more reason why' [NEB], 'therefore' [Herm, Hn, HNTC; NIV, RSV], 'so' [NJB, TNT], not explicit [NAB].

b. αἰτία (LN 89.15): 'cause' [BAGD, LN, Lns, WC; NASB], 'reason' [BAGD, LN; TEV].

c. pres. act. impera. of ἐλέγχω (LN 33.417): 'to rebuke' [KJV, NIV, RSV, TEV, TNT], 'to rebuke so as to convince' [WC], 'to convince' [BAGD], 'to reprove' [Hn, HNTC; NASB], 'to admonish' [Herm; NAB], 'to convict' [BAGD, Lns], 'to pull up' [NEB], 'to correct' [NJB].

d. ἀποτόμως (LN 88.74): 'sharply' [Hn, HNTC, Lns, WC; all versions except NASB, NJB], 'severely' [BAGD; NASB], 'strictly' [Herm], 'harshly' [LN]. The phrase ἔλεγχε αὐτοὺς ἀποτόμως 'reprove them sharply' is translated 'be severe in correcting them' [NJB].

QUESTION—What relationship is indicated by the phrase δι' ἣν αἰτίαν 'on account of which cause'?
  This phrase indicates an exhortation based on the situation described in 1:10 [EBC, El, SSA, TC]: because of the situation I have just described, therefore reprove them.
QUESTION—What is implied by ἐλέγχω 'reprove'?
  It implies an attempt to bring them to soundness in the faith [Alf, EGT, El, HNTC, NCB]: rebuke them in order to help them. It implies pointing out the error of the false teachings [EBC, SSA]. The present tense of the verb indicates that they are to keep on reproving them [Lns].
QUESTION—To whom does αὐτούς 'them' refer?
  1. It refers to the believers in general [Alf, Lns, My]: rebuke the believers. The believers were not resisting the false teachers as they should [My].
  2. It refers to the false teachers [HNTC, NCBC, TC, TG, TNTC]: rebuke the false teachers.
  3. It includes all who need reproving, both the teachers and the church members (who were listening to the false teachers) [EBC, El, GNC, Hn, SSA]: rebuke both the teachers and those who are listening to them. Some take this to be directed primarily the teachers [GNC]; others, primarily to those who were being influenced by the teachers [EBC, El].

**in-order-that[a] they-may-be-healthy[b] in[c] the faith,[d]**
LEXICON—a. ἵνα (LN 89.59): 'in order that' [BAGD, Hn, WC], 'so that' [BAGD, HNTC, Lns; NEB, NIV, TEV, TNT], 'that' [Herm; KJV, NASB, RSV], 'in an attempt to' [NAB], not explicit [NJB].
  b. pres. act. subj. of ὑγιαίνω (LN 23.129): 'to be healthy' [BAGD, LN, Lns], 'to be morally healthy' [WC], 'to be sound' [BAGD, Hn, HNTC; KJV, NASB, NIV, RSV], 'to remain sound' [TNT], 'to be well' [LN]. The phrase ὑγιαίνωσιν ἐν τῇ πίστει 'they may be healthy in the faith' is translated 'they may come to a sane belief' [NEB], 'they may come to the sound faith' [Herm], 'they may have a healthy faith' [TEV], 'to keep them close to sound faith' [NAB].
  c. ἐν with dative object (LN 89.5): 'in' [Hn, HNTC, Lns, WC; KJV, NASB, NIV, NJB, RSV, TNT], not explicit [NAB, TEV].
  d. πίστις (LN 31.104): 'faith' [BAGD, Hn, HNTC, LN, Lns, WC; all versions except NEB], 'belief' [NEB].
QUESTION—What relationship is indicated by ἵνα 'in order that'?
  It introduces the purpose (or contemplated result) of the rebuke [Alf, EBC, EGT, El, GNC, Lns, My, TC, TNTC]: rebuke them in order that they may be healthy in the faith.
QUESTION—What is implied by the present tense of the verb ὑγιαίνωσιν 'they may be healthy'?
  The present tense refers to continued spiritual health [EBC, Lns]: in order that they may continue to be healthy. However, some take the verb to imply that they are not spiritually healthy but should become so [Hn, NCB, TG].

QUESTION—What is implied by the phrase ἐν τῇ πίστει 'in the faith'?

It is in the area of Christian beliefs that they were to be healthy [Alf, EBC, El, Lg, Lns, My, NCB, SSA, TC, TNTC]. It refers to the true teachings of the gospel [EBC].

**1:14** not paying-attention[a] to-Jewish myths[b] and commandments[c] of-men[d] rejecting[e] the truth.

LEXICON—a. pres. act. participle of προσέχω (LN 30.35): 'to give heed' [BAGD, Lns; KJV, RSV], 'to pay heed' [HNTC], 'to pay attention' [BAGD, LN; NASB, NIV], 'to give attention' [WC], 'to take notice' [NJB, TNT], 'to lend ears' [NEB], 'to consider carefully' [LN], 'to hold on' [TEV], 'to follow' [BAGD, Herm], 'to be affected' [NAB], 'to devote oneself' [Hn]. The present tense indicates that they are people who habitually turn away [Alf, EBC, SSA] or who were in the process of turning away [Alf]. It means primarily that they should stop paying attention to these false teachings if they are listening to them, and also that they should not pay attention to them if they have not yet done so [SSA].

b. μῦθος (LN 33.13): 'fable' [BAGD, Herm, HNTC, LN, WC; KJV, TNT], 'myth' [BAGD, Hn, LN, Lns; NAB, NASB, NEB, NIV, NJB, RSV], 'legend' [LN; TEV], 'story' [LN].

c. ἐντολή (LN 33.330): 'commandment' [BAGD, Herm, LN, Lns; KJV, NASB, NEB, TEV], 'command' [BAGD; NIV, RSV], 'order' [LN; NJB], 'injunction' [Hn] 'rule' [HNTC; NAB], 'instruction' [TNT], 'precept' [WC].

d. ἄνθρωπος (LN 9.1): 'man' [Herm, Hn, HNTC, Lns, WC; KJV, NAB, NASB, RSV, TNT], 'mankind' [LN], 'people' [LN; NJB], 'those' [NIV], 'human' [TEV], 'merely human origin' [NEB].

e. pres. mid. participle of ἀποστρέφω (LN **31.62**): 'to turn from' [KJV], 'to turn aside from' [WC], 'to turn away from' [BAGD, Lns; NASB, NJB], 'to swerve from' [NAB], 'to turn one's back on' [Herm, Hn], 'to turn one's back upon' [NEB], 'to reject' [BAGD, HNTC, LN; NIV, RSV, TEV, TNT].

QUESTION—What does the phrase Ἰουδαϊκοῖς μύθοις 'Jewish myths' refer to?

It may refer to the beginnings of Gnostic mythologies [Alf, Brt, NCBC]. They are probably similar to the "interminable fables" referred to in 1 Tim. 1:4 [HNTC]. They may be gnostic or fanciful expansions of Old Testament stories [CBC, IB, TNTC], fanciful stories similar to those of apocryphal Judaism [EBC, MNTC, My] about Jewish ancestors [Hn, Lns], Jewish oral traditions [Rb], or other ascetic prohibitions [EGT, El]. They are contrasted with the truth [Bg, SSA].

QUESTION—How are the two nouns related in the genitive construction ἐντολαῖς ἀνθρώπων 'commandments of men'?

Men are the source or authors of the commands [EGT, Hn, MNTC, NCB, SSA, TG; NAB, NEB]: commands which have their source in men rather

TITUS 1:14

than in God/Scripture. They are commands imposed by men [GNC, HNTC], the interpretations of men [ICC] in the Jewish Halakah [NCBC].

QUESTION—What 'commandments of men' are meant?

The commandments are probably prohibitions concerning food, marriage, and other ritual observances [Alf, EBC, HNTC, IB, ICC, Lg(D), My, NCB, TC]. They are to be rejected because they are not in harmony with Scripture and because of the character of the teachers [EBC].

QUESTION—What relationship is indicated by the participial form ἀποστρεφομένων 'turning away'?

It describes the people referred to [Alf, Lg(D); all versions]: men who turn away from the truth. They habitually reject the truth of the gospel [EBC, Lns, MNTC, NCB], or they have rejected the truth [GNC, Lns].

QUESTION—What is 'the truth' mentioned here?

It is the truth taught in the gospel [EBC, Lns, MNTC, NCB, Rb, TG].

**1:15** All-things (are) pure[a] in-reference-to-the[b] pure-(persons);[c]

LEXICON—a. καθαρός (LN 53.29): 'pure' [BAGD, Herm, Hn, HNTC, LN; all versions except NAB], 'clean' [BAGD, LN, Lns, WC; NAB].
  b. dative case of τοῖς καθαροῖς 'the pure': 'in reference to', 'for' [Herm, HNTC, WC], 'to' [Hn, Lns; all versions except KJV], 'unto' [KJV].
  c. καθαρός (LN 53.29): 'pure'. The substantive τοῖς καθαροῖς 'the pure' is translated 'the pure' [HNTC; KJV, NASB, NEB, NIV, RSV], 'those who are pure' [Herm, Hn; NJB, TEV, TNT], 'the clean' [Lns, WC; NAB].

QUESTION—What is the significance of the dative case of τοῖς καθαροῖς 'in reference to the clean'?

  1. This dative of reference is translated by most as 'to' [Hn, Lns; all versions], and implies the meaning 'in the estimation of': all things are pure in the estimation of pure people, but in the estimation of defiled people nothing is pure.
  2. It means 'for the use of' [Alf, EGT, El, SSA, TC, WC]: all things used by pure people are pure, but nothing used by defiled people is pure.

QUESTION—What is meant by καθαρός 'pure'?

  1. It has two meanings: it has a ritual or ceremonial meaning when referring to all things, and a moral meaning when referring to people [Alf, Blm, EBC, GNC, Herm, Hn, HNTC, IB, Lg, MNTC, NCB, SSA, TG, WC]: all things are ritually pure/clean to/in reference to morally pure people, but nothing is ritually pure/clean to/in reference to morally defiled people. The things referred to are things connected with the commandments of men (1:14), such as clean and unclean categories of food, utensils, etc. [Alf, Blm, CBC, GNC, Hn, HNTC, IB, Lg, NCB, TG]. Some commentators think that in the contrast, the reference to things extends to both uses of pure [HNTC, SSA]: but nothing is ritually or morally pure to morally defiled people.

2. It means 'morally pure' in all cases [Lns]: all things are morally pure in reference to morally pure people, but to morally defiled people nothing is morally pure.

**but to-the defiled<sup>a</sup> and unbelieving<sup>b</sup> (persons) nothing (is) pure,<sup>c</sup>**

LEXICON—a. perf. pass. participle of μιαίνω (LN **88.260**): 'to defile' [BAGD]. The substantive τοῖς μεμιαμμένοις 'the defiled' is translated 'those who are defiled' [Herm, LN; KJV, NASB, TEV, TNT], 'defiled (unbelievers)' [NAB], 'the corrupt' [RSV], 'those who are corrupted' [NIV, NJB], 'those who are contaminated' [Hn], 'those who are polluted' [HNTC, WC], 'those who have been stained with filth' [Lns], 'tainted (minds)' [NEB].

b. ἄπιστος (LN 31.98): 'unbelieving' [BAGD], 'to be unbelieving' [LN]. The substantive phrase τοῖς…ἀπίστοις is translated 'the unbelieving' [Lns; RSV], 'unbelievers' [NAB, NEB], 'those who are unbelieving' [Hn, HNTC; KJV, TEV, TNT], 'those who do not believe' [Herm; NIV], 'those who are without faith' [WC], 'those who lack faith' [NJB].

c. καθαρός (LN 53.29): 'pure' [BAGD, Herm, Hn, HNTC, LN; all versions except NAB], 'clean' [BAGD, LN, Lns, WC; NAB].

QUESTION—What is implied by this clause?
Since uncleanness defiles their thoughts and actions, nothing is pure for them [Alf, Bg, Blm, EGT, Hn, HNTC, Lg, My]. Their calling morally neutral things impure reveals the impure character of the teachers [EBC].

QUESTION—Who are the ἀπίστοις 'unbelievers'?
1. They are those who reject Jesus and the gospel message [GNC, Lg(D), My, SSA, TNTC], or people who totally reject God, not merely unbelievers [MNTC], or people who have no faith [El]: to those who do not believe in Christ/God.
2. They are weak Jewish Christians who do not believe that Christ is the end of the law [ICC, NCB]: to those who lack faith to put aside Jewish ritual regulations about food.

**but is-defiled<sup>a</sup> of-them both the mind<sup>b</sup> and the conscience.<sup>c</sup>**

LEXICON—a. perf. pass. indic. of μιαίνω (LN 88.260): 'to be defiled' [BAGD, Herm, LN; KJV, NASB, TEV, TNT], 'to be corrupted' [NIV, RSV], 'to be polluted' [HNTC, WC], 'to be contaminated' [Hn, LN], 'to be stained with filth' [Lns], 'to be tainted' [NAB, NEB], 'to be morally filthy' [LN]. The verb is also translated as a noun: 'corruption' [NJB].

b. νοῦς (LN 26.14): 'mind' [BAGD, Herm, Hn, LN, Lns; all versions except NEB], 'intelligence' [HNTC], 'reason' [NEB]. It is the sphere of practical reason [My]; it includes the will as well as the thoughts [El, Hn, Lns, WC], the entire bent of a man's inner life [Lg].

c. συνείδησις (LN 26.13): 'conscience' [BAGD, Herm, Hn, HNTC, LN, Lns, WC; all versions], 'moral sensitivity' [LN]. It is the source of moral evaluation of an action [My].

QUESTION—What is implied by this clause?

Their ability to make judgments is perverted and their conscience is hardened [ICC]: their mind and conscience are defiled so that they are unable to make proper moral judgments.

**1:16 God they-profess<sup>a</sup> to-know,<sup>b</sup>**

LEXICON—a. pres. act. indic. of ὁμολογέω (LN 33.221; 33.274): 'to profess' [Hn, HNTC, Lns; KJV, NASB, NEB, RSV, TNT], 'to declare' [LN], 'to claim' [Herm; NAB, NIV, NJB, TEV], 'to assert' [LN], 'to confess outwardly and publicly' [BAGD, WC].

b. perf. (with pres. meaning) act. infin. of οἶδα (LN 28.1): 'to know' [BAGD, Herm, Hn, HNTC, LN, Lns, WC; all versions except NEB], 'to acknowledge' [NEB]. The verb indicates a claim to intuitive and direct knowledge [Hn].

QUESTION—What relationship is indicated by this clause?

This clause is an expansion of the preceding clause, showing that they are lying willfully [Alf]: (I will also say the following about these people). Or, it indicates the grounds for the charge that they are unbelievers (1:15) [Blm].

QUESTION—What is implied by the verb ὁμολογοῦσιν 'they confess/ profess'?

Some commentators say that this is a sincere profession, but that the behavior of these people shows that their sincerity is mistaken [Alf]. Other commentators say that this is a false profession intended to deceive others [TNTC]. Still others say that Paul does not intend to indicate the sincerity of their profession one way or the other [Lg, My].

QUESTION—What relationship is indicated by the infinitive form εἰδέναι 'to know'?

It expresses the indirect statement of what they profess [Rb]: they profess that they know God.

QUESTION—What is meant by θεὸν εἰδέναι 'to know God'?

It means to be intimately related to him [EBC], to be well informed about him [EBC, ICC], and to know all the truth relating to him [GNC].

**but by-the works<sup>a</sup> they-deny,<sup>b</sup>**

LEXICON—a. ἔργον (LN 42.11): 'work' [Herm, Lns, WC; KJV, NJB], 'action' [Hn, HNTC; NAB, NEB, NIV, TEV, TNT], 'deed' [LN; NASB, RSV], 'act' [LN].

b. pres. mid. (deponent = act.) indic. of ἀρνέομαι (LN 34.48; 36.43): 'to deny' [BAGD, Herm, Hn, HNTC, LN, Lns, WC; all versions], 'to reject' [LN]. The implied meaning is not that they are overtly denying God, but that their evil deeds are evidence that they do not actually know God [SSA].

QUESTION—What is the significance of the dative case of τοῖς ἔργοις 'by the works'?

This dative is instrumental [Rb]: they deny him/it by means of their works.

QUESTION—What is the implied object of the verb ἀρνοῦνται 'they deny'?
1. The object is God [Alf, Bg, El, Herm, Lg(D), Lns, SSA; all versions except TEV]: by their actions they deny God. One takes it to mean that they specifically deny the existence of God [NAB].
2. The object is their claim [GNC, Hn, IB, Lg, My, TG; TEV]: by their actions they deny that they know God.

**being abominable[a] and disobedient[b] and with-respect-to[c] every good work worthless.[d]**

LEXICON—a. βδελυκτός (LN **25.188**): 'abominable' [BAGD, Herm, Lns, WC; KJV], 'detestable' [BAGD, HNTC, LN, Lns; NASB, NIV, RSV], 'despicable' [Hn], 'disgusting' [NAB], 'hateful' [TEV]. The phrase βδελυκτοὶ ὄντες καὶ ἀπειθεῖς 'being abominable and disobedient' is translated 'they are outrageously rebellious' [NJB], 'They are thoroughly objectionable rebels' [TNT]. This entire phrase is translated 'Their detestable obstinacy disqualifies them for any good work' [NEB]. The word is used of something that is disgusting to God [El, GNC, HNTC, IB, Lg, My, TG], that which causes disgust because it is hypocritical [EBC, TNTC], despicable to God and to his people [Lns]; it describes the moral depravity of the heretics [My].

b. ἀπειθής (LN 36.24): 'disobedient' [BAGD, Herm, Hn, HNTC, LN, Lns, WC; KJV, NASB, NIV, RSV, TEV], 'intractable' [NAB].

c. πρός with accusative object (LN 89.7; 89.60): 'unto' [KJV], 'for' [Herm, Hn, HNTC, Lns; NASB, NIV, NJB, RSV, TNT], 'for the purpose of' [WC]. It means 'towards the accomplishing of' [Alf]. The phrase πρὸς πᾶν ἔργον ἀγαθὸν ἀδόκιμοι 'with respect to every good work rejected' is translated 'not fit to do anything good' [TEV], 'thoroughly incapable of any decent action' [NAB].

d. ἀδόκιμος (LN 65.13): 'worthless' [BAGD; NASB], 'valueless' [LN], 'useless' [Herm], 'quite useless' [TNT], 'unfit' [BAGD, Hn; NIV, RSV], 'quite untrustworthy' [NJB], 'disqualified' [HNTC], 'tested out as spurious' [Lns], 'reprobate' [KJV].

QUESTION—What relationship is indicated by the participle ὄντες 'being'?
1. It indicates the reason for their evil deeds [Hn]: they do evil deeds because they are abominable, disobedient and worthless with respect to every good work.
2. It indicates an additional evidential grounds for knowing that they do not know God [Lns, SSA]: it is true that they deny God, since they show it by their works and since they are abominable, disobedient, and worthless with respect to every good work.

QUESTION—In what way were they disobedient?
They disobeyed God [GNC, Herm, IB, TG, WC], God's word [EBC, HNTC, Lns, TC], God's law [Hn], the gospel [Lg], and church authority [IB].

TITUS 1:16 47

QUESTION—In what way were they worthless for every good work?
They were unfit for Christian service [Bg, HNTC, ICC] or for morally good works [EBC, GNC, MNTC, NCB, TG], unable to do anything that is based on faith [Hn].

**DISCOURSE UNIT: 2:1–3:11** [Alf]. The topic is various directions to Titus.

**DISCOURSE UNIT: 2:1–15** [EBC, GNT, ICC; NASB, NIV, TEV]. The topic is the natural groups among the believers [EBC], duties which must be taught to older and younger believers [NASB, NIV], teachings concerning sound doctrine [GNT; TEV].

**DISCOURSE UNIT: 2:1–10** [EBC, EGT, GNC, Herm, Hn, HNTC, IB, Lg, MNTC, NCBC, SSA, TC, TNTC, WC; NAB, NJB]. The topic is counsel on certain matters [NAB, NJB], instructions concerning duties of various groups of believers [EBC, EGT, GNC, Herm, Hn, HNTC, Lg, MNTC, TC, WC], rules governing the conduct of Christians [TNTC], qualities which various groups should have [NCBC], the minister's responsibilities to his people [IB].

**DISCOURSE UNIT: 2:1–8** [NCB]. The topic is instructions for the older and younger men and women.

**2:1** But$^a$ (as for) you, speak$^b$ the-things-which are-fitting$^c$ for-the being-healthy$^d$ teaching.$^e$

LEXICON—a. δέ (LN 89.124): 'But' [Herm, Hn, WC; KJV, NASB, RSV, TEV], 'now' [Lns], 'then' [NJB], not explicit [HNTC; NAB, NEB, NIV, TNT].
  b. pres. act. impera. of λαλέω (LN 33.70): 'to speak' [Hn, LN; KJV, NASB, TNT], 'to speak out' [WC], 'to utter' [Lns], 'to teach' [HNTC; NIV, RSV, TEV], 'to preach' [NJB], 'to proclaim' [Herm]. This verb is also translated as a noun phrase: 'your speech' [NAB], 'what you say' [NEB]. This verb indicates oral teaching [EBC, EGT], even informal conversation [Hn]. The present tense indicates that Titus has been teaching properly and that he is to continue to do so [Lns], or simply that he is to teach continually (with no reference to the past) [SSA].
  c. pres. act. indic. of πρέπω (LN 66.1): 'to be becoming (for)' [Lns, WC; KJV], 'to be fitting (for)' [BAGD, LN; NASB], 'to befit' [RSV], 'to be in accord (with)' [NIV], 'to be proper (to)' [Herm], 'to go (with)' [NJB], 'to agree (with)' [TEV], 'to be in keeping (with)' [HNTC; NEB, TNT], 'to be consistent (with)' [Hn; NAB]. The focus is to be on the side of behavior rather than mental knowledge [GNC, IB].
  d. pres. act. participle of ὑγιαίνω (LN 23.129): 'being healthy' [LN]. This participle is also translated as an adjective: 'sound' [Herm, Hn, HNTC; all versions except NEB, NJB], 'wholesome' [NEB], 'healthy' [BAGD, Lns, WC; NJB]. See this word at 1:9.
  e. διδασκαλία (LN 33.224; 33.236): 'doctrine' [Hn, HNTC, LN; all versions], 'teaching' [BAGD, Herm, LN, Lns, WC]. See this word at 1:9.

QUESTION—What relationship is indicated by σὺ δέ 'but you'?

This phrase indicates a contrast with the persons mentioned in the preceding verse [Alf, El, GNC, Hn, HNTC, IB, ICC, Lg, Lns, MNTC, My, Rb, SSA, TC, TNTC]: those people teach such things, but as for you, you are to speak the things that are in accord with sound teaching. The pronoun σύ 'you' emphasizes this contrast [EBC, Lns, MNTC, TNTC].

**2:2** Old-men[a] to-be sober,[b] serious,[c] sensible,[d]

LEXICON—a. πρεσβύτης (LN 9.31): 'old man' [BAGD, Herm, LN, Lns, WC], 'older man' [HNTC; all versions except KJV], 'aged man' [BAGD, Hn; KJV]. The word refers to age, not to the position of 'elder' in the church [Alf, EBC, EGT, El, GNC, Hn, IB, ICC, Lg, Lns, MNTC, My, NCBC, SSA, TC, TG, WC].

b. νηφάλιος (LN 88.87): 'sober' [BAGD, Herm, HNTC, LN, WC; KJV, NEB, TEV, TNT], 'temperate' [BAGD, Hn; NAB, NASB, NIV, RSV], 'reserved' [NJB], 'restrained' [LN]. The two adjectives νηφαλίους and σεμνούς together are translated 'temperate' [Lns].

c. σεμνός (LN 88.47): 'serious' [BAGD; RSV, TNT], 'serious-minded' [NAB], 'sensible' [TEV], 'dignified' [BAGD, Herm, Hn, HNTC, WC; NASB, NJB], 'grave' [KJV], 'high-principled' [NEB], 'honorable' [LN], 'worthy of respect' [LN; NIV], 'of good character' [LN]. It means to be dignified and serious in purpose [EBC], having moral qualities which other people respect [SSA].

d. σώφρων (LN 88.94): 'sensible' [LN; NASB, RSV], 'temperate' [KJV, NEB], 'self-controlled' [BAGD, Hn; NAB, NIV, TEV], 'self-restrained' [TNT], 'sober-minded' [Lns], 'moderate' [LN; NJB], 'circumspect' [HNTC], 'prudent' [BAGD, Herm], 'discreet' [WC].

QUESTION—How is this phrase related to the preceding clause?

It begins the list of those to whom Titus should speak or teach and specifies what he should teach them [Alf, El, Lg, SSA].

QUESTION—What verb is to be understood in this phrase?

Many translate with a form of 'to be' [Herm, HNTC, Lns; NASB, NJB]: old men should be sober, etc. Some begin this sentence by supplying a verb similar to the verb in 2:1 [Blm, EBC, SSA, WC; NAB, NIV, RSV, TEV, TNT]: tell/teach old men to be sober, etc. Others begin this sentence by supplying a verb similar to the verb in 2:6 [Bg, Hn]: exhort old men to be sober, etc.

QUESTION—What is meant by νηφαλίους 'sober'?

1. It means to be temperate and restrained in all areas of life [EBC, Hn, HNTC, Lns, SSA, TC, TNTC]: tell old men to be temperate. This includes being temperate in matters of drinking wine [Hn, TC, TNTC]. It refers to restraint regarding one's desires [HNTC], to being clear-headed in all situations [EBC], to having a well-balanced mind [SSA]. Both νηφαλίους and σεμνούς refer especially to being able to avoid being led astray by erroneous teachings [Lns].

2. It means to be temperate regarding strong drink [EGT, IB, NCBC]: tell old men not to drink much strong drink.

**being-healthy<sup>a</sup> in-the faith,<sup>b</sup> in-the love,<sup>c</sup> in-the endurance;<sup>d</sup>**
LEXICON—a. pres. act. participle of ὑγιαίνω (LN 23.129): 'to be healthy' [BAGD, LN], 'to be well' [LN]. This participle is also translated as an adjective: 'sound' [Herm, Hn, HNTC; all versions], 'healthy' [Lns, WC].
  b. πίστις (LN 31.104): 'faith' [BAGD, Herm, Hn, HNTC, LN, Lns, WC; all versions].
  c. ἀγάπη (LN 25.43): 'love' [BAGD, Herm, Hn, HNTC, LN, Lns, WC; NASB, NEB, NIV, NJB, RSV, TEV], 'charity' [KJV]. The phrase ὑγιαίνοντας τῇ ἀγάπῃ 'being healthy in the love' is translated 'loving' [NAB, TNT].
  d. ὑπομονή (LN 25.174): 'perseverance' [BAGD; NASB, NJB], 'endurance' [BAGD, Herm, Hn, LN, WC; NEB, NIV, TEV], 'steadfastness' [BAGD, HNTC; RSV], 'patience' [BAGD, Lns; KJV]. The phrase ὑγιαίνοντας...τῇ ὑπομονῇ 'being healthy in the endurance' is translated 'steadfast' [NAB], 'patient' [TNT]. It refers to the fortitude to endure [El].
QUESTION—What is the relationship between 'sound' and the nouns 'faith', 'love', and 'endurance'?
  1. All three nouns express elements in which the old men should be sound [Alf, EBC, EGT, El, GNC, Herm, Hn, HNTC, ICC, Lns, SSA, WC; KJV, NASB, NEB, NIV, NJB, RSV, TEV]: teach old men to be sound in their faith, in their love, and in their endurance.
  2. 'Sound' governs only 'faith'; the infinitive 'to be' is to be repeated before 'love' and 'patience' [Blm; NAB, TNT]: teach the old men to be sound in the faith, to be loving, and to be patient.
QUESTION—What is the significance of the definite article with each of the nouns 'faith', 'love', and 'endurance'?
  1. It relates these nouns to the person subjectively [Alf, EBC, Hn] and implies possession [EBC, Hn]: sound in the exercise of their faith, their love, their patience.
  2. The article indicates that all three nouns are used objectively [Lns]: sound in the faith, the love, and the patience which are set forth in God's Word.
QUESTION—What is meant by 'sound in faith'?
  1. The reference to faith is subjective, not objective as in 1:13; that is, it refers to the event of believing [Alf, EBC, EGT, GNC, Hn, HNTC, ICC, TC]: sound in the exercise of their faith/believing. It means that their faith must be vital [Hn, ICC] and that they must not hold to erroneous views [Hn, IB, ICC]. They should trust fully in God and his Word [Hn].
  2. The reference to faith is to an objective faith [IB, Lns, SSA]: believing in the correct doctrines. They must be sincere in their belief [SSA].
QUESTION—What is meant by 'sound in love'?
  It means that they must demonstrate genuine love, not being bitter nor vindictive [EBC]; they must sincerely love people. In addition to their love

for other people, their love for God may be intended as well [SSA]. It means that their love must not become faint because of wickedness around them, and it must be well-balanced [ICC]; it must avoid false sentimentality [WC].

QUESTION—What is meant by 'sound in endurance'?
1. It means that they must be able to endure bravely the problems or persecutions of their life [EBC, El, ICC, Lg, My, WC] yet not be callous, rash, or fanatical [ICC, WC]: they must bravely endure the trials of life.
2. It means that they must be loyal to the orthodox faith [IB, SSA]: steadfast in the Christian faith.

**2:3** old-women[a] likewise[b] in[c] conduct[d] befitting-holy-people,[e]

LEXICON—a. πρεσβῦτις (LN **9.37**): 'old women' [BAGD, Herm, Lns, WC], 'older women' [BAGD, HNTC, LN; all versions except KJV], 'aged women' [Hn; KJV].
  b. ὡσαύτως (LN 64.16): 'likewise' [BAGD, Lns; KJV, NASB, NIV, RSV], 'in like manner' [LN, WC], 'similarly' [BAGD, Hn, HNTC; NAB, NEB, NJB], 'in the same way' [BAGD, Herm, LN; TEV]; not translated [TNT].
  c. ἐν with dative object (LN 90.23): 'in' [KJV, NAB, NASB, NEB, NIV, RSV], not explicit [NAB, NJB, TEV, TNT].
  d. κατάστημα (LN 41.8): 'conduct' [Herm, LN], 'behavior' [BAGD, LN; KJV, NASB, RSV], 'bearing' [NEB], 'the way they live' [NIV], 'demeanor' [BAGD, Hn, HNTC, Lns, WC], 'deportment' [Blm]. This noun is also translated as verb: 'to behave' [NAB, NJB, TEV], 'to live lives' [TNT].
  e. ἱεροπρεπής (LN **53.6**): 'as becometh holiness' [KJV], 'as befits sacred persons' [Lns], 'as devout persons' [LN], 'reverent' [Hn, HNTC; NASB, NEB, NIV, RSV], 'reverend, i.e., worthy of the honor which is paid to sacred persons' [WC], 'worthy of reverence' [BAGD], 'priestly' [Herm]. The phrase ἐν καταστήματι ἱεροπρεπεῖς 'in behavior befitting holy people' is translated 'must behave in ways that befit those who belong to God' [NAB], 'should behave as befits religious people' [NJB], 'to behave as women should who live a holy life' [TEV], 'are to live lives of reverence to God' [TNT].

QUESTION—What is being compared by ὡσαύτως 'likewise'?
The aged women are expected to conduct themselves in a manner similar to that of the aged men [Alf, EBC, El, NCB]. The requirements for the aged women are somewhat similar to those for the aged men [Hn, SSA, TNTC]. The reference is general—as Paul has given some instructions for the aged men, he also gives some instructions for the aged women [Lns].

QUESTION—What is meant by καταστήματι ἱεροπρεπεῖς 'conduct befitting holy people'?
It implies that their conduct should be appropriate to their holy calling [Blm, EBC, ICC, TG], like that of people carrying out sacred duties [ICC, Rb], like that of a good priestess fulfilling her priestly duties [EBC, GNC, Herm, HNTC, IB, ICC, Lns]. Some commentators think that both dress and conduct

are in view here [CBC, EGT, Hn, Lg]. According to others, the set of the mind is in view rather than outward appearance [TC, TNTC, WC]. 'Conduct' includes both gestures and habits [Alf]; it implies conduct expressive of one's inner character [EBC, Herm, HNTC, SSA]; it includes both the external factor of dress and the internal aspects of character [El, Hn, Lg, MNTC].

**not slanderers,[a] not to-much wine enslaved,[b] teachers-of-what-is-good,[c]**
LEXICON—a. διάβολος (LN 33.397): 'slanderer' [BAGD, Hn, LN, Lns; NIV, RSV, TEV], 'gossip' [HNTC], 'given to gossip' [Herm], 'slanderous gossip' [NAB], 'malicious gossip' [NASB], 'scandal-monger' [NEB, TNT], 'false accuser' [KJV]. The phrase μὴ διαβόλους 'not slanderers' is translated 'with no scandal-mongering' [NJB], 'not prone to slander' [WC].
- b. perf. pass. participle of δουλόω (LN 87.82): 'to be enslaved (to)' [BAGD, Hn, HNTC, LN, WC; NASB], 'to be enslaved (by)' [Lns], 'to be addicted (to)' [NIV, TNT], 'to be given (to)' [Herm; KJV]. The phrase μὴ οἴνῳ πολλῷ δεδουλωμένας 'not to much wine enslaved' is translated 'not slaves to drink' [NAB, RSV], 'nor slaves to strong drink' [NEB], 'not slaves to wine' [TEV], 'with no addiction to wine' [NJB]. Wine is specified because hard liquor was not in use in Titus's day [Lg].
- c. καλοδιδάσκαλος (LN **33.249**): 'teacher of good things' [KJV], 'teacher of all good things' [Herm], 'teacher of goodness' [WC], 'one who teaches what is good' [LN], 'teacher of right behavior' [NJB], 'teacher of that which is excellent' [Hn], 'teacher of excellence' [Lns]. This noun is also translated as a participle: 'teaching what is good' [BAGD, HNTC; NASB]; it is also translated as a verb: 'to teach what is good' [NIV, RSV, TEV, TNT]. The phrase καλοδιδασκάλους, ἵνα σωφρονίζωσιν τὰς νέας 'teachers of what is good, in order that they may encourage the young women' is translated 'By their good example they must teach the younger women' [NAB], 'they must set a high standard, and school the younger women' [NEB].

QUESTION—What manner of teaching is implied by καλοδιδασκάλους 'teachers of what is good'?

Personal advice and encouragement, not formal teaching, is in view here [EBC, El, GNC, Hn, HNTC, SSA, TC, TNTC, WC]; it is teaching by words and by example [EGT, GNC, HNTC, IB, NCB, WC], perhaps by example only [MNTC, NCBC], or more by speech and teaching than by example [Lg, My, SSA]. The good things they are to teach are specified in the following verses [Bg, SSA, TG]. According to one commentator, this phrase instead 'one who is a good teacher' [CBC].

**2:4** in-order-that[a] they-may-train[b] the young-(women)[c] to-be husband-lovers,[d] child-lovers,[e]

LEXICON—a. ἵνα (LN 89.59): 'in order that' [BAGD, Lns], 'in order (to)' [TEV], 'so that' [Hn, HNTC, WC], 'that' [BAGD; KJV, NASB], 'and so' [RSV], 'then' [Herm; NIV], 'and' [NJB, TNT], not explicit [NAB, NEB].

    b. σωφρονίζω (LN **33.229**): 'to train' [Hn, HNTC; NIV, RSV, TEV, TNT], 'to discipline or control' [WC], 'to show (them how)' [NJB], 'to encourage' [BAGD; NASB], 'to advise' [BAGD, Herm], 'to teach' [LN; NAB], 'to make (them) sober-minded' [Lns], 'to teach (them) to be sober' [KJV], 'to school' [NEB]. The literal meaning of the word is to bring someone to his senses [GNC]. Some commentators take it to mean to instruct them to be temperate/sober [Lns, NCB; KJV]. Most take it to mean 'to admonish', the admonishment being the following words.

    c. νέος (LN 67.116): 'young women' [BAGD, Herm, Hn, Lns, WC; KJV, NASB, RSV], 'younger women' [HNTC; NAB, NEB, NIV, NJB, TEV], 'young wives' [TNT]. Paul says 'young' here, not the comparative 'younger', since he includes all of child-bearing age [LN (2.6)].

    d. φίλανδρος (LN 25.37): 'lover of her husband' [WC], 'loving her husband' [BAGD], 'having love for one's husband' [LN]. The phrase φιλάνδρους εἶναι 'to be husband-lovers' is translated 'to love their husbands' [Herm; all versions except NEB, NJB], 'to be loving toward their husbands' [Hn], 'to be devoted to their husbands' [HNTC], 'to be devoted to husbands' [Lns], 'how they should love their husbands' [NJB], 'to be loving wives' [NEB]. The exhortation here and in the following adjective refers to loving behavior rather than to the emotion of love [TG].

    e. φιλότεκνος (LN **25.38**): 'lover of one's children' [WC], 'loving one's children' [BAGD], 'loving one's own children' [LN]. The phrase εἶναι φιλοτέκνους 'to be child-lovers' is translated 'to love their children' [Herm; all versions except NEB, NJB], 'to be loving toward their children' [Hn], 'to be devoted to their children' [HNTC], 'to be devoted to children' [Lns], 'how they should love their children' [NJB], 'to be loving mothers' [NEB].

QUESTION—What relationship is indicated by ἵνα 'in order that'?

    1. It introduces the purpose of giving these instructions to the old women [Blm, Hn, TG]: tell the aged women to behave thus in order that they may teach the young women. It is the older women, not Titus himself, who are to instruct the young women [Bg, EBC, El (in 2:6), Lg (in 2:5)].

    2. It introduces the purpose of being καλοδιδασκάλους 'teachers of what is good' [ICC, SSA, TC]: they should be teachers of what is good in order that they may train the young women.

QUESTION—What is meant by τὰς νέας 'the young (women)'?

The word is literally 'new', probably referring primarily (or perhaps exclusively [EGT, Hn]) to newly married women [EBC, EGT, GNC, Hn, TC, WC]: that they may train the newly married women. Although it refers primarily to young married women, most of the words listed can apply to single women as well [El]: that they may train the young women.

QUESTION—What relationship is indicated by the infinitive εἶναι 'to be'?

It introduces the content (or the aim [My]) of the verb σωφρονίζωσιν 'they may train' [SSA]; it and the whole series of adjectives beginning with φιλάνδρους 'husband-lovers' are dependent on that verb [El]: train them to be husband-lovers, etc.

**2:5 sensible,ᵃ pure,ᵇ working-at-home,ᶜ good,ᵈ being-subjectᵉ to their-own husbands,**

TEXT—Some manuscripts read οἰκουρούς 'staying at home', instead of οἰκουργούς 'working at home'. GNT does not deal with this variant. 'Staying at home' is read by Blm, Brt, El, My, TC, and KJV.

LEXICON—a. σώφρων (LN 88.94): 'sensible' [LN; NAB, NASB, NJB, RSV], 'discreet' [WC; KJV], 'sober-minded' [Lns], 'circumspect' [HNTC], 'temperate' [NEB], 'moderate' [LN], 'self-controlled' [BAGD, Hn; NIV, TEV], 'self-restrained' [TNT]. This adjective is also translated as an adverb: '(live) prudently' [Herm]. 'Discreet', which implies spontaneity, is a better rendering than 'self-restraint', which implies effort [Alf]. This word and the following form a pair [EBC, GNC, HNTC, Lns, SSA]; both refer to sexual morality [GNC, Hn, HNTC, SSA]. The meaning is sobermindedness as a protection against deceivers [Lns]. It refers to being even-tempered, wise, and conscientious [MNTC].

b. ἁγνός (LN 88.28): 'chaste' [Hn, HNTC, Lns; KJV, NAB, NEB, NJB, RSV], 'pure' [BAGD, LN, WC; NASB, NIV, TEV, TNT], 'without defect' [LN], 'sincerity' [Herm]. This word refers to sexual purity [El, GNC, HNTC, ICC, My, TC, TG], and also purity of heart in all aspects of conduct [EBC].

c. οἰκουργός (LN 46.3): 'working at home' [BAGD], 'worker at home' [Hn; NASB], '(how) to work in one's home' [NJB], 'busy at home' [NAB, NEB, NIV], 'domestic' [BAGD, HNTC; RSV], 'housekeeper' [Lns], 'home-worker' [WC], 'homemaker' [LN], 'housewife' [TEV, TNT], 'to fulfill her household duties well' [Herm]. This and the following word are another pair [EBC, GNC, Lns], this word referring to their domestic duties [EBC, GNC]. She should not be a gadabout [HNTC].

d. ἀγαθός (LN 88.1): 'good' [BAGD, LN, Lns; KJV], 'good to others' [WC], 'kindly' [NAB], 'kind' [Hn, HNTC; NASB, NEB, NIV, RSV, TNT], 'gentle' [NJB].

e. pres. mid. or pass. participle of ὑποτάσσω (LN 36.18): (pass.) 'to be subject (to)' [BAGD; NASB, NIV]; (mid.) 'to submit oneself (to)' [LN; TEV], 'to subject oneself (to)' [BAGD, Lns, WC]. It is also translated with an active sense: 'to respect the authority (of)' [NEB], 'to obey' [Herm, LN; NJB]. This participle is also translated as an adjective: 'obedient' [KJV, TNT], 'submissive' [Hn, HNTC; NAB, RSV]. If it is middle voice, it expresses voluntary acceptance of the husband's headship [EBC]. The quality of submission is the other side of the coin to loving their husbands [My].

QUESTION—What is the function of ἀγαθάς 'good'?

1. This word is a separate quality [Alf, EBC, EGT, El, GNC, Hn, HNTC, ICC, Lns, MNTC, My, TC, TNTC, WC; all versions except TEV, TNT]: they must be busy at home and they must be good women.
2. This word is an attribute of the preceding word [Herm, NCBC; TEV, TNT]: they must be good workers at home, or they must do their housework well. It forms a pair with the preceding word and means 'good women' [GNC, Lns], those who benefit their husbands and children [Lns], who show kindness and sympathy to those in their households, including slaves [EBC, EGT, GNC, Hn, HNTC, MNTC] (especially to their servants [ICC, WC]) by not acting with undue austerity or miserliness [El].

**in-order-that[a] not the word of-the God might-be-blasphemed.[b]**

LEXICON—a. ἵνα (LN 89.59): 'in order that' [BAGD, Hn, Lns, WC], 'that' [BAGD, Herm; KJV, NASB, RSV], 'so that' [HNTC; NIV, NJB, TEV], 'so' [TNT], 'thus' [NAB, NEB].

b. pres. pass. subj. of βλασφημέω (LN 33.400): 'to be blasphemed' [BAGD, Herm, LN, Lns, WC; KJV], 'to be dishonored' [NASB], 'to be brought into disrepute' [NEB, TNT], 'to be discredited' [RSV], 'to be disgraced' [NJB], 'to be reviled' [Hn, LN]. It is also translated in an active sense: '(thus the word of God) will not fall into disrepute' [NAB], '(so that no one) will malign (the word of God)' [NIV], '(so that no one) will speak evil (of the message that comes from God)' [TEV], '(so that God's word) may suffer no scandal' [HNTC].

QUESTION—What relationship is implied by ἵνα 'in order that'?

1. It introduces the purpose for requiring such a high standard of conduct for the young women [EBC, EGT, GNC, Herm, Hn, HNTC, IB, ICC, Lg(D), SSA, TNTC]: they should conduct themselves in this way in order that the word of God may not be ill-spoken of. It relates to all the preceding items [EBC, Hn]
2. It introduces the purpose for requiring the young wives to be subject to their husbands [Brt, El, MNTC, My, WC]: they should be subject to their husbands in order that the gospel may not be discredited. Some critics of the gospel said that Christian women were taught to disobey their husbands [Brt].
3. The purpose clause extends back to include the conduct of the aged women as well as the young women [Lns]: the aged women and the young women must conduct themselves properly in order that the gospel may not be discredited.

QUESTION—Why might the word of God be blasphemed because of them?

The failure of Christian wives to live properly would subject the gospel to being discredited by non-Christians [EBC, EGT, Hn, SSA]. The expression is a litotes, Paul actually meaning that the word of God should be honored by their conduct [Hn].

**2:6 The younger-(men)ᵃ likewiseᵇ exhortᶜ to-be-sensibleᵈ**

LEXICON—a. νέος (LN 67.116): 'young man' [BAGD, Herm; KJV, NAB, NASB, NIV, TEV], 'younger man' [Hn, HNTC, Lns, WC; NEB, NJB, RSV, TNT]. 'Younger men' are in contrast with the 'aged men' in 2:1 [El]. This word may refer to men under 60 [Hn, Lns], or possibly under 50 [Hn], years of age. This is a comparative adjective, 'younger', whereas in referring to the women he does not use the comparative form [Lns].

b. ὡσαύτως (LN 64.16): 'likewise' [BAGD, Lns; KJV, NASB, RSV], 'similarly' [BAGD, Hn, HNTC; NEB, NIV, NJB], 'in the same way' [BAGD, Herm, LN; TEV], 'in like manner' [LN, WC], 'also' [TNT]; not explicit [NAB]. The young men are to exercise responsibility just as are the groups previously referred to [EBC, Hn, SSA]. The exhortation is similar to that in 2:3 [My].

c. pres. act. impera. of παρακαλέω (LN 25.150): 'to exhort' [BAGD, Herm, WC; KJV], 'to urge' [BAGD, Hn, HNTC; NASB, NEB, NJB, RSV, TEV, TNT], 'to admonish' [Lns], 'to encourage' [BAGD, LN; NIV], 'to tell' [NAB]. Here Paul uses an imperative verb for the first time in the exhortations which begin with 2:2 [EBC, HNTC]; it is more forceful than the verb in 2:1 [EBC, HNTC, TNTC] and appeals to the young men's moral responsibility [EBC, MNTC]. The present tense implies that Titus should continually exhort the younger men [Lns, SSA].

d. pres. act. infin. of σωφρονέω (LN **32.34**): 'to be sensible' [BAGD; NASB], 'to be wise and sensible' [LN], 'to be sober-minded' [Lns; KJV], 'to keep oneself under control' [NAB], 'to exercise self-control' [Hn, HNTC], 'to be self-controlled' [NIV, TEV], 'to control oneself' [RSV], 'to be self-restrained' [TNT], 'to be temperate' [NEB], 'to be moderate' [NJB], 'to conduct one's life prudently' [Herm], 'to be discreet' [WC].

QUESTION—What is meant by σωφρονεῖν 'to be sensible'?

The adjective related to this verb is used in 1:8 and 2:2, 4, 5 [Hn, HNTC, IB, Lns, SSA], which gives it special force here [Lns]. It means to practice habitual self-restraint [WC]. It implies clear-headed and self-restrained behavior in daily life [EBC, GNC], avoidance of the inclinations of the sinful nature [Hn, MNTC] and of erroneous ideas and customs [Hn]. The repetition of this word (in verbal and adjectival forms) in these verses shows the need of this quality in Crete [TC] and implies that immoderate affections were too common in Crete [El]. This verb sums up the conduct which the younger men were to be urged to observe [Lg, My]. This self-mastery is essentially a Christian concept including the aspect of humility, not the mere pagan Greek moralism [MNTC, TNTC].

## 2:7 in-regard-to[a] all-(things),[b]

LEXICON—a. περί with accusative object (LN 89.6): 'in regard to' [Lns], 'in' [Herm, Hn, WC; all versions except NAB]. The phrase περὶ πάντα 'in regard to all things' is translated 'at all points' [HNTC], 'completely' [NAB].

b. πᾶς (plural) (LN 59.23): 'all things' [Lns, WC; KJV, NASB, NEB, TEV], 'everything' [NIV, NJB, TNT], 'all respects' [Herm; RSV], 'every respect' [Hn], 'all matters' [Alf]. This phrase emphasizes the extent of the duty [EBC].

QUESTION—What is this phrase connected with?

1. It is connected with the preceding infinitive σωφρονεῖν 'to be sensible' (2:6) [GNC, Herm, Hn, HNTC, MNTC, NCB, SSA; NAB, NEB, NJB]: urge the younger men to be sensible in regard to all things. Those who hold this interpretation consider the following word σεαυτὸν 'yourself' to be in the initial position in its unit, which would make it parallel with all of the other major classes in this section [SSA].

2. It is connected with the following participle παρεχόμενος 'showing' [EBC, El, ICC, Lg, Lns, My, TC, TNTC, WC; KJV, NASB, NIV, RSV, TEV, TNT]: in regard to everything show yourself as a pattern. This connection gives the proper emphasis to 'yourself' [EBC]. Those who hold this interpretation consider the phrase emphatic by forefronting [Lg(D), My].

## yourself showing[a] (as) an-example[b] of-good works,[c]

LEXICON—a. pres. mid. participle of παρέχω (LN 13.26): 'to show' [BAGD, Herm, Hn, HNTC; KJV, NASB, RSV], 'to furnish' [Lns], 'to set (an example)' [NAB, NEB, NIV, NJB, TNT], 'to be (an example)' [TEV], 'to continue to be' [LN], 'to afford' [WC]. The present tense implies that Titus was to do continually the things mentioned [Lns, SSA]. Some commentators say that the middle voice implies the personal involvement of Titus [Alf, EBC, EGT], although another says that the middle voice has virtually the same meaning as the active voice [ICC], and another calls the middle voice redundant [Rb].

b. τύπος (LN 58.59): 'example' [Herm, LN, Lns; all versions except KJV, RSV], 'pattern' [BAGD; KJV], 'model' [BAGD, Hn, HNTC, LN; RSV], 'type' [BAGD, WC].

c. ἔργον (LN 42.11): 'work' [BAGD, Herm, Lns, WC; KJV, NJB], 'deed' [BAGD, Hn, LN; NASB, RSV], 'act' [LN], 'conduct' [HNTC], 'behavior' [TEV], 'what (is good)' [NIV], 'everything you do' [TNT], not explicit [NAB].

QUESTION—What relationship is indicated by the participial form παρεχόμενος 'showing'?

The participle is dependent upon the preceding imperative παρακάλει 'urge', and thus functions as an additional exhortation, 'show yourself as an example'; it also governs the characteristics which follow [SSA]. It makes what he now says about Titus subordinate to what precedes [Lns].

QUESTION—How are the noun σεαυτόν 'yourself' and the pronoun τύπον 'example' related?

'Example' is in apposition with 'yourself'; 'yourself' being the reflexive pronoun [EBC, El, TC] as the object of the participle. 'Yourself' is emphatic [El, HNTC, Lg(D)] as its forefronting shows [SSA]: show yourself as an example. Without 'yourself' the sense would be simply 'set an example' without necessarily specifying who was to be the example [Alf, El]. The reflexive pronoun with the middle voice of the participle gives more emphasis to the personal aspect [TC].

QUESTION—To whom is Titus to show himself as an example?

Some translate that he is to show himself as an example 'to them', implying the young men mentioned in the previous verse [HNTC; NAB, NEB, NIV]. Others think that this means that he is to show himself as an example to all believers [EBC, Hn, Lns, MNTC].

## in[a] the teaching[b] integrity,[c] seriousness,[d]

TEXT—Some manuscripts add ἀφθαρσίαν 'incorruptibility' following σεμνότητα 'seriousness'. GNT does not deal with this variant. Only KJV includes this word, translating it 'sincerity'.

LEXICON—a. ἐν with dative object (LN 89.5): 'in' [Hn, HNTC, Lns, WC; all versions except NAB, NJB], not explicit [NAB]. The phrase ἐν τῇ διδασκαλίᾳ 'in the teaching' is translated 'when you are teaching' [NJB].

b. διδασκαλία (LN 33.224; 33.236): 'doctrine' [LN; KJV, NASB], 'teaching' [BAGD, Hn, HNTC, LN, Lns, WC; NAB, NEB, NIV, RSV, TEV, TNT]. This noun is also translated as a verb: 'to teach' [NJB]. The reference is to public instruction [Bg]. It refers to the act of teaching [EGT, El, GNC, TC, TNTC].

c. ἀφθορία (LN **88.43**): 'integrity' [HNTC, LN; NEB, NIV, RSV], 'soundness' [BAGD], 'sincerity' [NJB], 'uncorruptness' [Lns, WC; KJV], 'incorruptibility' [Hn], 'purity' [NASB]. This noun is also translated as an adjective: 'sincere' [TEV, TNT], 'pure' [Herm]. This word means innocence [Herm], correctness of doctrine [IB, Lg, Lns, My, NCBC, TNTC], purity of both motive and doctrine [ICC], single-mindedness and sincerity of motive [MNTC, TC].

d. σεμνότης (LN 88.46): 'gravity' [HNTC, Lns; KJV, RSV], 'seriousness' [BAGD; NIV], 'dignity' [BAGD, Hn, WC], 'propriety' [LN], 'earnestness' [NJB], 'high principle' [NEB], 'befitting behavior' [LN]. This noun is also translated as an adjective: 'dignified' [Herm; NASB], 'serious' [TEV, TNT]. It means dignity in his speech and manner [ICC, Lg, Lns, MNTC, My, TC, TNTC, WC].

QUESTION—What is ἐν τῇ διδασκαλίᾳ 'in the teaching' connected with?

It is connected with the preceding participle παρεχόμενος 'showing' [Blm, Hn, Lg, Lns, My, TC; NEB, RSV]: and show in your teaching integrity and seriousness. The meaning is that integrity and seriousness should characterize Titus in his teaching [Bg, EBC, EGT, El, Hn, HNTC, IB, Lg(D), Lns, NCB, NCBC, SSA, TC, TG, TNTC, WC]: in your teaching you should show that you are incorruptible and serious.

**2:8 word<sup>a</sup> healthy<sup>b</sup> beyond-reproach,<sup>c</sup>**

LEXICON—a. λόγος (LN 33.98, 33.99): 'word' [LN; NAB, TEV]; 'speech' [Hn, HNTC; KJV, NASB, NEB, NIV, RSV], 'speaking' [BAGD, LN], 'statement' [Lns]. 'message' [LN; NJB], 'preaching' [Herm], 'word of preaching' [WC], 'whatever you say' [TNT]. One commentator thinks that this refers to preaching but not to private conversation [Lg]. Others think that this refers to both teaching and ordinary conversation [EBC, El]. This word and its two following modifiers are dependent on 'showing yourself' in 2:7 [Herm].

  b. ὑγιής (LN **72.14**): 'healthy' [BAGD, Lns, WC], 'sound' [BAGD, Herm, Hn, HNTC, LN; all versions except NEB, NIV], 'wholesome' [NEB]; 'pure and uncorrupted' [Blm], 'agreeable to the apostolic gospel' [HNTC, SSA], 'soundness' [NIV]. It must be in harmony with the true gospel [EBC, EGT, IB, TC], in opposition to the teachings of the heretical teachers [My].

  c. ἀκατάγνωστος (LN **33.415**): 'irreproachable' [Herm; NJB, TNT], 'which is beyond reproach' [BAGD; NASB], 'which are above criticism' [LN], 'that cannot be criticized' [TEV], 'incensurable' [Hn], 'that cannot be censured' [RSV], 'not to be condemned' [WC], 'that cannot be condemned' [KJV, NIV], 'not condemned' [BAGD], 'to which no one can take exception' [NAB], 'to which none can take exception' [NEB], 'to which no exception can be taken' [HNTC], 'nothing to be found against it' [Lns]. This word refers to the manner in which the message is presented [EGT]. What Titus says, publicly or privately, should not be open to hostile opposition [El]. It must be such that thinking persons will find it respectable [SSA].

**in-order-that<sup>a</sup> the (person) from<sup>b</sup> opposite<sup>c</sup> may-be-put-to-shame<sup>d</sup>**

LEXICON—a. ἵνα (LN 89.59): 'in order that' [WC; NASB], 'so that' [Herm, Hn, HNTC, Lns; NIV, NJB, RSV, TEV], 'that' [KJV, TNT], 'if it does' [NAB], not explicit [NEB].

  b. ἐκ with genitive object (LN 90.16): 'from'. The phrase ὁ ἐξ ἐναντίας 'the person from opposite' is translated 'the opponent' [Herm; NASB], 'an opponent' [RSV], 'any opponent' [HNTC; NJB, TNT], 'he who is opposed' [Lns], 'those who oppose you' [NIV], 'he that is on the opposite side' [Hn], 'he who is on the contrary side' [WC], 'he that is of the contrary part' [KJV], 'he who is hostile' [LN (39.6)], 'your enemies' [TEV].

  c. ἐναντίος (LN 39.6): 'opposite' [BAGD], 'hostile' [LN]. The word 'opinion' is to be supplied [Blm].

d. aorist pass. subj. of ἐντρέπω (LN 25.196): 'to be put to shame' [BAGD, Hn, HNTC, WC; NASB, RSV, TEV, TNT], 'to be shamed' [LN, Lns], 'to be converted' [Herm]. This verb is also translated with active meaning: 'to be ashamed' [BAGD; KJV, NIV], 'to be at a loss' [NJB]. This word is also paraphrased: 'and hostility will yield to shame' [NAB]. The opponent will be ashamed probably because it will be seen that he has no valid criticism [EBC, EGT, Hn]. He will be inclined to repent [IB]. In addition to shame, there is the element of frustration and defeat implied in this word [SSA].

QUESTION—What relationship is indicated by ἵνα 'in order that'?

This word introduces the purpose (or the intended result [Lns]) of the preceding comments [EBC, Herm, Hn, My, Rb, SSA]. One commentator calls it the motive [HNTC].

QUESTION—Who are the opponents referred to here?

The reference is intentionally vague [EBC, HNTC, MNTC]. Some commentators think it refers to heathen opponents [Alf, EGT, Lg(D), My]. Some think it refers primarily to opponents in the church [GNC, Hn, IB, Lg]. Others think that it refers to any opponents, in or outside the church [El, HNTC, ICC, MNTC, SSA, TG]. Another takes it to refer to Satan and the false teachers, who are Satan's servants [Lg].

**having nothing to-say<sup>a</sup> concerning<sup>b</sup> us evil.<sup>c</sup>**

TEXT—Some manuscripts read ὑμῶν 'you (plural)' instead of ἡμῶν 'us'. GNT does not deal with this variant, and only KJV reads 'you'.

LEXICON—a. pres. act. infin. of λέγω (LN 33.69): 'to say' [BAGD, Herm, HNTC, LN, Lns, WC; all versions except NEB, NJB], 'to report' [Hn]. The phrase μηδὲν ἔχων λέγειν 'having nothing to say' is translated 'when he finds not a word to say' [NEB], 'with no accusation to make' [NJB].

b. περί with genitive object (LN 90.24): 'concerning' [Hn, WC], 'about' [Herm, HNTC; NAB, NASB, NIV, TEV, TNT], 'in regard to' [Lns], 'of' [KJV, RSV]. The phrase περὶ ἡμῶν φαῦλον 'concerning us evil' is translated 'to our discredit' [NEB].

c. φαῦλος (LN 88.116): 'evil' [BAGD, Hn, LN; KJV, RSV], 'bad' [BAGD, Herm, LN, WC; NAB, NASB, NIV, TEV, TNT], 'discreditable' [HNTC], 'ill' [Lns]. In the NT this word is used to describe deeds, never words [Alf, EGT, GNC, TC, TNTC].

QUESTION—What relationship is indicated by the participial form ἔχων 'having'?

1. It is causal, giving the reason why the opponents will be put to shame [GNC, Hn, HNTC, SSA; NIV]: they will be ashamed because they have nothing bad to say about us.

2. It expresses the means by which the opponents will be put to shame [MNTC; TEV]: they will be put to shame by not having anything bad to say.

3. It is conditional [Herm]: the opponent may be converted if he cannot say anything bad.

**DISCOURSE UNIT: 2:9–10** [NCB]. The topic is slaves [NCB].

**2:9 Slaves to-their-own[a] masters[b] to-submit-themselves[c]**

LEXICON—a. ἴδιος (LN 57.4): 'their own' [Hn, Lns, WC; KJV, NASB], 'their' [Herm, HNTC; all versions except KJV, NASB]. It refers to the masters who are their legal owners [Lg, SSA]. It does not mean 'their own rather than someone else's' [SSA]. One commentator does not think that it is emphatic [TC].

b. δεσπότης (LN 57.13): 'master' [BAGD, Herm, Hn, HNTC, LN, Lns, WC; all versions], 'owner' [LN]. This word focuses on the complete authority of the owner over the slave [EBC].

c. pres. mid. infin. of ὑποτάσσω (LN **36.18**): 'to submit themselves' [TEV], 'to be submissive' [Hn, HNTC; NAB, RSV, TNT], 'to subject themselves' [BAGD, WC], 'to be subject' [NASB, NIV], 'to be in subjection' [Lns], 'to be obedient' [KJV, NJB], 'to obey' [Herm, LN], 'to respect (someone's) authority' [NEB]. This word is stronger than 'to obey' [TNTC]. 'To submit themselves' correctly renders the middle voice of the participle [GNC]. The present tense implies habitual conduct, although no commentary mentions this point.

QUESTION—What is this phrase connected with?

The verb παρακάλει 'exhort' (from 2:6) is to be supplied here [Alf, Bg, EBC, EGT, El, GNC, Hn, Lg, Lns, My, Rb, SSA, TC]: exhort slaves to submit themselves.

**in[a] all-things[b]**

LEXICON—a. ἐν with dative object (LN 89.5): 'in' [Herm, Hn, HNTC, Lns, WC; all versions].

b. πᾶς (plural): 'all things' [BAGD, WC; KJV, TEV, TNT], 'everything' [BAGD; NASB, NEB, NIV, NJB], 'every way' [NAB], 'every respect' [Hn; RSV], 'all respects' [Herm, HNTC, Lns].

QUESTION—What is this phrase connected with?

1. It is connected with the preceding phrase 'to submit themselves' [EBC, EGT, GNC, Herm, Hn, HNTC, ICC, Lns, NCB, SSA, WC; NASB, NEB, NIV, NJB, TNT]: exhort the slaves to submit themselves in everything. This alternative probably gives better balance with the identical phrase at the end of 2:10 [HNTC, ICC]. This phrase elsewhere in the pastoral Epistles is clause-final [EGT, SSA], and similar phrases are found elsewhere in Paul's letters with this and similar verbs [EGT]. Also, if 'in all things' goes with 'to be well-pleasing' it would be emphatic by forefronting, which is not likely in a list such as it is [SSA].

2. It is connected with the following phrase 'to be pleasing' [Alf, Lg, MNTC, My, TNTC; KJV, NAB, RSV, TEV]: exhort the slaves to submit themselves and to be pleasing in everything.

TITUS 2:9

QUESTION—What is meant by πᾶσιν 'all things'?
Paul is not saying that slaves should obey orders that are morally wrong [Hn, HNTC, WC]; a Christian slave could not obey a master's orders that violated his conscience [EBC, Lg, TNTC]. Some commentators think that Paul has Christian households in mind [GNC, HNTC, MNTC, TNTC]. However, Paul is not dealing with the limitation of conscience here [WC]. Paul does not distinguish between Christian and non-Christian masters here [EBC, Hn]. Some think that Paul is addressing slaves in pagan households, since the last part of 2:10 seems to refer to a Christian slave's behavior before unbelievers, and since no advice is given here to the masters [NCBC].

**to-be well-pleasing,**[a]
LEXICON—a. εὐάρεστος (LN 25.94): 'well-pleasing' [Herm, Lns, WC; NASB], 'pleasing, acceptable' [BAGD, LN], 'eager to please' [Hn]. The phrase εὐαρέστους εἶναι 'to be well-pleasing' is translated 'to please well' [KJV], 'to please' [NAB], '(they are) to please' [TEV], 'to comply with (someone's) demands' [NEB], '(they must) do what is wanted' [NJB], 'to try to please' [NIV], 'to give satisfaction' [HNTC; RSV], '(they must) try to give satisfaction' [TNT]. The meaning is to give their masters satisfaction by their work [Alf, EGT, WC]; they should actively try to please, as Christians rather than as slaves [HNTC]. This exhortation is general, with some specifics following [GNC, SSA]. It explains the preceding 'to submit themselves in everything' as meaning to please their masters well [Lns].
QUESTION—To whom were the slaves to be well-pleasing?
They were to please their masters [Alf, EBC, El, GNC, Hn, HNTC, Lg, Lns, SSA, TG, TNTC, WC; KJV, NAB, NEB, NIV, TEV]: to be well-pleasing to their masters.

**not contradicting,**[a]
LEXICON—a. pres. act. participle of ἀντιλέγω (LN 33.455): 'to contradict' [BAGD, Herm; NAB], 'to talk back' [Hn; NIV, TEV], 'to answer back' [HNTC, Lns; NEB, TNT], 'to answer again' [KJV], 'to gainsay' [WC], 'to be refractory' [RSV], 'to oppose' [LN]. This participle is also translated as an adjective: 'argumentative' [NASB]. It is also translated with the negative: 'without argument' [NJB]. It refers to arguing or complaining [TG]. It refers to more than contradiction by words; it includes actions as well [Alf, EGT, El, TC, TNTC]. It means not to be rebellious [Blm, Hn], not to argue against their master's orders or try to obstruct the master's will [EBC, EGT, El, Lg, SSA]. The present tense refers not to isolated instances but to habitual behavior [Lg, My].
QUESTION—What relationship is indicated by this participial phrase?
It gives an added exhortation [EBC, GNC, Herm; NIV]: they should be well-pleasing and they should not contradict. Some commentators take it to be a subordinate point to 'to be well-pleasing', giving a specific detail [Lns, My, SSA] in the form of the negative aspect [Hn].

QUESTION—Who were the slaves not to contradict?
They were not to contradict their masters [GNC, HNTC, TG, TNTC; NAB, NEB, NIV, TEV].

**2:10** **not stealing,**[a]

LEXICON—a. pres. mid. participle of νοσφίζω (LN 57.246): 'to steal' [NAB, NIV, TEV], 'to purloin' [KJV], 'to pilfer' [Herm, Hn, HNTC; NASB, NEB, NJB, RSV, TNT], 'to take things for oneself' [Lns], 'to embezzle' [LN], 'to put aside for oneself, to misappropriate' [BAGD], 'to misappropriate funds for oneself' [LN], 'to keep back perquisites for oneself' [WC]. The word refers to petty theft [EBC, TC, TNTC], stealing [MNTC], or misappropriation of things entrusted to them [EBC, EGT, GNC, Hn, HNTC].

QUESTION—What relationship is indicated by this participial phrase?
It is coordinate with the preceding participial phrase [HNTC; NAB, NIV, TEV, TNT]: not contradicting and not stealing.

**but**[a] **demonstrating**[b] **all**[c] **good**[d] **faithfulness,**[e]

LEXICON—a. ἀλλά (LN 89.125): 'but' [Herm, Hn, HNTC, Lns, WC; KJV, NAB, NASB, NEB, NIV, RSV], 'instead' [TEV]; not explicit [NJB, TNT].

b. pres. mid. participle of ἐνδείκνυμι (LN 28.51): 'to demonstrate' [LN], 'to show' [LN, Lns; KJV, NASB, NJB, RSV], 'to display' [HNTC], 'to exhibit' [WC], 'to evince' [Hn], 'to express' [NAB]. It means to provide proof [TNTC].

c. πᾶς (LN 58.28; 59.23): 'all' [HNTC, Lns; KJV, NASB], 'every kind of' [WC]. The two words πᾶσαν ἀγαθήν 'all good' are translated 'constant' [NAB], 'complete at all times' [NJB], 'entire and true' [RSV], 'utmost' [Hn]. The phrase πᾶσαν πίστιν ἐνδεικνυμένους ἀγαθήν 'demonstrating all good faithfulness' is translated 'to show themselves strictly honest and trustworthy' [NEB], 'to show that they can be fully trusted' [NIV], 'they must show that they are always good and faithful' [TEV], 'they must show that they are entirely trustworthy' [TNT], 'they should show that they are entirely faithful and worthy' [Herm]. 'All' means that the slaves should show fidelity at all times [SSA, TC]; they should demonstrate all possible fidelity [Alf].

d. ἀγαθός (LN 65.20; 88.1): 'good' [LN, Lns, WC; KJV, NASB], 'honest' [HNTC]. Some commentators say that it means that the 'fidelity' is genuine [El, SSA]. The double modifiers, 'all' and 'good' emphasize the importance of their showing fidelity [SSA]. This word implies that submission to their masters did not include obedience if their masters ordered them to do wrong [Bg, EBC, WC].

e. πίστις (LN 31.85; 31.88): 'faithfulness' [BAGD, LN, WC], 'trustworthiness' [Hn, HNTC, LN], 'faith' [LN; NASB], 'fidelity' [Lns; KJV, NAB, RSV], 'honesty' [NJB]. The meaning is not 'faith' *in* their masters but

TITUS 2:10

'fidelity' which they should show *to* their masters [EBC, EGT, Lns, SSA, TC]; faithfulness [GNC, Rb].

QUESTION—What relationship is indicated by this participial phrase?

It is in contrast with the preceding negative phrase or phrases [GNC, Herm, Hn, HNTC, Lns, My, WC; KJV, NAB, NASB, NEB, NIV, TEV]: not stealing, but on the contrary showing fidelity. It is an additional exhortation [NJB] and means more than merely refraining from stealing [My]. It is the generic restatement of the preceding specific 'not stealing' [SSA].

**in-order-that[a] the teaching[b] the/which-is of-the Savior[c] of-us God they-may-adorn[d] in[e] all-things.[f]**

LEXICON—a. ἵνα (LN 89.59): 'in order that' [Lns, WC], 'so that' [Herm, Hn, HNTC; NIV, NJB, RSV], 'that' [KJV, NASB], 'so as' [NAB, TEV], 'and so' [TNT], not explicit [NEB].

b. διδασκαλία (LN 33.236): 'teaching' [BAGD, Herm, HNTC, LN, Lns, WC; NIV, NJB, TEV, TNT], 'doctrine' [Hn, LN; KJV, NAB, NASB, NEB, RSV]. The reference is to the word of God [Lns, NCBC]. It refers specifically to the doctrines of salvation [El, SSA], the gospel [El, My], as the forefronted word 'Savior' indicates [SSA].

c. σωτήρ (LN 21.31): 'Savior' [Hn, HNTC, LN, Lns, WC; all versions], 'savior' [BAGD, Herm]. The reference is to the Father, not Christ [Alf, EGT, El, GNC, Herm, My, NCB, TC], or to the totality of the Godhead [Lg].

d. pres. act. subj. of κοσμέω (LN 79.12): 'to adorn' [BAGD, Hn, LN, Lns, WC; KJV, NASB, RSV], 'to embellish' [HNTC], 'to make attractive' [NIV], 'to beautify' [LN], 'to do credit to' [BAGD], 'to be a credit to' [Herm; NJB], 'to bring credit to' [TEV, TNT].

e. ἐν with dative object: 'in'. See in 2:9.

f. πᾶς (plural) (LN 59.23): 'all things' [WC; KJV], 'everything' [RSV], 'all they do' [TEV], 'every way' [Herm; NIV, NJB, TNT], 'every way possible' [NAB], 'all such ways' [NEB], 'every respect' [Hn; NASB], 'all respects' [HNTC, Lns]. This word is neuter, referring to 'things', not to persons [Alf, EBC, My, SSA]. 'All things' refers to every area of their work [TC]. The phrase 'in all things' is emphatic in its position at the end of the sentence [EBC].

QUESTION—What relationship is indicated by ἵνα 'in order that'?

It introduces the purpose for the good conduct the slaves are to show [El, Herm, Hn, Lns, SSA, WC; NIV, NJB, RSV]: they must be such people in order that they may adorn the teaching.

QUESTION—How are the noun and the noun phrase related in the genitive construction τὴν διδασκαλίαν τὴν τοῦ σωτῆρος ἡμῶν θεοῦ 'the doctrine/ teaching of our Savior God'?

1. God is the content of the teaching [Lns, TG; TEV]: the teaching about our Savior God. 'Savior' is attributive to 'God', indicating that God saves us [Lns].

2. God is the source of the teaching [NCB]: the teaching which comes from our Savior God.
3. God is both the source and content of the teaching [SSA]: the teaching which is about God and which also comes from him.

QUESTION— In what way would they adorn the teaching?
Their good behavior will give a favorable impression of the Christian faith to people [SSA, TC, TNTC, WC]. They would adorn the teaching by living good lives, showing the result of their following the teachings and causing their masters to value it and be attracted to it [EBC, GNC, HNTC, TNTC].

QUESTION—Who does ἡμῶν 'our' refer to?
'Our' includes all Christians [TG]: God the Savior of all Christians.

**DISCOURSE UNIT: 2:11–3:8** [NAB]. The topic is how life is transformed.

**DISCOURSE UNIT: 2:11–3:7** [TNTC]. The topic is the theological basis for living the Christian life.

**DISCOURSE UNIT: 2:11–3:2** [NCB]. The topic is God's grace and our obedience.

**DISCOURSE UNIT: 2:11–15** [EGT, GNC, Herm, Hn, HNTC, IB, Lg, MNTC, TNTC; NJB]. The topic is the basis for the Christian life [GNC, HNTC, MNTC; NJB], the history of salvation as the basis for Christian conduct [Herm], God's grace as the motivation for the Christian life [Hn], how God's grace can educate his people [TNTC], the necessity to work and wait [IB], God's purpose in revealing his grace, as the reason for the preceding exhortations [Lg].

**DISCOURSE UNIT: 2:11–14** [EBC, NCBC, SSA, TC, WC]. The topic is the basis for the Christian life [EBC], the moral reason for Christ's coming to earth [WC], the doctrinal basis for the exhortations in the preceding verses [TC], the return of Christ [NCBC].

**2:11** For

LEXICON—γάρ (LN 89.23; 91.1): 'for' [Herm, Hn, HNTC, Lns, WC; all versions except NAB, NJB], 'you see' [NJB], not explicit [NAB].

QUESTION—What relationship is indicated by this word?
It introduces an expanded comment on the topic of 'God our savior' (2:10) [Alf, EBC, El, Lns, MNTC, NCBC, TNTC]. One commentator calls it a digression [NCB]. Most find a relationship.
1. It indicates the grounds for referring to God as savior [Lns]: I am correct in saying that God is our savior since his grace appeared for the salvation of all men.
2. It indicates the grounds for the exhortations in the preceding verses [Alf, Blm, EBC, EGT, El, GNC, Herm, HNTC, ICC, Lg, MNTC, My, SSA, TG, WC]: you should do and be such things since the grace of God has appeared. It is not limited to the exhortations to slaves (2:9–10) but applies to all classes (2:1–10) [Blm, EBC, GNC, Herm, ICC, Lg, MNTC,

SSA]. One commentator refers it to all the exhortations from 1:10–2:10 [Alf].

**has-appeared<sup>a</sup> the grace<sup>b</sup> of-the God**

LEXICON—a. aorist pass. indic. of ἐπιφαίνω (LN 24.21): 'to appear' [BAGD, Herm, Hn, LN, Lns; KJV, NAB, NASB, NIV, RSV], 'to be revealed' [NJB, TNT], 'to be manifested' [HNTC], 'to dawn upon the world' [NEB]. This verb is also translated with an active meaning: '(God) has revealed' [TEV]. It is also translated as a phrase: 'there was a glorious appearance, an Epiphany' [WC]. This word is emphatic [MNTC] by forefronting, stressing the historical reality [EBC].

b. χάρις (LN 88.66): 'grace' [BAGD, Herm, Hn, HNTC, LN, Lns, WC; all versions].

QUESTION—How are the two nouns related in the genitive construction ἡ χάρις τοῦ θεοῦ 'the grace of God', and how did God's grace appear?

'Grace' is the expression of God's favor to mankind [Alf, EBC, Hn, HNTC, ICC]: the grace which God has granted to mankind. Grace appeared as the effect of a gracious act of God. He intervened for mankind's salvation [MNTC, My, SSA, TNTC]. God graciously sent his Son, and some commentators think that the incarnation is the primary reference [El, TC]. Others refer the appearance of grace to Christ's entire life, death, and resurrection [EBC, Hn, HNTC, ICC, Lg, Lns, MNTC, SSA]. Others think it refers to God's gracious action in the entirety of redemption [Alf, HNTC, IB, Lg, My, TC, TNTC]. Others think that grace appeared to the people of Crete when the gospel was preached there [Blm, GNC]. Grace is God's spontaneous favor in delivering people [EBC, HNTC], his kindness and love for mankind [EGT, Lns, TG], his giving the greatest gift to those who deserved the greatest punishment [Hn].

**related-to-salvation<sup>a</sup> to-all persons<sup>b</sup>**

TEXT—Some manuscripts add the article ἡ 'the' before σωτήριος 'related-to-salvation'. This variant is not discussed by GNT; it would make σωτήριος attributive ('the grace of God which brings salvation') instead of predicative ('the grace of God has appeared, related to salvation'). The article is included by Blm, El, and KJV.

LEXICON—a. σωτήριος (LN **21.28**): 'saving' [BAGD, Lns, WC], 'healing' [NEB]. This word is also translated as a phrase: 'offering salvation' [NAB], 'bringing salvation' [BAGD, Herm, Hn, LN; NASB, TNT], 'to save' [NJB], 'for the salvation of' [HNTC; RSV, TEV]. This word is also translated as a clause: 'that brings salvation' [KJV, NIV].

b. ἄνθρωπος (LN 9.1): 'men' [Herm, Hn, HNTC, Lns, WC; KJV, NAB, NASB, NIV, RSV, TNT], 'persons' [LN], 'mankind' [LN; NEB, TEV], 'human race' [NJB].

QUESTION—How is this phrase related to the preceding clause?

It is related to its subject, 'grace' [Alf] in a predicative relation, not attributive [Lns, TC]: God's grace appeared, bringing salvation for all men.

The sense is that God's grace produces salvation [WC]. It offers salvation to everyone [Blm, EGT, HNTC, IB, ICC, Lns, MNTC, SSA, WC], salvation from the power of sin [ICC]. This phrase describes the grace referred to as the sole means for salvation for mankind [El].

QUESTION—What is the phrase πᾶσιν ἀνθρώποις 'to all persons' connected with?

1. It is connected with σωτήριος 'related to salvation' [Alf, Blm, Brt, CBC, EBC, EGT, El, GNC, Herm, Hn, HNTC, Lg, Lns, My, SSA, TC, TG, TNTC, WC; all versions except KJV, NIV]: God's grace makes salvation available to all persons. The author emphasizes the universal offer of salvation [CBC, Lns, My, NCB, NCBC, TC].
2. It is connected with ἐπεφάνη 'it has appeared' [KJV, NIV]: God's grace has appeared to all persons.

**2:12 instructing[a] us,**

LEXICON—a. pres. act. participle of παιδεύω (LN 33.226): 'to instruct' [LN; NASB, TEV], 'to teach' [LN; KJV, NIV, NJB, TNT], 'to train' [HNTC, LN; NAB, RSV], 'to educate' [Herm, Lns, MNTC, WC], 'to correct, give guidance' [BAGD]. This participle is also translated with passive meaning: '(by it) we are disciplined' [NEB]. The present tense implies that the education is a continuing process [Lns, MNTC, SSA].

QUESTION—What relationship is indicated by the participial form παιδεύουσα 'instructing'?

It states what the grace of God does [Herm, SSA; NAB, NEB, NIV, NJB, TEV, TNT]: the grace of God has arrived, and it teaches us.

QUESTION—What is meant by παιδεύουσα 'instructing'?

The participle is comprehensive in meaning, including teaching, discipline, correction, etc. [EBC, Hn]. Some think that the emphasis is upon education [GNC, Herm, IB, ICC, Lns, MNTC, NCBC, TG, TNTC]. Others think that the meaning is to discipline, not merely to teach [Alf, EGT, El, HNTC, My, NCB, SSA, TC, WC; NEB].

QUESTION—Who is referred to by the pronoun ἡμᾶς 'us'?

'Us' is inclusive [SSA], and includes all Christians [TG].

**that**

LEXICON—ἵνα (LN 90.22): 'that' [Lns; KJV, NJB], 'in order that' [Hn], 'to the end that' [WC], not explicit [Herm, HNTC; NAB, NEB, NIV, RSV, TEV, TNT].

QUESTION—What relationship is indicated by this word?

1. It indicates the content of παιδεύουσα 'instructing' [GNC, Herm, HNTC, Lg, MNTC, My, SSA; all versions]: teaching us that we should live thus.
2. It introduces the purpose of παιδεύουσα 'instructing' [Alf, EBC, El, Hn, Lns, TC]: it instructs us in order that we may live thus.
3. It introduces the purpose of the appearance of the grace of God through Christ [EGT]: the grace of God appeared in order that we might live thus.

## TITUS 2:12

**having-renounced<sup>a</sup> the ungodliness<sup>b</sup> and the worldly<sup>c</sup> desires<sup>d</sup>**

LEXICON—a. aorist mid. (deponent = act.) participle of ἀρνέομαι (LN 30.52): 'to renounce' [Herm, Hn, HNTC; NEB, RSV], 'to deny' [BAGD, Lns, WC; KJV, NASB], 'to say "No" to' [LN; NIV], 'to reject' [NAB], 'to give up' [NJB, TEV, TNT].

b. ἀσέβεια (LN 53.10): 'ungodliness' [Hn, Lns; KJV, NASB, NIV, TNT], 'impiety' [BAGD], 'ungodliness' [WC], 'godlessness' [BAGD, Herm, LN], 'ungodly living' [TEV], 'godless ways' [NAB, NEB], 'irreligion' [HNTC; RSV], 'everything contrary to true religion' [NJB]. It includes worship of false gods, denial of God's existence or of his attributes, ungodly behavior, or disobedience to God's will [Blm], false ideas of God [HNTC, ICC]. It refers to heathen and immoral conduct [EGT, Hn, IB, ICC], actions contrary to God's will [SSA], anything which is dishonorable or offensive to God [El, ICC], failure to worship God [WC], the totality of life lived in opposition to God's law [Lg]. It is the opposite of εὐσεβῶς 'godily' [El, GNC, ICC, My, SSA, TC, TG, TNTC]. This term is the generic of which the following term is a specific [Lns]. The definite article indicates that this quality is well known [Lns].

c. κοσμικός (LN **41.39**): 'worldly' [BAGD, Herm, Hn, HNTC, LN, Lns; all versions]. This word is translated as a phrase: 'of the world' [WC]. The reference is to the world system which is under Satan's control and is without God [Alf, EBC, My], actions which are opposed to God [SSA], desires directed solely to the present world [HNTC, Lg, Lns, TNTC].

d. ἐπιθυμία (LN 25.12; 25.20): 'desire' [BAGD, Herm, HNTC, LN, WC; NAB, NASB, NEB, TNT], 'evil desire' [LN], 'passion' [Hn; NIV, NJB, RSV, TEV], 'lust' [LN, Lns; KJV]. The definite article with this noun makes it comprehensive, referring to all worldly desires [Alf]. The article is used because these desires are well known [Lns]. The combination of the two negative qualities adds emphasis [Lns]. 'Worldly desires' is a specific of the general term 'ungodliness' [Lns].

QUESTION—What relationship is indicated by the participial form ἀρνησάμενοι 'having renounced', and what is the significance of the aorist tense?

1. The participle is directly connected to the following verb and is subordinate to it [Alf, EGT, El, Lns, TC; KJV]: God's grace instructs us that, having renounced ungodliness and worldly desire, we should live soberly, righteously, and godlily. The action of this aorist participle is prior to the main verb [EBC, El, Lns, SSA, TC]: after renouncing, we should live soberly, etc. This may be a reference to the time of baptism [HNTC, ICC, Lns, NCBC, TC]. Or, the action of the aorist participle occurs at the time of the main verb, the aorist summing up the whole life [Alf]: renouncing, we should live, etc. The use of a participle here shows that the negative effect is less prominent than the positive effect [Lns].

2. The participle is the object of ἵνα 'that' and is coordinate with the following verb [EBC, GNC, Herm, Hn, HNTC, ICC, TNTC, WC; all

versions except KJV]: God's grace instructs us that we should renounce ungodliness and worldly desires and that we should live soberly, righteously, and godlily. The participle gives the negative contrast to the following positive effect [EBC, GNC, Herm, Hn, HNTC, Lg, TNTC, WC].

**soberly[a] and righteously[b] and godlily[c] we-should-live[d] in[e] the present[f] age,[g]**
LEXICON—a. σωφρόνως (LN 88.94): 'soberly' [BAGD, HNTC; KJV], 'sober-mindedly' [Lns], 'sensibly' 2:13 [LN; NASB], 'temperately' [NAB], 'self-restrained' [NJB]. This adverb is also translated as an attribute of 'a life': 'self-controlled' [NIV], 'disciplined' [TNT], 'sober' [WC; RSV], 'prudent' [Herm], 'of self-mastery' [Hn], 'of temperance' [NEB]. 'Soberly' refers to our relations to ourselves [Blm, EBC, EGT, El, Hn, HNTC, ICC, Lg, MNTC, TC, TNTC, WC], to self-control [My].

b. δικαίως (LN 88.15): 'righteously' [LN, Lns; KJV, NASB], 'justly' [BAGD, LN; NAB], 'uprightly' [BAGD, HNTC]. This adverb is also translated as an attribute of 'a life': 'upright' [Herm; NIV, NJB, RSV, TEV], 'righteous' [WC; TNT], 'of honesty' [NEB], 'of fairness' [Hn]. This word refers to our relations with other persons [Blm, EBC, EGT, El, Hn, HNTC, ICC, Lg, MNTC, My, TC, TNTC, WC]. It means a life of which God approves [Lns, My], a life of obeying God's and man's laws [SSA].

c. εὐσεβῶς (LN 53.6): 'godlily' [Lns], 'godly' [Lns; KJV, NASB], 'in a godly manner' [BAGD], 'devoutly' [NAB], 'in a devout manner' [LN], 'religiously' [HNTC]. This adverb is also translated as an attribute of 'a life': 'godly' [WC; NIV, RSV, TEV, TNT], 'religious' [NJB], 'pious' [Herm], 'of godliness' [NEB], 'of devotion' [Hn]. This word refers to our behavior toward God [Blm, EBC, EGT, El, Hn, HNTC, ICC, Lg, MNTC, TC, TNTC, WC], holy thoughts and conduct [My], pious worship and communion with God [Lns], Christian conduct based on a proper relationship with God [EGT, SSA], living as God requires [TNTC]. It is the opposite of ἀσέβεια 'ungodliness' [GNC, Lns, TNTC].

d. aorist act. subj. of ζάω (LN 41.2): 'to live' [BAGD, LN, Lns, WC; KJV, NAB, NASB], 'to live lives' [Hn; NIV, NJB, RSV, TEV, TNT], 'to live a life' [WC; NEB], 'to lead a life' [Herm], 'to conduct oneself' [LN]. The aorist tense probably is comprehensive, referring to our entire life [EBC].

e. ἐν with dative object (LN 67.136): 'in' [Herm, HNTC, Lns, WC; all versions except TNT]. The phrase ἐν τῷ νῦν αἰῶνι 'in the present age' is also translated 'here and now' [TNT], 'in the here and now' [Hn].

f. νῦν (LN 67.38): 'present' [HNTC, WC; KJV, NASB, NEB], 'this' [Herm; NAB, RSV, TEV], 'this present' [Lns; NIV, NJB], 'now' [LN].

g. αἰών (LN 67.143): 'age' [BAGD, Herm, HNTC, LN, WC; NAB, NASB, NEB, NIV], 'eon' [Lns], 'world' [KJV, NJB, RSV, TEV].

TITUS 2:12 69

QUESTION—How are these three qualities related?
The two instances of καί 'and' connecting these three words gives added emphasis by calling attention to each adverb separately [SSA]. These three adverbs are forefronted for emphasis [EBC]. 'Soberly' is the first of the three; it gives the contrast to 'worldly desires' and is the chief characteristic of the chapter [ICC].

**2:13** awaiting[a] the blessed[b] hope[c]
LEXICON—a. pres. mid. (deponent = act.) participle of προσδέχομαι (LN 85.60): 'to await' [Herm, LN; NAB, RSV], 'to wait for' [BAGD, Hn, LN; NIV, NJB, TEV], 'to look forward to' [HNTC; NEB], 'to look for' [KJV, NASB, TNT], 'to expect' [BAGD, Lns, WC]. It is a joyful expectation [Bg, EBC, EGT]. The present tense shows that this expectation is a continuing state [Alf, EBC].
   b. μακάριος (LN 25.119): 'blessed' [BAGD, Herm, Hn, HNTC, Lns, WC; KJV, NAB, NASB, NIV, RSV, TEV], 'happy' [LN]. The phrase τὴν μακαρίαν ἐλπίδα 'the blessed hope' is translated 'the happy fulfillment of our hope' [NEB], 'the fulfillment of our blessed hope' [TNT], 'in hope (for) the blessing which will come' [NJB].
   c. ἐλπίς (LN 25.61): 'hope' [BAGD, Herm, Hn, HNTC, Lns, WC; KJV, NAB, NASB, NIV, RSV], 'what is hoped for' [LN], 'day we hope for' [TEV]. The sense is objective, referring to the object which is hoped for, the realization of the hope [Alf, El, Hn, HNTC, IB, Lg, Lns, MNTC, My, NCB, NCBC, SSA, TC, TG, TNTC].
QUESTION—What relationship is indicated by the participial form προσδεχ-όμενοι 'awaiting'?
   1. It indicates a temporal circumstance [GNC, Hn, HNTC, TG; NAB, NIV, TEV, TNT]: we should live righteously while we await the blessed hope.
   2. It indicates the reason or grounds for ζήσωμεν 'we should live' [Herm, ICC]: we should live righteously, because we await the blessed hope.
QUESTION—What is meant by calling the hope 'blessed'?
Some commentators explain it to mean that the hope brings blessing [GNC, Hn, My, SSA, TC]. Others take blessedness to be the object of the hope: we hope for blessings [Herm; NJB], or we hope for the blessed day of the appearing [TEV].

**and[a] appearing[b] of-the glory[c] of-the great[d] God and Savior of-us Jesus Christ,**
TEXT—Some manuscripts read 'Christ Jesus' instead of 'Jesus Christ'. GNT does not deal with this variant. 'Christ Jesus' is read by Herm, Hn, HNTC, NCB, TC, WC, NAB, NASB, NEB, and NJB.
LEXICON—a. καί (LN 89.92): 'and' [Herm, HNTC, Lns, WC; KJV, NASB], 'with' [NJB], not explicit [Hn; NAB, NEB, NIV, RSV, TEV, TNT].
   b. ἐπιφάνεια (LN 24.21): 'appearing' [BAGD, LN; KJV, NAB, NASB, NIV, NJB, RSV, TNT], 'appearance' [BAGD, Herm, LN], 'manifestation' [HNTC], 'epiphany' [Lns, WC]. This noun is also translated as a

verb: 'to appear' [NEB, TEV]. This will be a second appearing, the previous one being mentioned in 2:11 [Alf, Hn, IB, Lns, My, Rb, SSA, TC].

   c. δόξα (LN 79.18): 'glory' [Herm, Hn, HNTC, LN, Lns, WC; NAB, NASB, NJB, RSV, TNT], 'splendor' [LN]. This noun is also translated as an adjective: 'glorious' [KJV, NIV]. This word refers to the awesome radiance that surrounds God [HNTC]. It is God's saving presence [TG]. It refers to the totality of Christ's attributes in himself and in those who believe in him [ICC, Lns]. It refers to the splendor which will accompany Christ when he appears [SSA]. It is the glory both of the Father and of the Son [Alf].

   d. μέγας (LN 87.22): 'great' [BAGD, Herm, Hn, HNTC, LN, Lns, WC; all versions], 'important' [LN].

QUESTION—How are the two nouns 'hope' and 'appearing' related?

   1. The content of the 'hope' is explained as being the appearing of Jesus Christ [Blm, EBC, GNC, Hn, HNTC, Lg, Lns, My, NCB, SSA, TNTC, WC; NAB, NIV, RSV, TEV, TNT]: our blessed hope, (namely) the appearing. Both terms are governed by one definite article, which implies that the two are one event from two points of view [EBC, Lns]. The καί 'and' between these two nouns has the sense of 'even' or 'namely' [GNC].

   2. 'Hope' and 'appearing' are separate events [Alf, Herm; KJV, NASB]: awaiting the blessed hope and the appearing.

   3. 'Hope' is fulfilled when the glory appears [NEB].

QUESTION—How are event word and the attribute word related in the genitive construction ἐπιφάνειαν τῆς δόξης τοῦ μεγάλου θεοῦ καὶ σωτῆρος 'appearance of the glory of the great God and Savior'?

   1. God's glory is what will appear [Alf, Bg, EBC, EGT, El, GNC, Herm, Hn, HNTC, Lns, TNTC, WC; NAB, NASB, NEB, NJB, RSV, TEV]: the appearing of the glory belonging to the great God and Savior. The glory which Christ now has in heaven will be manifested on earth at his appearing [EBC]. Glory is related to both 'hope' and 'appearing', since they are both governed by the same definite article [El].

   2. 'Glory' describes the manner of the appearing [Blm, SSA; KJV, NIV, TNT]: the glorious appearing of our great God and Savior. He will come gloriously [SSA].

QUESTION—What is the phrase Ἰησοῦ Χριστοῦ 'Jesus Christ' connected with?

   1. It is in apposition with the whole preceding phrase, 'the great God and Savior of us' [Bg, Blm, Brt, EBC, El, GNC, Hn, IB, ICC, Lg, Lns, NCB, NCBC, Rb, SSA, TC, TG, TNTC, WC; all versions except KJV, NAB]: the appearing of our great God and Savior, (namely) Jesus Christ. In the NT the word ἐπιφάνειαν 'appearing' always refers to Christ, never to God the Father; the NT does not teach an appearing of the Father [Blm, CBC, EGT, El, GNC, Hn, IB, Lg, SSA, TC, TNTC, WC]. Nowhere else

TITUS 2:13

in the NT is God described as 'great' [SSA, TNTC]. Both God and Savior are governed by one article, which indicates unity of reference of the two parts [Brt, EBC, GNC, Hn, IB, ICC, Lns, NCB, Rb, WC]; and since the following verse refers to Christ alone [El] it is logical to refer this phrase to Christ alone as its antecedent [EBC]. The adjective 'great' is connected with both God and Savior [Blm, EBC, El, Lg]: Christ who is the great God and great Savior. The genitive ἡμῶν 'of us' is to be taken with both God and Savior [Blm, Hn, IB, ICC, Lg, Lns, NCB, NCBC, WC; all versions except KJV, NAB]: of him who is our great God and Savior.

2. It is in apposition with only 'our Savior'; 'the great God' refers to the Father [Alf, EGT, Herm, HNTC, MNTC, My; KJV, NAB]: the appearing of the great God (the Father), and of our Savior Jesus Christ. Two glories will be manifested when Christ comes again, the Father's and the Son's [Alf, EGT]. Paul does not elsewhere clearly call Christ 'God' [HNTC, My], and in the pastoral Epistles Christ is generally presented as dependent upon God [HNTC]. The use of the adjective 'great' shows that God is distinct from Savior [My]. The article is sometimes omitted before σωτῆρος 'Savior' [EGT, TC].

3. It is possibly in apposition with 'the glory' [GNC]: the appearance of our Savior God's glory, (namely, the appearance of) Jesus Christ. This interpretation avoids the problems of the other interpretations [GNC].

QUESTION—To whom does ἡμῶν 'of us' refer?

It refers to all Christians in general [Hn]: the Savior of all Christians.

**2:14** who gave[a] himself in-behalf-of[b] us

LEXICON—a. pres. act. indic. of δίδωμι (LN 23.100): 'to give' [Herm, Hn, HNTC, Lns, WC; KJV, NASB, NIV, RSV, TEV, TNT], 'to give up' [BAGD], 'to offer' [NJB], 'to give one's life' [LN], 'to sacrifice' [BAGD; NAB, NEB], 'to die for' [LN]. He gave himself to death [Blm], and the word (or the whole phrase [My]) implies that he did it freely and willingly [Blm, EBC, Hn, Lg, Lns, SSA]. The following pronoun 'himself' is emphatic—his whole self, the greatest gift of all [El].

b. ὑπέρ with genitive object (LN 90.36): 'for' [BAGD, Herm, Hn, HNTC, Lns, WC; all versions], 'on behalf of' [Alf, BAGD, My, SSA]. Some commentators think that it includes the meaning 'in our stead' [Hn, ICC, Lg, Lns, TNTC]; substitution is involved [Lg].

QUESTION—Who does ὅς 'who' refer to?

It refers to Jesus Christ (2:13) [Alf, Hn, HNTC, IB, Lg, Lns, MNTC, My, SSA]: Jesus Christ gave himself.

**in-order-that[a] he-might-redeem[b] us from[c] all lawlessness[d]**

LEXICON—a. ἵνα (LN 89.59): 'in order (to)' [Herm, Hn; NJB], 'that' [WC; KJV, NASB, TNT], 'so as' [Lns], 'to' [HNTC; NAB, NEB, NIV, RSV, TEV].

b. aorist mid. subj. of λυτρόω (LN 37.128): 'to redeem' [BAGD, Herm, Hn; KJV, NAB, NASB, NIV, RSV], 'to ransom' [El, HNTC, Lns, WC; NJB], 'to set free' [BAGD, LN; NEB, TNT], 'to liberate' [LN], 'to deliver' [LN], 'to rescue' [BAGD; TEV]. This word is used of ransoming from slavery [Bg]. The basic sense is to buy off with a price [Alf, Lns, My], paying the ransom to deliver from sin's penalty [Blm] or bondage [IB], to deliver from the bondage to lawlessness [EBC, El, Hn, Lg, Lns, My, SSA]. The ransom was his blood [El, Hn, My]. The middle voice indicates personal interest by Christ [Alf, Lns, My]. Since there is no indication of the one to whom the ransom was paid, the focus is upon the deliverance of the ransomed ones rather than upon the full figure of ransom [SSA].

c. ἀπό with genitive object (LN 89.122): 'from' [Herm, Hn, HNTC, Lns, WC; all versions]. It implies being effectively removed from the vicinity of lawlessness [EBC, TC, TNTC], not merely 'out' as ὦκ would imply [TC, TNTC].

d. ἀνομία (LN 88.139): 'unrighteousness' [NAB], 'iniquity' [HNTC; KJV, RSV], 'wickedness' [NEB, NIV, TEV, TNT], 'injustice' [Herm], 'lawlessness' [BAGD, El, Hn, LN, Lns, WC], 'lawless deed' [NASB], 'lawless living' [LN], 'fault' [NJB]. The principal thought is deliverance from the power of sin rather than from the guilt of sin [ICC, NCB].

QUESTION—What relationship is indicated by ἵνα 'in order that'?

It indicates the purpose for which Christ gave himself [GNC, Hn, Lg, MNTC, My, SSA, TC]: he gave himself in order to redeem and purify us.

## and might-cleanse[a] for-himself a-people[b] special,[c]

LEXICON—a. aorist act. subj. of καθαρίζω (LN 53.28): 'to cleanse' [BAGD, LN, Lns, WC; NAB], 'to purify' [BAGD, Hn, LN; KJV, NASB, NIV, NJB, RSV, TNT], 'to make pure' [NEB, TEV], 'to consecrate' [Herm]. This cleansing follows the redemption; Christ's people are cleansed by his blood [EBC, HNTC, ICC, Lg].

b. λαός (LN 11.12): 'people' [BAGD, Herm, Hn, HNTC, Lns, WC; all versions], 'people of God' [LN].

c. περιούσιος (LN **57.5; 58.48**): 'of his own' [HNTC; NAB, RSV], 'for his own possession' [NASB], 'marked out for his own' [NEB], 'his very own' [Hn], 'that are his very own' [EBC; NIV], 'to be his very own' [NJB], 'who belong to him alone' [LN; TEV], 'set apart for himself' [GNC], 'select' [Lns], 'his chosen' [BAGD; TNT], 'his special' [Herm], 'special' [BAGD, LN], 'peculiar' [KJV], 'peculiarly his own' [WC]. Some commentators think that the word implies belonging to one's household [Alf, El], but not 'chosen out from among other things' [Alf]. Others think that it does mean 'chosen out from among other things' [Blm]; especially God's own people above all other nations [Bg, Lns]; a valued property [EGT]; what remains over, hence one's special possession [MNTC], a special treasure, one's own in a special sense [TNTC].

QUESTION—Who are the special people?
The special people are the ones referred to by 'us' in the preceding clause [EGT; NEB, TEV, TNT]: that he might purify us to make us fit to be his special people.

**a-zealot<sup>a</sup> of-good<sup>b</sup> works.<sup>c</sup>**

LEXICON—a. ζηλωτής (LN 25.77): 'zealous seeker' [WC], 'enthusiast' [LN], 'zealous person' [LN]. This noun is also translated as an adjective: 'zealous' [HNTC, Lns; KJV, NASB, RSV], 'eager' [Herm]. The phrase ζηλωτὴν καλῶν ἔργων 'a zealot of good works' is translated 'eager to do what is good' [NIV], 'eager to do good' [NEB, NJB, TEV], 'eager to do what is right' [NAB], 'with a zest for noble deeds' [Hn], 'and (that he might) inspire us to do good' [TNT]. The word used means 'a zealot' [BAGD, EBC].

b. καλός (LN 65.22; 88.4): 'good' [Herm, HNTC, LN; KJV, NASB, NEB, NJB, RSV, TEV, TNT], 'fine' [LN, WC], 'excellent' [Lns], 'noble' [Hn], 'what is good' [NIV], 'what is right' [NAB]. The reference to good works is general, including both help to others and right actions [SSA].

c. ἔργον (LN 42.11): 'work' [BAGD, Herm, HNTC, Lns, WC; KJV], 'deed' [Hn, LN; NASB, RSV], 'act' [LN]. This noun is also translated as a verb: 'to do' [NEB, NIV, NJB, TEV, TNT].

QUESTION—How is this phrase related to what precedes?
It indicates the characteristic which the 'special people' should have [GNC, My, SSA, TNTC]: a special people who are characterized by a zeal to do good works.

QUESTION—How are the two nouns related in the genitive construction ζηλωτὴν καλῶν ἔργων 'zealot of good works'?
'Good works' indicates the object for which the zeal is manifested [El, Rb]: zealous to do good works.

**DISCOURSE UNIT: 2:15–3:11** [WC]. The topic is instructions to emphasize the moral purpose of Christ's incarnation, with special emphasis upon maintaining a spirit of love [WC].

**DISCOURSE UNIT: 2:15** [EBC, NCBC, SSA, TC]. The topic is a summary of Titus's responsibilities [EBC], exhortation to Titus to speak with authority [TC]. It is a verse of transition [NCBC].

**2:15** **These-things speak<sup>a</sup> and exhort<sup>b</sup> and reprove<sup>c</sup>**

LEXICON—a. pres. act. impera. of λαλέω (LN 33.70): 'to speak' [LN, WC; KJV, NASB], 'to say' [LN; NAB, NJB, TNT], 'to tell' [Hn, LN], 'to utter' [Lns], 'to declare' [RSV], 'to teach' [Herm, HNTC; NIV, TEV]. The phrase ταῦτα λάλει 'these things speak' is translated 'these, then, are your themes' [NEB]. This word refers to declaring his message [HNTC], or to teaching [My]. The present tense implies continuing to do what he has already been doing [EBC, Hn, Lns].

b. pres. act. impera. of παρακαλέω (LN 25.150): 'to exhort' [BAGD, Herm, HNTC; KJV, NASB, RSV], 'to urge' [Hn; NEB], 'to encourage' [BAGD, LN, WC; NIV, NJB, TEV, TNT], 'to admonish' [Lns], 'to make appeals' [BAGD; NAB]. This word means to encourage believers to practice the teachings [Alf, Blm, EBC, El, GNC, IB], to urge the people to accept them [HNTC], or to exhort them strongly [My]. The present tense implies continual exhortation [EBC, Hn, Lns].

c. pres. act. impera. of ἐλέγχω (LN 33.417): 'to reprove' [Herm, Hn, HNTC; NASB, RSV, TNT], 'to rebuke' [LN, WC; KJV, NIV, TEV], 'to reproach' [LN], 'to impress with conviction' [Lns], 'to argue' [NEB, NJB], 'to make corrections' [NAB], 'to bring to light, to expose, to set forth' [BAGD]. This word means to reprove those who oppose or neglect the teachings [Alf, Blm, EBC, El, GNC, HNTC, IB, My]. The present tense implies continual reproving [EBC, Hn, Lns]. See this word at 1:13.

QUESTION—What does ταῦτα 'these things' refer to?

1. It refers to what precedes [Alf, Blm, EBC, EGT, El, GNC, Herm, HNTC, IB, My, TC, TNTC; NASB, NIV, NJB, TEV, TNT]: speak the things which I have mentioned. There is a special reference to 2:1 where the same verb is used concerning the things that are fitting for healthy teaching [Alf, EBC, El, HNTC]. It refers to all the exhortations in chapter 2 [TNTC], or to everything from 1:10 [GNC, Hn, Lg, SSA].

2. It refers to the following verses [CBC]: speak the things which I am about to mention.

QUESTION—To what verbs is ταῦτα 'these things' related?

1. It is related to all three verbs: 'speak', 'exhort', and 'reprove' [Herm, Hn, SSA]: speak these things and exhort these things and reprove the believers regarding these things.

2. It is related only to 'speak' [EGT, El, GNC, TC]: speak these things, and also exhort and reprove the believers.

**with[a] all authority;[b]**

a. μετά with genitive object (LN 89.79): 'with' [Herm, Hn, HNTC, Lns, WC; all versions except TEV, TNT]. The phrase μετὰ πάσης ἐπιταγῆς 'with all authority' is translated 'use your full authority' [TEV], 'you have full authority' [TNT]. The phrase relates to the manner in which Titus is to speak [SSA].

b. ἐπιταγή (LN 37.42): 'authority' [Hn, HNTC, LN; all versions], 'command' [BAGD, WC], 'impressiveness' [Herm], 'imperativeness' [Lns]. The meaning is that Titus can and must speak with authority (in a highly authoritative manner [EGT]) as God's minister [Bg, Blm, EBC, HNTC, MNTC], or as Christ's representative [Hn]. He is not to let the church decide whether or not to obey his teaching [My]. His authority comes from his relationship with Paul [GNC]. He has a message from God and a commission as an apostle [HNTC, IB, SSA, TNTC].

TITUS 2:15

QUESTION—What is this phrase connected with?
1. It is connected with all three preceding verbs [Blm, EBC, Herm, Hn, HNTC, IB, Lns, SSA]: speak, exhort, and reprove with all authoritativeness. The three verbs are closely connected by καί 'and' [SSA] and form a climax to what Paul has said: Titus is to say these things; more than this, he is to urge them; even more than this, he is to emphasize them so as to convict the careless or disobedient [EBC, Lns].
2. It is connected with παρακάλει καὶ ἔλεγχε 'exhort and reprove' only [EGT, TC, TG; NAB, NIV, NJB, RSV, TNT]: exhort and reprove with all authority. 'Speak' is a general term, which is to be carried out by 'exhort' and 'rebuke' as pastoral functions; the authoritativeness is not to be restricted to 'reprove' only [EGT].
3. It is connected with ἔλεγχε 'reprove' only [Blm, El, ICC]: reprove with all authority. It thus corresponds with 'sharply' in ἔλεγχε αὐτοὺς ἀποτόμως 'reprove them sharply' (1:13) [El, ICC].

**(let) no-one despise[a] you.**
LEXICON—a. pres. act. impera. of περιφρονέω (LN **76.25**): 'to despise' [BAGD, Rb, WC; KJV, NIV, NJB], 'to look down on' [BAGD, Herm; NAB, TEV], 'to underrate' [HNTC], 'to disregard' [Lns; NASB, RSV], 'to slight' [Hn; NEB], 'to ignore' [TNT], 'to invalidate one's authority' [LN]. It is a third person imperative, stating positively what is implied by the preceding phrase 'with all authority' concerning the manner of Titus's teaching [SSA, TC]. This word does not refer to avoiding justified criticism, but rather to speaking and acting in an authoritative manner that will not be disregarded [El, My]. It does not mean to despise, but rather to disregard [Lns].
QUESTION—How is this clause, a third person command, related to what precedes?
It is addressed to Titus [TG], urging him so to conduct himself in these exhortations and rebukes that no one will be able to criticize him for lack of authoritativeness [Alf, Blm, EGT] or to question his right to speak [MNTC]: carry out these instructions authoritatively so that no one will be able to criticize or disregard you. He must behave in a consistent manner so that his authority will not be despised [EGT]. The meaning is that no one will be permitted to disregard him, because of his divine message and his apostolic commission [IB]. Some think that it is also intended for the churches to hear in order to remind them of Titus's authority [EBC, GNC, Hn, HNTC, IB, ICC, NCBB, SSA]: I remind the churches that the people must not disregard your authority.

**DISCOURSE UNIT: 3:1–11** [EBC, GNT, HNTC, Lg; NJB]. The topic is instructions for the Christians [NJB], the maintaining of good deeds [GNT], the social challenge to believers [HNTC], Christians' relationships to other persons [EBC], opposition to the false teachers [Lg].

**DISCOURSE UNIT: 3:1–8** [Hn, ICC]. The topic is duties to authorities and to other people.

**DISCOURSE UNIT: 3:1–8a** [GNC, Herm, IB, SSA]. The topic is instructions for believers in their relationships to government and society [GNC], general admonitions based on the salvation which God has provided [Herm], how Christians should live in a non-Christian society [IB].

**DISCOURSE UNIT: 3:1–2** [Alf, EBC, EGT, MNTC, NCBC, SSA, TC, TNTC]. The topic is believers' duties as citizens [EBC, MNTC, NCBC], believers' attitude in society [Alf, TC, TNTC].

**3:1** Remind[a] them to-be-subject[b] to-rulers,[c] to-authorities,[d]

TEXT—Instead of ἀρχαῖς ἐξουσίαις 'rulers, authorities', some manuscripts have ἀρχαῖς καὶ ἐξουσίαις 'rulers and authorities'. GNT omits the καί 'and' with a C rating, indicating a considerable degree of doubt. 'And' is omitted by Alf, EGT, El, Hn, Lg(D), Lns, My, Rb, SSA, WC, and NASB. 'And' is included by Blm and Lg. The reading of others is uncertain, since some doubtless include 'and' stylistically without reading it in the Greek text.

LEXICON—a. pres. act. impera. of ὑπομιμνῄσκω (LN 29.10): 'to remind' [BAGD, Hn, HNTC, LN, WC; all versions except KJV], 'to put in mind' [KJV], 'to put in remembrance' [Lns], 'to cause to remember' [LN], 'to admonish' [Herm]. The meaning is to remind the people of things they had known but which might be forgotten [Alf, EBC, GNC, Hn, ICC, My, NCB, TNTC], or at least things which they would recognize as legitimate aspects of the gospel [GNC]. The present tense of the imperative mood means that Titus is to remind the people regularly [EBC, HNTC, SSA] and probably was already doing so [SSA].

  b. pres. mid. infin. of ὑποτάσσω (LN 36.18): 'to be subject' [Herm; KJV, NASB, NIV], 'to be in subjection' [Hn, Lns], 'to be loyally subject' [NAB], 'to subject oneself' [BAGD], 'to obey'.[LN], 'to be submissive' [HNTC; NEB, RSV], 'to submit' LN; [TEV, TNT], 'to submit themselves' [WC]. The two verbs ὑποτάσσεσθαι, πειθαρχεῖν 'to be subject, to obey' are translated 'to be obedient' [NJB]. The middle voice implies that the Christians should voluntarily submit themselves [EBC, WC]. It refers to a general attitude toward those in authority over them [ICC, Lg, Lns, NCB].

  c. ἀρχή (LN 37.56): 'ruler' [BAGD, Hn, HNTC, LN, WC; NASB, NIV, RSV, TEV, TNT], 'rulership' [Lns], 'authority' [BAGD], 'magistrate' [Herm], 'principality' [KJV], 'government' [NEB]. The phrase ἀρχαῖς ἐξουσίαις 'to rulers, authorities' is translated 'to the government and its officials' [NAB], 'to the officials in authority' [NJB].

  d. ἐξουσία (LN 37.38): 'authority' [BAGD, Herm, Hn, HNTC, LN, Lns, WC; NASB, NEB, NIV, RSV, TEV, TNT], 'power' [KJV], 'ruler' [LN].

TITUS 3:1    77

QUESTION—How is this clause related to what precedes?
After giving instructions concerning Christian conduct in church and family life [MNTC], the discussion now turns to Christian conduct in public life [Hn, MNTC, My], especially to relations with non-Christians [Lg] in government and society [Lns].

QUESTION—To whom does αὐτούς 'them' refer?
It refers to the Christian believers, not to all Cretans in general [EBC, MNTC, My, SSA, TG, TNTC]: remind the Christians to be subject, etc.

QUESTION—What relationship is indicated by the five infinitives in this and the following verse?
They give the content of what Titus is to remind the believers [SSA]: remind them to do the following things.

QUESTION—What is the relationship between the two nouns ἀρχαῖς 'rulers' and ἐξουσίαις 'authorities'?
These two abstract nouns [EBC, EGT, Lns] are essentially synonymous [TG]. They refer not to individual rulers but to a type of government [EBC, Lns, SSA]. They refer to civil authorities, not to church leaders [Bg, SSA, TNTC, WC].

**to-obey,**
LEXICON—pres. act. infin. of πειθαρχέω (LN 36.12): 'to obey' [BAGD, LN; KJV, NAB, NEB, TEV, TNT], 'to be obedient' [BAGD, Herm, Hn, Lns, WC; NASB, NIV, RSV], 'to show them obedience' [HNTC]. The reference is to obedience to the rulers and authorities [Alf, El, GNC, Hn, My, NCB, SSA, TC, TNTC; KJV, NEB, TEV, TNT], obedience to specific commands [ICC, Lg, Lns; NAB]. Some commentators think that the verb implies obedience in general, not just to rulers and authorities [EGT, Herm].

QUESTION—How is the verb πειθαρχεῖν 'to obey' related to the preceding verb ὑποτάσσεσθαι 'to be subject'?
1. 'To obey' is the result and evidence of 'to be subject' [EBC, My]: to be subject, and therefore to obey. It is implied that the obedience will not violate Christian conscience [EBC, Lg].
2. The two verbs are independent [Herm, My(D), SSA, TC; NASB]: remind them to be subject and to be obedient.
3. The two verbs are essentially synonyms [MNTC, TG; NJB], giving the active and passive sense of submission [MNTC]: to be subject, that is, to obey.

**for[a] every good[b] work[c] to-be prepared,[d]**
LEXICON—a. πρός with accusative object (LN 89.7): 'for' [Herm, Hn, HNTC, Lns, WC; NASB, NEB, RSV, TNT], 'to' [KJV], not explicit [NAB, NIV, NJB, TEV].
b. ἀγαθός (LN 65.20): 'good' [BAGD, Herm, Hn, LN, WC; KJV, NASB, NIV, NJB, TEV, TNT], 'honest' [NAB, RSV], 'honorable' [HNTC;

NEB], 'beneficial' [Lns]. This word limits 'work' to works which are good [ICC, Lns, My].
   c. ἔργον (LN 42.11): 'work' [Herm, Hn, Lns, WC; KJV, NEB, RSV, TNT], 'deed' [LN; NASB], 'act' [LN], 'task' [HNTC], 'employment' [NAB]. The reference is to everything which is a part of being a good citizen [EBC, Hn, HNTC, IB, ICC, Lns, MNTC, My(D), TNTC]; in particular, works which the government requires from citizens [Lg, My], or to activities by the government which Christians can and should support [TG], provided no violation of Christian conscience is involved [TNTC]. Others take this to be doing good to others in general [GNC, SSA].
   d. ἕτοιμος (LN 77.2): 'ready' [BAGD, Hn, HNTC, LN, Lns, WC; all versions], 'prepared' [Herm, LN].
QUESTION—What is this phrase related to?
   1. It is coordinate to what precedes and follows [EBC, Hn, IB, ICC, Lg, Lns, MNTC, My, TC, TG, TNTC; NAB, NEB, NJB, TEV, TNT]: to obey and to be ready to do any good work and to speak evil of no one.
   2. It is a generic statement of what follows [Blm, GNC, My(D)]: to be ready to do every good work such as the following three duties.

**3:2** **to-speak-evil-of**[a] **no-one,**
LEXICON—a. pres. act. infin. of βλασφημέω (LN **33.400**): 'to speak evil of' [HNTC; KJV, NAB, RSV, TEV], 'to malign' [NASB], 'to slander' [NEB, NIV, TNT], 'to go slandering' [NJB], 'to defame' [BAGD, Herm, LN], 'to revile' [BAGD, Hn], 'to blaspheme' [Lns], 'to abuse' [WC]. It means that they are not to use reviling language [Blm] against persons who hurt or offended them [EBC].

**to-be not-fighting**[a], **kind,**[b]
LEXICON—a. ἄμαχος (LN 39.24): 'not quarrelsome' [HNTC; NAB, TNT], 'uncontentious' [NASB], 'not contentious' [Hn, LN], 'unaggressive' [WC], 'peaceable' [BAGD, Herm; NIV, NJB], 'peaceful' [LN; TEV]. This adjective is also translated as a noun: 'no brawler' [KJV], 'non-fighter' [Lns]; and as a verb: 'to pick quarrels' [NEB], 'to quarrel' [RSV]. It means not attacking others [Bg], not engaging in quarrelsome conduct [Blm, EBC].
   b. ἐπιεικής (LN **88.63**): 'kind' [BAGD, Herm], 'gentle' [BAGD; KJV, NASB, NJB, RSV], 'genial' [Hn], 'forbearing' [LN; NAB], 'yielding' [BAGD, Lns], 'considerate' [WC; NIV, TNT], 'friendly' [TEV], 'conciliatory' [GNC, HNTC]. This adjective is also translated as a verb phrase: 'to show forbearance' [NEB]. It means not to resist those who attack them [Bg], not to insist on one's rights [EBC, Hn, ICC, Lns]. It is the positive counterpart of the negative 'not fighting' [Lg, Lns, My, NCB].

**showing<sup>a</sup> all gentleness<sup>b</sup> to<sup>c</sup> all persons.**

LEXICON—a. pres. mid. participle of ἐνδείκνυμι (LN 28.51): 'to show' [BAGD, Herm, Hn, HNTC, LN, Lns; KJV, NASB, NEB, NIV, RSV, TEV], 'to display' [NAB], 'to exhibit' [WC], 'to demonstrate' [LN], 'to be' [NJB]. The present tense refers to continuous demonstration of this attitude [EBC].

b. πραΰτης (LN 88.59): 'gentleness' [BAGD, Herm, HNTC, LN, TNTC], 'gentle attitude' [TEV], 'gentle disposition' [NEB], 'humility' [BAGD; NIV], 'courtesy' [BAGD; NAB, RSV], 'polite' [NJB], 'consideration' [BAGD; NASB], 'meekness' [BAGD, LN, Lns, WC; KJV], 'mildness' [Hn, LN]. It means 'courteous consideration' [HNTC], 'true humility', the opposite of promoting oneself [EBC, Lns]; the adjective 'all' refers to the full manifestation of humility [EBC, EGT, Hn], at all times [SSA].

c. πρός with accusative object (LN 90.58): 'to' [Herm, WC; NJB, TNT], 'toward' [Hn, Lns; NAB, NIV, RSV, TEV], 'towards' [HNTC; NEB], 'unto' [KJV], 'for' [NASB].

QUESTION—What relationship is indicated by the participial form ἐνδεικνυμένους 'showing'?

It is a further admonition [EBC, Herm, Hn; all versions except KJV, NASB]: be kind, and also show gentleness.

QUESTION—To whom does πάντας ἀνθρώπους 'all persons' refer?

It refers to people in general, including the heathen [Alf, Blm, EBC, HNTC, ICC, MNTC, My, NCB, TC, WC]: to everyone.

**DISCOURSE UNIT: 3:3–11** [NCB]. The topic is salvation.

**DISCOURSE UNIT: 3:3–8** [EBC, MNTC]. The topic is the motives for godly behavior [EBC], the contrast between Christianity and paganism [MNTC].

**DISCOURSE UNIT: 3:3–7** [EGT, NCBC, TC]. The topic is the same as 2:11–14 (from a liturgical fragment) with an added reference to baptism [NCBC], the fact that we have no reason to be proud, but rather that we should be thankful to God [TC].

## 3:3 **For**

LEXICON—γάρ (LN 89.23): 'for' [Hn, HNTC, Lns, WC; KJV, NASB, NEB, RSV, TEV]; not explicit [Herm; NAB, NIV, NJB, TNT].

QUESTION—What relationship is indicated by this word?

It indicates the grounds for the exhortation to show kindness and gentleness [Alf, Blm, CBC, EBC, El, GNC, Hn, HNTC, ICC, Lg, My, SSA]: they should be kind and gentle to others, since they themselves once were as bad, and God was kind, loving, and merciful to them when they were in that condition. It also indicates grounds for believing that these Cretans can be redeemed [EGT, WC]: we should show kindness and gentleness to them, since they can be redeemed.

80                                TITUS 3:3

**we-were at-one-time we also foolish,**[a] **disobedient,**[b] **going-astray,**[c]
LEXICON—a. ἀνόητος (LN 32.50): 'foolish' [BAGD, HNTC, LN, WC; all versions except NEB, NJB], 'stupid' [LN], 'ignorant' [NJB], 'without understanding' [Hn, LN], 'devoid of understanding' [Lns], 'in our folly' [NEB], 'in foolishness' [Herm]. This means to be without understanding of spiritual matters [Alf, EBC, EGT, Hn, My, SSA, TNTC, WC], without knowledge of God [Bg, Blm, HNTC, TG].
  b. ἀπειθής (LN 36.24): 'disobedient' [BAGD, Hn, HNTC, LN, Lns, WC; all versions except NEB], 'in disobedience' [Herm], 'in our obstinacy' [NEB]. The reference is disobedience to God [Alf, Bg, GNC, Lg, My, TC, TG, TNTC] and a refusal to believe in him [Blm], or it is a rebellious attitude against both God's and man's authority [EBC, Hn, HNTC, IB, ICC, SSA, WC].
  c. pres. pass. participle of πλανάω (LN 31.8): 'to be deceived' [LN, Lns, WC; KJV, NASB, NIV], 'to be deluded' [BAGD, Hn], 'to be misled' [BAGD, LN; NJB], 'to be led astray' [RSV], 'to be misguided' [HNTC], 'to be caught in error' [Herm]. It is also translated with an active sense: 'to lose one's way' [TNT], 'to be astray' [NEB]. It is also translated as an adjective: 'wrong' [TEV]. It is also translated as a phrase: 'far from true faith' [NAB]. Most commentators think that it should be given the passive sense, 'to be led astray by others' [Alf, EBC, EGT, HNTC, MNTC, My, TC, TNTC, WC] or by Satan [GNC, WC]. It may mean 'to be self-deceived', implying willful self-deception [Blm]. Others think that it has the neutral sense, 'to go astray' [El; NEB, TNT].
QUESTION—What is implied by the forefronting of ἦμεν 'we were'?
  It implies that the Christians were no longer in their former condition [EBC, El, GNC, Hn, Lg, Lns, My, TG]: we were formerly, but are not now, in that condition.
QUESTION—What is implied by the imperfect tense of ἦμεν 'we were'?
  The imperfect tense implies that the items following were continuing or repeated conditions [SSA]: we were continually being such people.
QUESTION—What relationship is indicated by καί 'also'?
  It expresses a comparison with unbelievers [SSA]: we also, like the unbelievers, were in such a condition.
QUESTION—To whom does ἡμεῖς 'we' refer?
  1. It is inclusive, referring to the writer and the recipients: Paul, Titus, and the Cretan Christians [GNC, Herm, HNTC, Lg, Lns, TG], and all Christians everywhere [Alf, CBC, EBC, El, Hn, IB, My, SSA]: we Christians were once foolish and disobedient.
  2. Paul includes himself with the Cretan Christians only to soften the reference [Blm, Brt]: we (actually, you Cretan Christians) were once foolish and disobedient. The description does not apply to Paul [Brt].

## TITUS 3:3

**being-slaves[a] to-desires[b] and to-pleasures[c] various[d]**
LEXICON—a. pres. act. participle of δουλεύω (LN 37.25): 'to be a slave' [BAGD, Herm, LN; NAB, NEB, RSV, TEV], 'to slave' [Lns, WC], 'to serve' [BAGD; KJV]. It is also translated with a passive sense: 'to be enslaved' [Hn, HNTC; NASB, NIV, NJB, TNT], 'to be controlled by' [LN].
    b. ἐπιθυμία (LN 25.20): 'desire' [BAGD, Herm, LN, WC; TNT], 'passion' [Hn; NAB, NEB, NIV, NJB, RSV, TEV], 'lust' [HNTC, LN, Lns; KJV, NASB].
    c. ἡδονή (LN 25.27): 'pleasure' [BAGD, Hn, HNTC, Lns, WC; all versions except NJB], 'desire' [LN], 'dissipation' [NJB], 'lust' [Herm], 'passion' [LN]. This word includes evil speaking as well as pleasures of taste [Bg].
    d. ποικίλος (LN 58.45): 'various' [BAGD, Hn; NASB, RSV], 'manifold' [BAGD, WC], 'divers' [KJV], 'diversified' [LN], 'of various kinds' [LN; NAB, TNT], 'of every kind' [NEB], 'all kinds of' [Herm; NIV], 'of all kinds' [Lns; TEV], 'all sorts of' [HNTC], 'different' [NJB].
QUESTION—What is the word ποικίλαις 'various' connected with?
    1. It is connected with both 'desires' and 'pleasures' [EBC, Herm, Hn, HNTC, Lg, MNTC, SSA, TC; KJV, NASB, NIV, NJB, RSV]: we were slaves to various desires and pleasures.
    2. It is connected with 'pleasures' only [NAB]: we were slaves to desires and to various pleasures.

**in[a] evil[b] and envy[c] living,[d]**
LEXICON—a. ἐν with dative object (LN 13.8): 'in' [Herm, Hn, HNTC, Lns, WC; all versions].
    b. κακία (LN 88.105): 'evil' [LN], 'wickedness' [LN; NJB], 'malice' [Herm, Hn, HNTC, WC; all versions except NJB], 'badness' [BAGD, LN], 'faultiness' [BAGD], 'baseness' [Lns]. It refers to an evil mind-set rather than to evil activity [El, Hn, TC], all that is morally inferior [Lns].
    c. φθόνος (LN 88.160): 'envy' [BAGD, Herm, Hn, HNTC, LN, Lns, WC; all versions except NJB], 'malice' [NJB], 'jealousy' [BAGD, LN].
    d. pres. act. participle of διάγω (LN **41.3**): 'to live' [Hn, LN; KJV, NIV, NJB], 'to spend one's life' [Herm, WC; NASB, TEV], 'to pass one's life' [TNT], 'to lead a life' [Lns], 'to pass one's days' [RSV], 'to pass the time' [HNTC], 'to go one's way' [NAB]. It is also translated with a passive sense: 'our days were passed' [NEB].

**hateful,[a] hating[b] one-another.**
LEXICON—a. στυγητός (LN 88.204): 'hateful' [BAGD, Herm; KJV, NAB, NASB, NJB, TNT], 'detestable' [Hn, HNTC, WC], 'detested' [Lns], 'hated' [BAGD, LN; RSV, TEV], 'being hated' [NIV], 'odious' [NEB]. It means that their conduct deserved man's hatred [Hn, SSA] and God's [Blm, My]; it was 'detestable' to other people [EBC, HNTC, Lg, SSA]. They were hated by other people [El, GNC, Lns].

b. pres. act. participle of μισέω (LN 88.198): 'to hate' [BAGD, Herm, Hn, LN, Lns, WC; all versions], 'to loathe' [HNTC], 'to detest' [LN].

## 3:4 But[a]

LEXICON—a. δέ (LN 89.124): 'but' [Herm, Hn, HNTC, WC; all versions], 'however' [Lns].

QUESTION—What relationship is indicated by this word?

It introduces a contraexpectation to 3:3 [GNC, SSA]: although we were formerly sinful, nevertheless God saved us. Some find contrasts: God's kindness contrasted with man's inhumanity to man [Hn, My], and our past spiritual darkness contrasted with the light of God's kindness and mercy [Hn, Lg]. The ὅτε 'when' is contrasted with ποτέ 'formerly' of 3:3 [My(D)].

**when the kindness[a] and the love-for-mankind[b] of-our Savior God appeared,[c]**

LEXICON—a. χρηστότης (LN 88.67): 'kindness' [BAGD, Hn, LN; all versions except RSV], 'goodness' [BAGD, HNTC; RSV], 'benignity' [Lns], 'generosity' [BAGD, Herm], 'sweet graciousness' [WBC]. It implies God's merciful concern [HNTC] which motivates his forgiveness and blessings [EBC, ICC, My, NCBC], the graciousness of his love [TC]. It means benevolence in general [Lg].

b. φιλανθρωπία (LN **25.36**): 'love for mankind' [BAGD; NASB, NJB], 'love toward man' [Hn; KJV], 'love for men' [Lns; TNT], 'love' [NAB, NIV, TEV], 'loving kindness' [BAGD, Herm; RSV], 'affection for mankind' [LN], 'generosity' [HNTC; NEB], 'humanity' [WC]. The meaning is God's love towards men [Alf, Bg, El, TNTC], his respect for or benevolence toward mankind [HNTC] demonstrated in his love and pity for us in our sinfulness [EBC, ICC], his compassion for mankind [Lg].

c. aorist pass. indic. of ἐπιφαίνω (LN 24.21; 14.39): 'to show oneself, to make an appearance' [BAGD], 'to appear' [LN], 'to be revealed' [NJB, TEV], 'to be manifested' [HNTC]. This passive verb is also translated in the active voice: 'to appear' [Herm, Hn, Lns; KJV, NAB, NASB, NIV, RSV], 'to dawn upon the world' [NEB], 'to make its glorious appearance' [WC], '(God) revealed (his kindness)' [TNT]. See this word at 2:11.

QUESTION—What relationship is indicated by ὅτε 'when'?

It indicates the time of ἔσωσεν ἡμᾶς 'he saved us' in the following clause [SSA]: when God's kindness and love appeared, God saved us. This does not mean that these events occurred simultaneously. After God's kindness and love appeared in the ministry of Christ, God saved people one by one as they put their faith in Christ [Lns, SSA].

QUESTION—In what way did God's kindness and love for mankind appear?

1. These attributes were manifested in the coming and person of Christ [EBC, HNTC, IB, ICC, Lns, MNTC, Rb, SSA, TC, TG, WC], that is, in Christ's incarnation [EBC, HNTC, IB, ICC, MNTC, Rb, TC, WC]. The aorist tense of the verb ἐπεφάνη 'appeared' implies that God's kindness

TITUS 3:4 83

and love were suddenly made visible at Christ's incarnation. Others speak of the manifestation covering Christ's whole redeeming work [Alf, ICC, Lns].

2. Although God's kindness and love were revealed historically in Christ's redeeming work, the emphasis in the present passage is on the event of each believer's new birth by faith in Jesus Christ [GNC].

QUESTION—How are the two nouns 'kindness' and 'love' related to the genitive phrase 'of the Savior of us, God'?

The two nouns are distinct, each having its definite article [EBC, El, Lns, My]; however, the verb ἐπεφάνη 'appeared' is singular, indicating that they are closely associated [EBC, ICC, Lns]; consequently the genitive phrase 'of the Savior of us, God' refers to both nouns. They are forms of God's ἀγάπη 'love' [Lns]. The two nouns are closely associated [Alf, CBC, EGT, GNC, HNTC]. The two nouns form one concept, as the singular verb indicates [Hn]. The two terms together are the equivalent of 'grace' [Lg].

QUESTION—To whom does τοῦ σωτῆρος ἡμῶν θεοῦ 'our Savior God' refer?

It refers to God the Father [Alf, Blm, EBC, EGT, El, Hn, ICC, Lg, Lns, NCB, Rb, SSA, TC, TG].

QUESTION—To whom does ἡμῶν 'our' refer?

It refers to Paul and to all who have received Christ as Savior [EBC, Hn, ICC, Lns].

**3:5** not because-of[a] works[b] the-ones in[c] righteousness[d] which we have-done,[e]

LEXICON—a. ἐκ with genitive object (LN 89.25): 'because of' [Herm; NAB, NIV, NJB, RSV, TEV, TNT], 'by' [KJV], 'on the basis of' [NASB], 'for' [NEB], 'in recognition of' [HNTC], 'by virtue of' [Hn], 'as a result of' [Lns], 'in consequence of' [WC].

b. ἔργον (LN 42.11): 'work' [BAGD, Herm, Hn, Lns, WC; KJV], 'deed' [BAGD, HNTC, LN; NAB, NASB, NEB, RSV, TEV], 'act' [LN; TNT], 'action' [BAGD; NJB], 'thing (we had done)' [NIV].

c. ἐν with dative object (LN 89.5): 'in' [HNTC, WC; NASB, RSV], 'in a state of' [Hn], 'in connection with' [Lns], 'of' [Herm; KJV], not explicit [NAB, NEB, NIV, NJB, TEV, TNT]. The sense of ἐν here is 'wrought in', while 'righteousness' is the element or sphere in which these works were done [EGT, El, Lg], or the state of the person's life [My]; and the article τῶν preceding the prepositional phrase 'in righteousness' specifies which works are being referred to [Alf]. The phrase means 'of a righteous nature' [MNTC].

d. δικαιοσύνη (LN 88.13): 'righteousness' [BAGD, Herm, Hn, HNTC, LN, Lns, WC; KJV, NASB, RSV]. This noun is also translated as an adjective: 'righteous' [NAB, NIV, TNT], 'upright' [NJB], 'good' [NEB, TEV]. The reference is probably to upright conduct rather than to strict observance of the Mosaic law [HNTC, My]. It refers to righteousness by any standard whatever [Lns], deeds of general morality [MNTC]. It refers to strict observance of the Mosaic law [TNTC]. Whether we did or did not do works of righteousness is not in view, but merely that any such works would have no saving merit [EGT]. One commentator thinks the implication is that such works can be done but cannot effect salvation [WC], but others think that no one has ever been able to do such works [Hn, Lg, My].

  e. aorist act. indic. of ποιέω (LN 42.7): 'to do' [Herm, LN, Lns, WC; all versions except NEB, TNT], 'to accomplish' [HNTC, LN], 'to perform' [Hn]. The meaning is 'we did', not 'we had done', which would imply works done prior to God's saving action [Alf, Lg], It could even mean that God saved us because of future righteous deeds which he foresaw we would do [Lg]. The translation 'have done' might erroneously seem to refer to works done after the new birth [EGT]. This verb, as well as its subject 'we', is emphatic, since it precedes the emphatic subject [Lns].

QUESTION—What relationship is indicated by ἐκ 'because of'?

It indicates a reason for being saved [Alf, Bg, CBC, EGT, El, GNC, Herm, Hn, Lns, MNTC]: we have not been saved because we have done righteous works. This implies that we have not done any works that merit our being saved [Bg, EBC, Hn, Lg, Lns, MNTC, My].

QUESTION—What is implied by the use of ἡμεῖς 'we'?

This pronoun is emphatic, stressing our personal involvement [El, Lns, My, SSA]: works which we personally have done. The emphatic 'we' is contrasted with the emphatic 'his mercy' [El, HNTC, Lns, TC], αὐτοῦ 'his' being forefronted for emphasis [SSA, TC]. 'We' includes Paul and his fellow Christians [EGT, TG].

**but[a] according-to[b] his mercy[c] he-saved[d] us**

LEXICON—a. ἀλλά (LN 89.125): 'but' [Herm, Hn, HNTC, Lns, WC; all versions except NJB]. The phrase ἀλλὰ κατὰ τὰὐτοῦ ἔλεος 'but according to his mercy' is translated 'it was for no reason except his own faithful love' [NJB]. The conjunction ἀλλά is a strong adversative, introducing and giving emphasis to the positive aspect [SSA].

  b. κατά with accusative object (LN 89.8): 'according to' [BAGD, Herm, Hn, WC; KJV, NASB], 'in accord with' [BAGD, Lns], 'because of' [NAB, NIV, TEV], 'because' [NEB, TNT], 'in virtue of' [HNTC; RSV], 'for (no) reason except' [NJB].

  c. ἔλεος (LN 88.76): 'mercy' [BAGD, Herm, Hn, LN, Lns, WC; KJV, NAB, NASB, NIV, RSV, TEV], 'compassion' [BAGD, HNTC], 'faithful love' [NJB]. This noun is also translated as a verb phrase: 'to be merciful' [NEB, TNT].

  d. aorist act. indic. of σῴζω (LN 21.27): 'to save' [BAGD, Herm, Hn, HNTC, LN, Lns, WC; all versions]. The aorist tense indicates that it is one past act [Alf, EBC, HNTC], but refers to many acts as it is applied to individuals at different times [Alf]. The verb means salvation from sin [El] at baptism [Brt]. Paul is here dealing with God's part in salvation; he is not dealing with man's part [EGT, El]. This is the main verb of the entire sentence [GNC].

QUESTION—What relationship is indicated by κατά 'according to'?

The preposition κατά 'according to' indicates that God's mercy is the standard for measuring his great grace [Alf, EBC, Hn, Lns]. The preposition indicates that God acted in accordance with his nature [MNTC]. Others take it to mean the moving cause [EGT, El, GNC, HNTC, My(D); all versions except KJV, NASB].

QUESTION—To whom does ἡμᾶς 'us' refer?

It refers specifically to Paul, Titus, and the Cretan Christians [Alf], or to Paul and Christians generally [EGT, Lg, My].

**through[a] washing[b] of-regeneration[c] and renewing[d] of-Holy Spirit,**

LEXICON—a. διά with genitive object (LN 89.76): 'through' [Herm, Hn; NAB, NEB, NIV, TEV, TNT], 'by' [KJV, NASB, RSV], 'by means of' [HNTC, Lns, WC; NJB].

b. λουτρόν (LN **53.43**): 'washing' [BAGD, Hn, HNTC, LN; KJV, NASB, NIV, RSV], 'baptism' [**LN**; NAB], 'water' [NEB, TNT], 'cleansing water' [NJB], 'bath' [BAGD, Herm, Lns], 'laver' [WC], This noun is also translated as a verb: 'to wash' [TEV].

c. παλιγγενεσία (LN **41.53**): 'regeneration' [BAGD, Hn, Lns, WC; KJV, NASB, RSV], 'new birth' [LN; NAB, TEV], 'rebirth' [BAGD, Herm, HNTC; NEB, NIV, NJB, TNT].

d. ἀνακαίνωσις (LN 58.72): 'renewing' [Hn, Lns; KJV, NASB], 'renewal' [BAGD, Herm, HNTC, LN; NAB, NIV, NJB, RSV, TNT], 'renewing power' [NEB], 'renovation' [WC], 'new life' [TEV]. The meaning is 'making new', not renewal of powers previously possessed [TNTC]. Some think that it refers to the transformation which the Holy Spirit produces at baptism [Brt, HNTC, My, TNTC]. Others think it refers to the lifelong renewing process by the Holy Spirit following regeneration [Alf, EBC, EGT, Hn, Lg, Lns].

QUESTION—What relationship is indicated by διά 'through'?

It indicates the means by which God saved us [Alf, EBC, Hn, Lg, Lns, My, SSA, TC; KJV, NASB, NJB, RSV]: God saved us by means of the washing of regeneration and renewal of the Holy Spirit.

QUESTION—How are the event words 'washing', 'regeneration', and 'renewing' related in this phrase?

    1. 'Regeneration' and 'renewal' are both results of the 'washing' and both are caused by the Holy Spirit [Alf, El, Hn, Lg, Lns, NCB, SSA, TC]: God saved us by means of washing us with the result that we were both regenerated and renewed by the Holy Spirit. The Holy Spirit may also be considered as the agent of regeneration [Lg].

    2. 'Washing' and 'renewal' are both means by which God saves [Blm, EBC, EGT; TNT]: God saved us by means of washing us with the result that we

were regenerated (or, which consisted of regeneration [EGT]) and by means of our being renewed by the Holy Spirit.
3. 'Regeneration' is explained as 'renewal' [GNC, Herm, HNTC, MNTC]: God saved us by means of washing us with the result that we were regenerated, that is, we were renewed by the Holy Spirit.

QUESTION—What is meant by λουτροῦ 'washing'?
1. 'Washing' is a metaphor for spiritual cleansing [EBC, EGT, GNC, Hn, Lns, SSA; TNT]: we were washed from our sins.
2. 'Washing' is a metaphor for baptism [Alf, Blm, El, Herm, HNTC, Lg, MNTC, NCB, TC]: we were baptized. Instead of an event, some commentators take λουτρόν to mean 'laver' or 'baptismal font' where the event takes place [Alf, Lg].

**3:6** whom he-poured-out[a] upon[b] us richly[c] through[d] Jesus Christ our Savior,

LEXICON—a. aorist act. indic. of ἐκχέω (LN 59.50): 'to pour out' [BAGD, Herm, Hn, HNTC, Lns, WC; NASB, NIV, RSV, TEV, TNT], 'to pour' [NJB], 'to shed' [KJV], 'to send down' [NEB], 'to give in abundance' [LN], 'to bestow generously' [LN]. The phrase ἐξέχεεν πλουσίως 'he poured out richly' is translated 'he lavished' [NAB].
b. ἐπί with accusative object (LN 90.57): 'upon' [BAGD, Hn, Lns, WC; NASB, NEB, RSV], 'on' [BAGD, HNTC; KJV, NAB, NIV, TEV, TNT], 'over' [BAGD, Herm; NJB].
c. πλουσίως (LN 59.57): 'richly' [BAGD, Herm, Hn, HNTC, LN, Lns, WC; NASB, RSV], 'abundantly' [BAGD; KJV, TEV], 'in abundance' [LN], 'in large amount' [LN], 'plentifully' [NEB], 'generously' [NIV], 'so generously' [NJB], 'freely' [TNT]. The word implies sufficiency for all people and for all of their needs [ICC], or sufficient to bring about our salvation [Lns].
d. διά with genitive object (LN 90.4): 'through' [Herm, Hn, HNTC, Lns; all versions], 'by means of' [WC].

QUESTION—To whom does the pronoun οὗ 'whom' refer?
It refers to the Holy Spirit [Alf, Bg, CBC, EGT, El, GNC, Hn, IB, Lg, Lns, My, NCB, Rb, SSA, TC, TG; NAB, NASB, NEB, NIV, TEV, TNT]: God poured out the Holy Spirit upon us.

QUESTION—What event is referred to by the aorist tense verb ἐξέχεεν 'he poured out'?
1. It refers to the outpouring of the Holy Spirit on individuals at their conversion or baptism [El, HNTC, Lns, My, SSA, TC, TNTC]: he poured out the Holy Spirit individually upon us at the time of our conversion or baptism. The basis of these individual outpourings is the outpouring at Pentecost [Lns, TNTC].
2. It refers to the outpouring at Pentecost [Hn, ICC]: God poured out the Holy Spirit upon the church (of which we are members) at Pentecost. At Pentecost the Holy Spirit was poured out on the church for all time [Hn].

3. It refers both to God's outpouring of the Holy Spirit at Pentecost and also to the outpourings of the Holy Spirit upon individuals subsequently [Alf, CBC, EBC, EGT, Rb]: whom he poured out at Pentecost and on individuals subsequently. The aorist tense shows that the author is thinking of the Pentecostal outpouring, but ἐφ' ἡμᾶς 'upon us' shows that he is thinking in particular of the outpouring of the Holy Spirit upon Christians [EGT].

QUESTION—What is the phrase διὰ Ἰησοῦ Χριστοῦ τοῦ σωτῆρος ἡμῶν 'through Jesus Christ our Savior' connected with?

1. It is connected with ἐξέχεεν 'he poured out' in 3:6 [EBC, EGT, El, GNC, HNTC, IB, Lg, Lns, MNTC, My, NCB, TC, TG, TNTC, WC]: he poured out the Holy Spirit through Jesus Christ. Jesus was the channel through whom God poured out the Holy Spirit [Alf, EBC, My, SSA]. Some commentators explain this as being the mediate agency [MNTC, SSA]: God poured out the Holy Spirit by having Jesus pour him out. Others take it to mean that our union with Christ [HNTC] or Christ's saving work [EBC, El, NCB] was what made it possible for God to pour out the Holy Spirit.

2. It is connected with ἔσωσεν 'he saved' in 3:5 [Bg]: he saved us through Jesus Christ.

**3:7** in-order-that[a]

LEXICON—a. ἵνα (LN 89.59): 'in order that' [BAGD, Hn, WC], 'that' [BAGD; KJV, NAB, NASB], 'so that' [HNTC, Lns; NEB, NIV, NJB, RSV, TEV], 'so' [TNT], 'thus' [Herm].

QUESTION—What relationship is indicated by this word?

1. It indicates God's purpose in pouring out the Holy Spirit [Alf, EGT, HNTC, My, SSA, TC, TG]: God poured out the Holy Spirit upon us in order that we might become heirs.

2. It indicates God's purpose in saving us (3:5) [Bg, El, Hn, NCB, TNTC]: God saved us in order that we might become heirs.

3. It indicates the result of God's pouring out the Holy Spirit [EBC, Lns]: God poured out the Holy Spirit upon us, and as a result we have become heirs. (However, the subjunctive mood does not seem to be explained adequately by this interpretation.)

**having-been-justified[a] by-the grace[b] of-that-one**

LEXICON—a. aorist pass. indic. of δικαιόω (LN 34.46): 'to be justified' [Herm, Hn, HNTC, WC; all versions except TEV, TNT], 'to be acquitted, to be pronounced and treated as righteous' [BAGD], 'to be put right with' [LN], 'to be put right with God' [TEV], 'to be made right with God' [TNT], 'to be declared righteous' [Lns]. The sense is 'to be declared righteous', not 'to be made upright' [Hn]. But perhaps it means both 'declared righteous' and 'made upright' [IB]. It means acquitted from our sins [Lg, My, TG] and put right with God [TG]. The passive voice implies 'to be made' rather than merely 'to become' [Alf]. The aorist tense indicates that the action of the participle is prior to the verb γενηθῶμεν 'we might become' [Alf, SSA]

b. χάρις (LN 88.66): 'grace' [BAGD, Herm, Hn, HNTC, LN, Lns, WC; all versions], 'kindness' [LN].

QUESTION—What relationship is indicated by the participial form δικαιωθέντες 'having been justified'?

1. It is coordinate with the verb γενηθῶμεν 'we might become' [EBC, NCBC; NAB, RSV, TEV, TNT]: in order that we might become justified and become heirs.
2. It gives a reason for our becoming heirs [SSA]: in order that we may become heirs because we have been justified.

QUESTION—What relationship is indicated by the dative phrase τῇ ἐκείνου χάριτι 'by that one's grace'?

It indicates that grace is the cause, motivation, or means of our becoming justified [Alf, EBC, GNC, Hn]: justified because of God's grace.

QUESTION—To whom does ἐκείνου 'of that one' refer?

1. It refers to the more remote antecedent, 'God' [Alf, Bg, Blm, EBC, EGT, El, IB, Lg, Lns, NCB, SSA, WC]: justified by God's grace.
2. It refers to 'Christ' [GNC, My]: justified by Christ's grace.

**we-might-become heirs[a] in-accordance-with[b] hope of-life eternal.**

LEXICON—a. κληρονόμος (LN 57.133): 'heir' [BAGD, Herm, Hn, HNTC, LN, Lns, WC; all versions except TEV, TNT], 'one who receives' [LN]. The phrase κληρονόμοι γενηθῶμεν 'we might become heirs' is translated 'we might come into possession' [TEV].

b. κατά with accusative object (LN 89.8): 'according to' [WC; KJV, NASB], 'in accord with' [Lns], 'in' [Hn, HNTC; NAB, NEB, NJB, RSV]. The phrase κατ' ἐλπίδα 'in accordance with hope' is translated 'having the hope' [NIV], 'as we hope' [Herm]. The phrase κατ' ἐλπίδα ζωῆς αἰωνίου 'in accordance with the hope of life eternal' is translated 'of the eternal life we hope for' [TEV]. The sense of the preposition is 'consistent with', that is, the hope is fully satisfied by the inheritance [Alf].

QUESTION—What is the genitive phrase ζωῆς αἰωνίου 'of life eternal' connected with?

1. It is connected with ἐλπίδα 'hope' and indicates its content [Alf, EBC, EGT, Herm, Lg, Lns, NCBC, TC, TNTC; KJV, NASB, NIV, TNT]: according to hope for life eternal.
2. It is connected with κληρονόμοι 'heirs' [Bg, El, GNC, Hn, HNTC, MNTC, My, NCB, WC; NAB, NEB, TEV]: heirs of life eternal, based on hope.

**DISCOURSE UNIT: 3:8–11** [EGT, TC, TNTC]. The topic is final instructions to do good deeds, avoid arguments, and avoid people who persist in heresy [TC], instructions concerning good deeds and concerning heretical teachers [TNTC].

**DISCOURSE UNIT: 3:8** [NCBC]. The topic is that Christians should do good works because of what God has done for them through Christ.

### 3:8a Faithful[a] the word,[b]

LEXICON—a. πιστός (LN 31.87): 'faithful' [BAGD, LN, Lns, WC; KJV], 'trustworthy' [BAGD, HNTC, LN; NASB, NIV], 'reliable' [Hn, LN], 'true' [TEV, TNT], 'sure' [RSV]. The phrase πιστὸς ὁ λόγος 'faithful the word' is translated 'you can depend on this to be true' [NAB], 'these are words you may trust' [NEB], 'this is doctrine that you can rely on' [NJB], 'the word stands firm!' [Herm].

b. λόγος (LN 33.98): 'word' [Herm, LN, WC; NEB], 'saying' [Hn, HNTC; KJV, NIV, RSV, TEV], 'statement' [Lns; NASB], 'doctrine' [NJB], 'all this' [TNT].

QUESTION—How are the adjective and noun related in the phrase πιστὸς ὁ λόγος 'faithful the word'?

1. 'Faithful' is the predicate and 'word' is the subject [Blm, El, Herm, Hn, Lns, WC; RSV, TNT]: the word is faithful.
2. 'Faithful' is an attributive modifier of 'word' [HNTC; KJV, NASB, NIV, TEV]: this is a faithful word. (Note that this rendering is grammatically inadmissible since the definite article makes 'word' definite, 'the word' and puts 'faithful' in predicate position.)

QUESTION—What word is meant?

1. 'Word' refers to what precedes [Alf, Bg, Blm, CBC, EBC, EGT, El, GNC, Herm, Hn, HNTC, IB, ICC, Lg, Lns, My, Rb, SSA, TC, TG, TNTC, WC; NAB, NEB, NJB, RSV, TEV, TNT]: what I have said is trustworthy. It refers specifically to 3:4–7 [EBC, EGT, GNC, Hn, Lg, My, Rb, TC, TG, TNTC, WC], 3:4–6 [Alf], 3:3–7 [SSA], 3:1–7 [IB].
2. 'Word' refers both to what precedes and to what follows, since this is a transitional statement [NCBC]: what I have said and what I am about to say is trustworthy.
3. 'Word' refers to what follows [MNTC]: What I am about to say is trustworthy.

**DISCOURSE UNIT: 3:8b–11** [GNC, Herm, IB, MNTC; NAB]. The topic is counsel to Titus [MNTC; NAB], the evidence for faith in Christ is deeds, not words [IB], a final appeal urging good works and warning against errors [GNC], appeals, and warning against heretics [Herm].

### 3:8b and

LEXICON—a. καί (LN 89.92): 'and' [Hn, HNTC, Lns, WC; KJV, NASB, NIV, TNT]; not explicit [Herm; NAB, NEB, NJB, RSV, TEV].

QUESTION—What relationship is indicated by this word?

1. It indicates a close connection between 'faithful is the word' and the following admonition [GNC, IB]: this word is faithful, and I want you to insist concerning these things.

2. It introduces the conclusion to the grounds 'faithful is the word' [SSA]: this word is faithful, and therefore I want you to insist concerning these things.

**concerning[a] these-things I-wish[b] you to-insist,[c]**

LEXICON—a. περί with genitive object (LN 89.6): 'concerning' [Lns, WC; NASB], 'about' [Herm, Hn], not explicit [HNTC; KJV, NAB, NIV, RSV, TEV, TNT]. The phrase περὶ τούτων is translated 'such are the points' [NEB], 'in teaching all this' [NJB]. The preposition focuses on the reference rather than the content [SSA]: speak confidently about these things.

b. pres. mid. (deponent = act.) indic. of βούλομαι (LN 25.3): 'to wish' [BAGD, HNTC; NEB], 'to will' [LN; KJV], 'to want' [Hn, LN; NAB, NASB, NIV, NJB, TEV, TNT], 'to desire' [LN; RSV], 'to intend' [Lns], 'my will is' [WC]. The phrase βούλομαί σε διαβεβαιοῦσθαι 'I wish you to insist' is translated 'you must speak firmly' [Herm].

c. pres. mid. (deponent = act.) infin. of διαβεβαιόομαι (LN 33.322): 'to insist (on)' [BAGD, HNTC, LN; NEB, RSV, TNT], 'to insist constantly' [WC], 'to affirm' [KJV], 'to speak confidently' [BAGD; NASB], 'to speak firmly' [Herm], 'to speak with confidence' [Hn, Lns], 'to state with confidence' [LN], 'to stress' [NIV], 'to lay great weight (on)' [NAB], 'to be quite uncompromising' [NJB], 'to give special emphasis (to)' [TEV]. The prefix δια- is an intensifier, implying persistent affirmation [Alf]. The prepositional phrase following implies that this verb means to speak confidently [SSA].

QUESTION—To what does τούτων 'these things' refer?

It refers to the things mentioned in 3:4–7 [Alf, EBC, HNTC] and may even include all of 3:1–7 [GNC, IB] or everything from 2:1 [ICC]: concerning the things I have just now mentioned.

**in-order-that[a] the-ones who-have-believed[b] God may-be-careful[c] to-engage-in[d] good works.**

LEXICON—a. ἵνα (LN 89.59): 'in order that' [Herm, Hn, WC], 'so that' [HNTC, Lns; all versions except KJV, NEB], 'that' [KJV], not explicit [NEB].

b. perf. act. participle of πιστεύω (LN 31.102): 'to believe' [Lns, WC; NASB], 'to believe in' [BAGD, HNTC, LN; KJV, NJB, RSV, TEV, TNT], 'to trust in' [BAGD; NIV], 'to put one's confidence in' [Herm], 'to commit oneself to' [NAB], 'to fix one's faith on' [Hn], 'to put faith on' [WC]. The perfect tense implies continuance in faith [Alf, EBC].

c. pres. act. subj. of φροντίζω (LN **30.20**): 'to be careful' [BAGD, Hn, HNTC; KJV, NAB, NASB, NIV, RSV], 'to devote care' [Lns], 'to give careful thought' [WC], 'to keep one's mind constantly occupied' [NJB], 'to fix one's attention on' [LN], 'to be concerned (with)' [TEV], 'to make up one's mind' [TNT], 'to learn' [Herm].

TITUS 3.8

d. pres. mid. infin. of προΐστημι (LN **35.12**): 'to engage in' [BAGD; NASB, TNT], 'to maintain' [KJV], 'to devote oneself (to)' [NIV], 'to apply oneself (to)' [Hn; RSV], 'to give one's time to do' [TEV], 'to be active in providing/giving' [LN], 'to busy oneself with' [BAGD, HNTC], 'to be concerned with' [Herm], 'to do' [NAB, NJB], 'to take the lead' [Lns], 'to engage in honorable occupations' [CBC; NEB]. The meaning 'to engage in honorable occupations' may be included [ICC], but it introduces a new and irrelevant topic which is inappropriate here [EBC, HNTC] and does not harmonize with the general NT sense of good works [EBC, EGT, TC]; the more general sense is preferable [IB, ICC, TC]. This word together with the preceding verb indicate emphasis [Blm, SSA].

QUESTION—What relationship is indicated by ἵνα 'in order that'?

It introduces the purpose or anticipated result of strongly affirming the thoughts of 3:4–6 [Alf, EGT, HNTC, Lg, Lns, My]: do this in order that Christians may do good works.

QUESTION—What is the significance of the dative θεῷ 'God' following the verb 'to believe'?

1. It indicates a saving faith, believing in God [CBC, EBC, GNC, Herm, HNTC, IB, Lg, My, NCBC, TG]: they who have believed in God for salvation. It means the same as εἰς τὸν θεόν '(to believe) in God' [My]. This phrase is emphatic by its position in the sentence [EBC].
2. It indicates that they have trusted that what God says is true; it is to be distinguished from εἰς τὸν θεόν '(to believe) in God' [Alf, Lns]: they who trust God's truthfulness.

**These-things are good and profitable[a] to-(the) mankind;**

TEXT—Some manuscripts add τά 'the' before καλά 'good', giving the sense 'these are the good and profitable things for mankind'. GNT does not deal with this variant. 'The' is included only by Alf.

LEXICON—a. ὠφέλιμος (LN 65.40): 'profitable' [Lns; KJV, NASB, NIV, RSV], 'beneficial' [BAGD, Herm, Hn, LN], 'useful' [BAGD, HNTC; NEB, NJB, TEV, TNT], 'advantageous' [BAGD; NAB].

QUESTION—To what does ταῦτα 'these things' refer?

1. It refers to the things mentioned in 3:4–7, as did τούτων 'these things' earlier in this verse [Alf, EBC, EGT, Hn, HNTC, IB, Lg, MNTC, NCB, TC, WC; TNT]: these things which I mentioned (in 3:4–7).
2. It refers to 'good deeds' in the preceding clause [GNC, TG; TEV]: it is good and profitable to do good deeds.
3. It refers to διαβεβαιοῦσθαι 'to insist on', or possibly to the ἵνα clause of the present verse [My]: it is good and profitable for the people that you insist on these things/that they should be diligent to do good deeds.

**DISCOURSE UNIT: 3:9–11** [EBC, Hn, ICC, NCBC]. The topic is avoiding controversy, admonishing heretical teachers and avoiding such people if admonishing fails [ICC], how Titus should respond to heretical teachers [EBC, NCBC].

**3:9 But**[a]

LEXICON—a. δέ (LN 89.124): 'but' [Herm, Hn, HNTC, Lns, WC; all versions except NAB]; not explicit [NAB].

QUESTION—What relationship is indicated by this word?

It indicates a contrast with the preceding verse [EBC, GNC, Hn, My, SSA]: but. The contrast is between following the preceding instructions and avoiding the following actions [Alf, GNC, Hn]. There is also a contrast between the profitableness of the preceding things and unprofitableness of the arguments about genealogies and the law [NCB, SSA].

**foolish**[a] **questionings**[b] **and genealogies**[c] **and arguments**[d] **and quarrels**[e] **pertaining-to-the-law**[f] **avoid;**[g]

LEXICON—a. μωρός (LN 32.55): 'foolish' [BAGD, Herm, Hn, HNTC, LN, WC; KJV, NASB, NEB, NIV, NJB, TNT], 'unwise' [LN], 'stupid' [NAB, RSV, TEV], 'silly' [Lns].

b. ζήτησις (LN 33.440): 'question' [KJV], 'questioning' [WC], 'questing' [Lns], 'inquiry' [Hn], 'investigation' [BAGD, Herm], 'speculation' [HNTC; NEB, NJB], 'argument' [NAB, TEV, TNT], 'controversy' [BAGD; NASB, NIV, RSV], 'dispute' [LN].

c. γενεαλογία (LN 10.26): 'genealogy' [BAGD, Herm, Hn, HNTC, LN, Lns, WC; all versions except TEV, TNT], 'the study of genealogies' [TNT], 'long list of ancestors' [LN; TEV]. This probably has the same reference as Ἰουδαϊκοῖς μύθοις 'Jewish fables' in 1:14 [HNTC]. It relates to fables based on Old Testament genealogies [SSA]. It may relate to the Gnostic idea of emanations of beings from the eternal Deity [Blm, Brt].

d. ἔρις (LN 33.447): 'contention' [BAGD; KJV], 'controversy' [NAB], 'strife' [BAGD, Lns; NASB], 'quarrel' [Herm, LN; NEB, TEV, TNT], 'dissension' [HNTC; RSV], 'argument' [NIV], 'dispute' [LN], 'quibble' [NJB], 'wrangling' [Hn]. The phrase ἔρεις καὶ μάχας 'arguments and quarrels' is translated 'fights' [WC]. ἔρις 'arguments' refers to a contentious spirit [EGT].

e. μάχη (LN 39.23): 'fight' [TEV], 'battle' [Lns], 'striving' [KJV], 'dispute' [BAGD, Herm; NASB, NJB, TNT], 'controversy' [HNTC; NEB], 'quarrel' [BAGD; NAB, NIV, RSV], 'fight' [LN], 'skirmish' [Hn]. This word refers to the quarrels as they are seen and heard [EGT]. The disputes would deal with interpretations of the law, or possibly the mystical meaning of parts of the law as affecting the genealogies [Alf].

f. νομικός (LN 33.337): 'pertaining to the law' [BAGD], 'about the law' [BAGD, Herm, Hn, HNTC, Lns, WC; KJV, NAB, NIV], 'about the Law' [NASB, NJB, TEV, TNT], 'about laws' [LN], 'over the Law' [NEB], 'over the law' [RSV]. This term relates to the law of Moses [SSA, TG], to the Gnostic mixture of heathenism with the law of Moses [Brt, NCB, Rb]. It relates to attempts to make permanent the transient aspects of the law of

Moses [EGT], or to what authority some aspects of the law had and how they were to be applied [El, Lg, My, NCBC].
g. pres. mid. impera. of περιΐστημι (LN **13.157**): 'to avoid' [BAGD, Herm, LN; KJV, NIV, NJB, RSV, TEV, TNT], 'to shun' [BAGD, Hn; NASB], 'to abstain from' [NAB], 'to keep clear of' [HNTC], 'to steer clear of' [NEB], 'to stand aside from' [WC], 'to turn one's back on' [Lns]. The verb means that Titus is not to permit these things to occur where he is in charge [SSA]. The imperative verb is addressed to Titus but is intended to be heeded by the church as well [GNC]. The fact that the extensive predicate of this verb is forefronted indicates that the predicate is emphatic [Hn, SSA], and also indicates a change of subject [SSA].

QUESTION—What does μωράς 'foolish' modify?
1. It modifies only the first noun, 'questionings' [GNC, Hn; NJB, TEV, TNT].
2. It modifies the first two nouns, 'questionings' and 'genealogies' [ICC, TNTC; NAB].
3. It modifies all four nouns, 'questionings', 'genealogies', 'arguments', and 'quarrels' [EBC].
4. It modifies the three event words, 'questionings', 'arguments', and 'quarrels' [SSA].

QUESTION—How are the first two nouns 'questionings' and 'genealogies' related?
1. They are separate things to avoid [HNTC, WC; all versions]: avoid questioning and avoid ideas about genealogies.
2. 'Genealogies' are the topic of 'questionings' [Herm, Hn, Lns, SSA]: avoid questioning about genealogies.

QUESTION—What does νομικάς 'pertaining to the law' modify?
1. It modifies only 'quarreling' [Herm, HNTC; all versions]: avoid arguing and avoid quarreling about the law.
2. It modifies both 'quarreling' and 'arguing' [Hn, Lns, SSA, WC]: avoid arguing and quarreling about the law.

**for[a] they-are unprofitable[b] and useless.[c]**

LEXICON—a. γάρ (LN 89.23): 'for' [Hn, HNTC, Lns, WC; KJV, NASB, RSV, TNT], 'because' [Herm; NIV]; not explicit [NAB, NEB, NJB, TEV].
b. ἀνωφελής (LN 65.50): 'unprofitable' [Hn, Lns, WC; KJV, NASB, NEB, NIV, RSV], 'of no special benefit' [LN], 'profitless' [HNTC], 'useless' [Herm; NAB, NJB, TEV, TNT], 'without advantage' [LN], 'harmful' [BAGD]. This word is the opposite of ὠφέλιμος 'profitable' in 3:8 [Bg, HNTC, SSA]. This and the following word focus on behavior that is useless rather than specifically heretical theologically [GNC].
c. μάταιος (LN 65.37): 'useless' [BAGD, LN; NIV], 'in vain' [Lns], 'have no point' [NAB], 'pointless' [NEB], 'worthless' [NASB, TEV], 'futile' [Hn, HNTC, LN; NJB, RSV, TNT], 'fruitless' [BAGD, Herm, WC],

'vain' [KJV]. This word is the opposite of καλός 'good' in 3:8 [Bg, El, SSA]. It means that it results in no real value [El].

QUESTION—What relationship is indicated by γάρ 'for'?

It indicates the grounds for the preceding instruction [SSA]: avoid such things, since they are unprofitable and useless.

**3:10** **A-factious[a] person after[b] one and a-second admonition[c] have-nothing-to-do-with,[d]**

LEXICON—a. αἱρετικός (LN 39.17): 'factious' [BAGD, Herm, Hn, WC; NASB, RSV], 'divisive' [NIV], 'heretical' [Lns], 'that is a heretic' [KJV]. The phrase αἱρετικὸν ἄνθρωπον 'a factious person' is translated 'a heretic' [KJV, NAB, NEB], 'a separatist' [HNTC], 'a trouble-maker' [TNT], 'a person who causes divisions' [LN; TEV], '(if) someone disputes what you teach' [NJB].

b. μετά with accusative object (LN 67.48): 'after' [BAGD, Herm, Hn, HNTC, Lns, WC; all versions except TEV], not explicit [TEV].

c. νουθεσία (LN 33.424): 'admonition' [BAGD, Lns, WC; KJV], 'warning' [BAGD, Hn, LN; NASB, NJB]. This noun is also translated as a verb: 'to warn' [Herm; NAB, NEB, NIV, TNT], 'to give a warning' [HNTC; TEV], 'to admonish' [RSV]. The admonition would consist of pointing out the wrong of the separation [EGT] or of the teaching [My, SSA], either private or public admonition [ICC], earnest and thorough exhorting [Lns, My] or instruction [SSA]. It means to admonish in a faithful and caring way [EBC].

d. pres. mid. (deponent = act.) impera. of παραιτέομαι (LN **34.41**): 'to reject' [BAGD, Herm; KJV, NASB], 'to shun' [WC], 'to have nothing to do with' [HNTC; NAB, NIV], 'to have nothing more to do with' [LN; RSV, TEV, TNT], 'to have nothing further to do with' [Hn], 'to have no more to do with' [NJB], 'to have done with' [NEB], 'to disdain to be bothered with' [Lns].

QUESTION—In what way is such a person factious?

He stirs up divisions within the church with his different views of questions [EBC, EGT, El, GNC, Hn, HNTC, NCB, SSA, TC, TNTC, WC]. He teaches such things as mentioned in 3:9 [Bg, El, GNC, Hn, Lns, SSA]. Some think that the false teachings are serious enough to classify as heresies [Alf, Blm, IB, Lg, Lns, NCBC; KJV, NAB, NEB].

QUESTION—What is meant by 'have nothing to do with' such a person?

Some commentators think that it means to cease to admonish him since admonition has proven useless [Bg, Lg]. Others think that it means not to bother with him any more [EBC, NCB], not to speak to him [Alf], to have nothing more to do with him [EGT, GNC, Lns, MNTC, TC, TNTC, WC]. It forbids such a person to teach in church [SSA]. Some think that this refers to excommunication from church [Hn], but many think that it does not mean to go so far as excommunication [EGT, El, Lg, MNTC, My, NCB, TC, TNTC, WC].

TITUS 3:11 95

**3:11** knowing[a] that perverted[b] (is) the such-a-person[c]
LEXICON—a. perf. (used as pres.) act. participle of οἶδα (LN 28.1): 'to know' [Herm, Hn, LN, Lns, WC; KJV, NASB, NJB, RSV, TEV], 'to be sure' [NIV, TNT], 'to rest assured' [HNTC], 'to recognize' [NAB, NEB].

b. perf. pass. indic. of ἐκστρέφω (LN **88.265**): 'to be perverted' [BAGD, HNTC, Lns; NAB, NASB, RSV], 'to be hopelessly perverted' [Herm], 'to be morally perverted' [WC], 'to have a perverted mind' [TNT], 'to be distorted' [Hn], 'to have a distorted mind' [NEB], 'to be warped' [NIV, NJB], 'to be corrupt' [LN; TEV], 'to be subverted' [KJV]. The perfect tense indicates a state resulting from having become perverted [EBC, GNC, Lns, SSA]. The passive voice implies that Satan is the source of the perversion [EBC, Lns]. The prefix ἐκ- implies complete corruption of his mind [El]. The verb is forefronted for emphasis [Lns].

c. τοιοῦτος (LN 64.2; 92.31): 'such a person' [Herm; NAB, RSV, TEV], 'such an individual' [Hn], 'such a man' [NASB, NIV], 'a man of that sort' [NEB], 'anyone of that sort' [NJB], 'a man like that' [HNTC; TNT], 'the man who is such' [WC], 'such a one' [Lns], 'he that is such' [KJV].

QUESTION—What relationship is indicated by the participial form εἰδώς 'knowing'?

It indicates the grounds for the command to reject the factious person (3:10) [Blm, EGT, El, GNC, Herm, Lns, SSA]: reject a factious person, since you know that he is perverted and is sinning. The man's refusal to listen would indicate this [EBC, El, MNTC], and it would be obvious that he had departed from the true doctrine [Lns].

QUESTION—In what way was such a person perverted?

Such a person willfully rejects the truth [EBC, El, Lns, MNTC] and holds wrong doctrine [SSA]. Some point to the rest of the verse as defining this perversion; he sins against his own knowledge and conscience [Blm, My].

**and he-is-sinning**[a]
LEXICON—a. pres. act. indic. of ἁμαρτάνω (LN 88.289): 'to sin' [BAGD, Hn, LN, Lns; KJV, NASB], 'to sin deliberately' [WC], 'to do wrong' [BAGD; TNT], 'to engage in wrongdoing' [LN]. This verb is also translated as an adjective: 'sinful' [NAB, NIV, RSV]. The phrase ἁμαρτάνει ὢν αὐτοκατάκριτος 'he is sinning, being self-condemned' is translated '(he) stands self-condemned in his sin' [NEB], '(he) is self-condemned in his sin' [HNTC], '(he) is self-condemned as a sinner' [NJB], '(he) has condemned himself through his sin' [Herm], 'his sins prove that he is wrong' [TEV]. The present tense indicates that the person is continuing in sin [Alf, EBC, GNC, Hn]. He is sinning by being factious [TNTC] and also by rejecting counsel [ICC].

**being self-condemned.**[a]
LEXICON—a. αὐτοκατάκριτος (LN **30.119**): 'self-condemned' [BAGD, Hn, HNTC, Lns, WC; NAB, NASB, NEB, NIV, NJB, RSV], 'condemned of himself' [KJV], 'condemned by what he himself has done' [LN]. The

phrase ὢν αὐτοκατάκριτος 'being self-condemned' is translated 'and he knows it' [TNT].

QUESTION—What relationship is indicated by the participial form ὢν 'being'?
1. It indicates the grounds for saying that such a man is a sinner [SSA]: it is true that he is sinning, since he is self-condemned.
2. It indicates the grounds for rejecting the man [El]: reject him, since he is self-condemned.
3. It indicates in what way the factious person is sinning [Lns]: he is sinning as being self-condemned.

QUESTION—What is meant by being self-condemned?
He is condemned by his own conscience [Alf, Blm, EBC, HNTC, ICC, Lg, MNTC, My]. He does not outwardly condemn himself, which might be a step toward reformation; but indirectly, by acting against his own conscience [El]. He knows that his present views are different from the orthodox teaching he formerly held [EBC, EGT, GNC, HNTC, Lg, MNTC, My]. He has brought about his own judgment by refusing to listen [Herm]. His actions automatically show that he is guilty of sin by not heeding the admonitions [ICC].

QUESTION—What is the phrase ὢν αὐτοκατάκριτος 'being self-condemned' connected with?
It is connected with ἁμαρτάνει 'he is sinning', but not with ἐξέστραπται 'he is perverted' [My]: he is sinning, being self-condemned.

**DISCOURSE UNIT: 3:12–15** [EBC, GNC, GNT, Hn, HNTC, IB, Lg, NCB, TNTC; NAB, NASB, NJB]. The topic is practical counsel, farewells, and good wishes [NAB, NJB], personal comments and farewells [HNTC, TNTC], personal matters [NASB], closing counsel and greetings [GNC, GNT, IB, Lg], conclusion [EBC, NCB].

**DISCOURSE UNIT: 3:12–14** [EBC, EGT, Herm, MNTC, WC]. The topic is personal counsel and further exhortation concerning good works [WC], directions concerning messengers, and greetings [Herm], personal information and greetings [MNTC], several concluding instructions [Alf, EBC].

**DISCOURSE UNIT: 3:12–13** [ICC, NCBC, TC]. The topic is an invitation to Titus to come to Paul, and a request to help expedite the journey of Zenas and Apollos [TC], instructions concerning co-workers [NCBC], personal comments [ICC].

**3:12 When I-send[a] Artemas to[b] you or Tychicus,**
LEXICON—a. aorist act. subj. of πέμπω (LN 15.66): 'to send' [BAGD, Herm, Hn, HNTC, LN, Lns; all versions].
  b. πρός with accusative object (LN 84.18): 'to' [Herm, Hn, HNTC, Lns; all versions except KJV], 'unto' [KJV].

TITUS 3:12 97

QUESTION—What is implied by this clause?
1. It implies that the person whom Paul will send is to replace Titus [EBC, EGT, El, GNC, Hn, HNTC, IB, ICC, Lns, MNTC, NCB, TC, TG, TNTC]: when I send Artemas or Tychicus to take your place.
2. It implies merely that Titus is to be brought to Nicopolis by whomever Paul sends to him; if that person were to take over Titus's work, Paul surely would have mentioned it more specifically [My]: when I send Artemas or Tychicus to bring you.

QUESTION—What does the form ὅταν 'when' and the subjunctive mood of the verb πέμπω 'send' indicate?
It indicates that the action has not yet occurred [Lns, TC]: When I send him (later).

QUESTION—What is the phrase ἢ Τύχικον 'or Tychicus' connected with?
This phrase in which Τύχικον 'Tychicus' is accusative is connected with the more remote accusative Ἀρτεμᾶν 'Artemas', not with the nearer accusative σέ 'you' [all commentaries and versions].

QUESTION—What is implied by the phrase 'Artemas or Tychicus'?
It implies that Paul has not yet decided which man he will send [EBC, GNC, Hn, HNTC, IB, Lns, MNTC, TG]: When I send Artemas, or possibly Tychicus.

**be-diligent/hurry<sup>a</sup> to-come to<sup>b</sup> me into<sup>c</sup> Nicopolis;**
LEXICON—a. aorist act. impera. of σπουδάζω (LN 68.63): 'to be diligent' [Lns; KJV], 'to endeavor' [LN], 'to make every effort' [Herm; NASB], 'to work hard' [LN], 'to do one's best' [Hn, HNTC; NIV, NJB, RSV, TEV], 'to do one's utmost' [TNT], 'to hurry' [BAGD; NAB], 'to hasten' [BAGD], 'to make haste' [NEB].
b. πρός with accusative object (LN 84.18): 'to' [Herm, Hn, HNTC, Lns; NAB, NASB, NIV, RSV, TEV, TNT], 'unto' [KJV]. The phrase ἐλθεῖν πρός με 'to come to me' is translated 'to join me' [NEB, NJB].
c. εἰς with accusative object (LN 84.22): 'at' [Hn, HNTC; all versions except KJV, TEV], 'in' [Herm; TEV], 'to' [Lns; KJV].

QUESTION—What is meant by σπούδασον 'be diligent/hurry'?
1. It refers to the effort Titus is to make [Alf, Herm, Hn, HNTC, Lg, Lns; all versions except NAB, NEB]: be diligent to come.
2. It refers to the speed with which Titus is to come [NAB, NEB]: hurry and come.

**for<sup>a</sup> there I-have-decided<sup>b</sup> to-pass-the-winter.<sup>c</sup>**
LEXICON—a. γάρ (LN 89.23): 'for' [Hn, HNTC, Lns; KJV, NASB, NEB, RSV, TNT], 'because' [Herm; NIV, TEV], not explicit [NAB, NJB].
b. perf. act. indic. of κρίνω (LN 30.75): 'to decide' [BAGD, Herm, Hn, HNTC, LN, Lns; all versions except KJV, NEB], 'to determine' [KJV, NEB], 'to make up one's mind' [LN].
c. aorist act. infin. of παραχειμάζω (LN 67.166): 'to spend the winter' [BAGD, Herm, Hn, LN; all versions except KJV, NIV], 'to winter'

[BAGD, HNTC, Lns; KJV, NIV]. The prefix παρα- indicates locality [El].

QUESTION: What relationship is indicated by γάρ 'for'?

It introduces the reason why Titus should go to Nicopolis [SSA]: go to Nicopolis, because I will spend the winter there.

QUESTION—What is implied by ἐκεῖ 'there'?

It implies that Paul was not at Nicopolis when he wrote to Titus [Bg, EBC, EGT, El, GNC, Herm, Hn, HNTC, Lns, MNTC, My, SSA, TC]: I have decided to go there. If Paul had been at Nicopolis when he wrote this letter, he would have said ὧδε 'here' [Bg, SSA, TC].

**3:13** **Zenas the lawyer[a] and Apollos diligently[b] send-forth,[c]**

LEXICON—a. νομικός (LN 56.37): 'lawyer' [BAGD, Herm, HNTC, LN, WC; all versions], 'law-expert' [Hn], 'jurist' [BAGD, Lns]. Some commentators think that he was probably a converted Jewish scribe or expert in the law of Moses [Alf, EGT, El, ICC, Rb]. Others think that »e was a civil lawyer [CBC, Herm, HNTC, Lg, Lns, MNTC, My, NCB, NCBC, WC]. This designation is perhaps given here to distinguish him from another man of the same name [HNTC, Lns, MNTC, SSA] and his profession is not in focus [SSA].

b. σπουδαίως (LN **68.65**): 'diligently' [BAGD, WC; KJV, NASB], 'with diligence' [Lns], 'eagerly' [NJB]. This adverb is also translated as a verb phrase: 'do your best' [HNTC, LN; RSV, TEV, TNT], 'do your utmost' [NEB], 'do everything you can' [NIV], 'do all you can' [Hn]. This is also combined with the verb: 'speed on their journey' [NAB].

c. aorist act. impera. of προπέμπω (LN 15.72): 'to send forth on one's journey' [Lns]; 'to send forward on one's journey' [WC], 'to send on one's way' [LN], 'to bring on one's journey' [KJV], 'to help on one's way' [HNTC, LN; NASB, NIV, NJB], 'to help on one's travels' [NEB], 'to help along on one's journey' [BAGD, Hn], 'to help forward on one's way' [TNT], 'to help get started on one's travels' [TEV], 'to speed on one's way' [RSV], 'to equip for a journey' [Herm]. The meaning is to enable them to go forward [Alf]. 'To send them forth' implies supplying their needs [EBC, El, Herm, Hn, LN, Lns, MNTC, My].

QUESTION—What is implied by the forefronting of the phrase 'Zenas the lawyer and Apollos'?

The forefronting calls attention to them as the new topic [SSA]: speaking now of Zenas and Apollos.

QUESTION—Why are Zenas and Apollos mentioned?

1. They are probably the bearers of this letter [EBC, GNC, Hn, Lns]. They were probably not with Titus when this letter was written, or Paul would have included greetings to them in the letter [Lns].
2. They were both in Crete when Paul wrote this letter, but were preparing to leave [Bg, Lg, MNTC]. This is why they are mentioned separately from

Artemas and Tychicus, who came later [Bg]. They were probably not bearers of the letter [MNTC].

**in-order-that/that**[a] **nothing to-them may-be-lacking.**[b]
LEXICON—a. ἵνα (LN 89.59, 90.22): 'in order that' [WC]; 'so that' [Herm, Hn; NASB], 'that' [Lns; all versions except NASB, NJB]; not explicit [HNTC; NJB].
  b. pres. act. subj. of λείπω (LN 57.43): 'to lack' [BAGD, Herm, Hn, LN, Lns, WC; NASB, RSV], 'to lack for' [HNTC], 'to be short of' [NEB], 'to be wanting' [KJV]. The phrase μηδὲν αὐτοῖς λείπῃ 'nothing be lacking to them' is translated 'they have everything they need' [NAB, NIV, NJB, TEV], 'they have all they need' [TNT].
QUESTION—What relationship is indicated by ἵνα 'in order that/that'?
  1. It indicates the purpose or anticipated result of sending the men [Herm, Hn, Lns, My, Rb, TG, WC]: send them forth diligently, in order that they may lack nothing. It is not an independent sentence with imperative sense [My].
  2. It indicates the content of the implied verb 'see to it' [HNTC, ICC; all versions except KJV, NASB]: see to it that they lack nothing.

**DISCOURSE UNIT: 3:14** [ICC, NCBC, TC]. The topic is a concluding exhortation to the believers [TC], a concluding exhortation to live useful lives [ICC], readiness to help people in need [NCBC].

**3:14** **And/But**[a]
LEXICON—a. δέ (LN 89.87, 89.124): 'and' [KJV, NASB, NEB, RSV, TNT], 'but' [WC], 'besides' [Hn, Lns]; not explicit [Herm, HNTC; NAB, NIV, NJB, TEV].
QUESTION—What relationship is indicated by this word?
  1. It indicates a resumption [EGT, Hn, Lns; KJV, NASB, NEB, RSV, TNT]: as I said previously, our people must learn to devote themselves to good works. This resumes the thought in 3:8 [EGT].
  2. It indicates a contrast [Alf, Bg, WC]: not only should you supply their wants, but let our people learn to do good [Alf, Bg].

**let-learn**[a] **our-(people)**[b] **also**[c] **to-devote-themselves-to**[d] **good**[e] **works**[f]
LEXICON—a. pres. act. impera. of μανθάνω (LN 27.12): 'to learn' [BAGD, Herm, Hn, HNTC, LN, Lns, WC; all versions except NAB, NEB]. This active verb is translated as a passive voice: 'to be taught' [LN; NEB]. The phrase μανθανέτωσαν προΐστασθαι 'let (them) learn to devote themselves to' is translated 'Let (them) devote themselves to' [NAB]. The present tense of the verb indicates continuous action; they had evidently not yet learned sufficiently well [SSA]. They are to learn by Titus's teaching and example; evidently the Christians had not aided Zenas and Apollos as they should have done [Bg].
  b. ἡμέτερος (LN 92.5): 'our people' [BAGD, Herm, Hn, HNTC, Lns, WC; NAB, NASB, NIV, NJB, RSV, TEV], 'our own people' [NEB, TNT],

'ours' [BAGD; KJV]. The reference is to the Christians around Titus in Crete [Alf, Bg, Blm, El, Hn, HNTC, IB, ICC, Lg, MNTC, My, Rb, SSA, TC, TG, TNTC, WC]. This is not intended to be a contrast with non-Christians [Lns].
   c. καί (LN 89.93): 'also' [Hn, Lns, WC; KJV, NASB, NJB], 'too' [HNTC], 'anyway' [Herm]; not explicit [NAB, NEB, NIV, RSV, TEV, TNT].
   d. pres. mid. infin. of προΐστημι (LN **68.67**): 'to devote oneself to' [NAB, NIV], 'to occupy oneself in doing' [NJB], 'to apply oneself to' [Hn; RSV], 'to busy oneself with' [HNTC], 'to strive to do' [LN], 'to engage in' [NASB, NEB], 'to spend one's time' [TEV], 'to take the lead in' [Lns, WC], 'to maintain' [KJV], 'to be concerned about, to care for, to give aid' [BAGD].
   e. καλός (LN 88.4): 'good' [Herm, HNTC, LN; all versions except NAB, NEB], 'noble' [Hn], 'excellent' [Lns], 'honest' [NAB, NEB].
   f. ἔργον (LN 42.11): 'work' [Herm, HNTC, Lns; KJV, NAB, NJB, TNT], 'deed' [Hn, LN; NASB, RSV], 'employment' [NEB]. This noun is also translated as a verb: 'to do' [NIV, TEV].

QUESTION—What is meant by καί 'also'?
This means that the other Christians in addition to Titus himself should be involved [Alf, EBC, El, HNTC, ICC, SSA, TC, WC]: let our people also, as well as you, learn to devote themselves to good deeds. Some commentators take this to mean that the Cretan Christians should be as involved as the non-Christians [MNTC, My]. One translation takes this to modify the verb, indicating another thing Christians should do [NJB]: our people must also learn to do the following. (However, this last interpretation violates the Greek syntax; καί meaning 'also' precedes the word to which it refers.)

QUESTION—What is meant by καλῶν ἔργων 'good works'?
   1. These are good deeds done to help others [Blm, EBC, El, GNC, Hn, HNTC, Lg, Lns, My, NCBC, TNTC].
   2. These are honorable occupations [ICC, NCB, TG; NEB].

**for[a] the necessary[b] needs,[c]**

LEXICON—a. εἰς (LN 89.57, 89.48): 'for' [Hn, Lns; KJV, NJB], 'in' [HNTC], 'in order to take care of' [NAB], 'in order to provide for' [NIV, TEV], 'so as to help' [RSV], 'to take care of' [Herm], 'to meet' [NASB], 'to produce' [NEB].
   b. ἀναγκαῖος (LN 71.39): 'necessary' [BAGD, LN; KJV], 'indispensable' [LN], 'imperative' [Hn, Lns], 'urgent' [HNTC; RSV], 'practical' [NJB], 'pressing' [BAGD; NASB], 'real' [TEV], 'genuine' [TNT]. This adjective is also conflated with χρείας 'needs': 'needs' [NAB], 'daily necessities' [NIV], 'necessities of life' [Herm; NEB].
   c. χρεία (LN 57.40): 'need' [BAGD, Hn, HNTC, LN, Lns; NASB, NJB, TEV, TNT], 'use' [KJV], 'cases of need' [HNTC; RSV], 'occasions of need' [Hn].

TITUS 3:14

QUESTION—What relationship is indicated by εἰς 'for'?

It indicates what type of good works are intended [Blm, Lns, My, SSA, TC]: let them learn to do good works to meet the needs which arise.

QUESTION—What are 'necessary needs'?

This refers to helping others who are in need [Alf, Bg, Blm, EBC, El, GNC, Hn, HNTC, IB, Lg, Lns, My, SSA, TC, TNTC; RSV, TEV, TNT]. It includes their teachers' needs as well [WC]. The bond of Christian fellowship makes it a spiritual necessity to help fellow believers [Bg]. It refers to help in general where there is a need, including non believers as well as fellow Christians [SSA]. The definite article implies wants which are known to exist from time to time [El, TC]. Some restrict it to the needs of one's own family [NAB, NEB, NIV, NJB]. Others think it refers both to providing for oneself and one's family and helping needy fellow Christians as such needs arise [EGT, ICC]

**in-order-that**[a] **not they-may-be fruitless.**[b]

LEXICON—a. ἵνα (LN 89.59): 'in order that' [Hn, WC; NIV], 'so that' [Herm, Lns; NAB], 'that' [KJV, NASB], 'so as' [RSV]; not explicit [NEB, NJB, TEV]. The phrase ἵνα μὴ ὦσιν ἄκαρποι 'in order that they may not be unfruitful' is translated 'otherwise they will be good for nothing' [HNTC], 'they should not live useless lives' [TEV], 'They must not waste their efforts' [TNT]. The reference is to indications of their faith by their deeds of love and mercy [El].

b. ἄκαρπος (LN 65.34): 'unfruitful' [BAGD, Hn, Lns, WC; KJV, NASB, RSV], 'unproductive' [BAGD, LN; NEB, NJB], 'useless' [LN]. The phrase μὴ ὦσιν ἄκαρποι 'they may not be unfruitful' is translated 'they may not live unproductive lives' [NIV], 'they do not lead an unproductive life' [Herm], 'they may be in a position to live fruitful lives' [NAB]. The reference may be to the claim of Roman pagans that Christians were unprofitable to the state, since they refused to work at certain trades [ICC], or that their religion made them dreamers who neglected the responsibilities and courtesies of ordinary life [MNTC].

QUESTION—What relationship is indicated by ἵνα 'in order that'?

It indicates the purpose or anticipated result of ministering to these needs [Blm, EBC, EGT, GNC, Hn, SSA]: the Christians there should minister in this way in order to bear fruit for God. This implies that ministering to such needs constitutes bearing fruit for God [Alf, EBC, Hn].

**DISCOURSE UNIT: 3:15** [EGT, Herm, ICC, MNTC, NCBC, WC. The topic is closing greetings [EGT, Herm, ICC, MNTC, NCBC], greetings and benediction [WC].

**DISCOURSE UNIT: 3:15a** [EBC, TC]. The topic is personal greetings [EBC], greetings [TC].

**3:15a** All greet[a] you the-(ones) with[b] me.

LEXICON—a. pres. mid. (deponent = act.) indic. of ἀσπάζομαι (LN 33.20): 'to greet' [BAGD, LN, WC; NASB, TNT], 'to send greetings' [Herm, Hn, LN; NAB, NEB, NIV, NJB, RSV, TEV], 'to send regards' [HNTC], 'to salute' [Lns; KJV].

    b. μετά with genitive object (LN 89.108): 'with' [Herm, Hn; all versions]. The phrase οἱ μετ' ἐμοῦ πάντες 'all the ones with me' is translated 'all my companions' [HNTC], 'all those in my company' [Lns].

QUESTION—Who are the people with Paul?

They are Paul's associates [EBC, Hn, HNTC, Lns, My] or the Christians who are around Paul [TG]. Some commentators think that it cannot be determined who are included in this greeting [Lg, SSA, TNTC]. The phrase is probably merely conventional [IB].

**Greet[a] the-(ones) loving[b] us in[c] faith.[d]**

LEXICON—a. aorist mid. (deponent = active) impera. of ἀσπάζομαι (LN 33.20): 'to greet' [BAGD, Herm, Hn, LN, WC; KJV, NAB, NASB, NIV, RSV, TNT], 'to give greetings to' [TEV], 'to give regards to' [HNTC], 'to salute' [Lns]. This verb is also translated as a noun: 'greetings' [NEB, NJB].

    b. pres. act. participle of φιλέω (LN 25.33): 'to love' [BAGD, Herm, Hn, HNTC, LN, Lns, WC; KJV, NAB, NASB, NIV, NJB, RSV], 'to have affection for' [LN]. The phrase τοὺς φιλοῦντας ἡμᾶς 'the ones loving us' is translated 'our friends' [TEV, TNT], 'those who are our friends' [NEB]. Φιλοῦντας 'loving' is the love of affection [EBC, Hn, Lns, My].

    c. ἐν with dative object (LN 13.8; 89.84): 'in' [Herm, Hn, HNTC, Lns, WC; all versions].

    d. πίστις (LN 31.102): 'faith' [BAGD, Herm, Hn, Lns, WC], 'the faith' [HNTC; all versions except NEB], 'truth' [NEB], 'Christian faith' [LN]. The sense of the phrase is their common faith or loyalty to Christ [ICC, TC]; 'in the faith', not 'in faith' [HNTC], since the article is commonly omitted in prepositional phrases in the pastoral Epistles [Alf, EGT, SSA]. 'In the faith' refers to the sphere within which the 'love' occurs [EBC, HNTC]. The absence of the article may give the sense of 'faithfully' [TNTC].

QUESTION—What is implied by the phrase τοὺς φιλοῦντας ἡμᾶς ἐν πίστει 'the ones loving us in faith'?

This phrase may refer to the fact that some have proved disloyal [GNC]; it probably implies that his greetings do not include the false teachers and those who are causing divisions [HNTC, IB, ICC, Lg]: those who love us in the sphere of the Christian faith. The phrase implies that all of the Christians in Crete love Paul and his co-workers in this way [Lns]. However, the phrase 'those who love us' may be merely a conventional expression, with 'in faith' added to give it a Christian element [Herm].

**DISCOURSE UNIT: 3:15b** [EBC, TC]. The topic is a closing benediction [EBC, TC].

**3:15b** The grace[a] with[b] you all.

TEXT—Some manuscripts add ἀμήν 'amen' after 'you all'. GNT omits 'amen' with a B rating, indicating some degree of doubt. 'Amen' is included by KJV.

LEXICON—a. χάρις (LN 88.66): 'grace' [BAGD, Herm, Hn, HNTC, LN, Lns, WC; all versions].

b. μετά with genitive object (LN 89.108): 'with' [Herm, Hn, HNTC, Lns, WC; all versions]. This preposition means that God's grace is to be in their midst [Hn]. The phrase 'with you all' includes the entire Christian community around Titus [HNTC, My], even those to whom he could not send warm greetings [ICC]. It implies that the letter was to be read to the churches [EBC, HNTC, ICC, Lg, MNTC, NCBC]. This closing phrase does not imply that the letter was written to the church as well as to Titus [El, My]; it is merely an inclusive benediction [El].

# EXEGETICAL SUMMARY OF PHILEMON

**INTRODUCTION**—This is a personal letter from Paul to a Christian named Philemon. It is occasioned by Paul's desire to intercede in behalf of Philemon's runaway slave, Onesimus, who had gone to Rome and been converted under Paul's ministry. Paul now writes to Philemon urging him to receive Onesimus back with forgiveness.

**DISCOURSE UNIT: 1–7** [TNTC]. These verses give the introduction to the letter.

**DISCOURSE UNIT: 1–3** [Alf, Bg, CBC, CGTC, EBC, EPC, GNT, Herm, Hn, ICC, Lg, Lt, MNTC, My, NCBC, NIC, TH, TNTC, WBC, WPC; NAB, NIV, NJB, TEV]. The topic is Paul's greeting [CGTC, EBC, EPC, GNT, Hn, ICC, NCBC, TNTC, WBC, WPC; NAB, NIV], the address [Bg; NJB], Paul's greeting and address [Alf, Lg, My], introduction [Herm; TEV].

**1** **Paul, a-prisoner[a] of-Christ Jesus**

LEXICON—a. δέσμιος (LN 37.117): 'prisoner' [BAGD, Herm, Hn, ICC, LN, Lns, WBC; all versions except TNT]. This noun is also translated as a descriptive phrase: '(one who is) in prison' [TNT].

QUESTION—Why does Paul call himself a prisoner rather than his usual self-designation, ἀπόστολος 'apostle'?

Paul is writing merely as a friend [Alf, ICC], to request a favor [ICC, Lg, NIC]. The designation, 'prisoner', is meant to touch Philemon's heart as a basis for Paul's entreaty [Bg, CBC, CGTC, EBC, Lg, Lns, Lt, MNTC, My, WBC]. Paul may be implying that the favor he is requesting is not as great a sacrifice as his own sacrifice in being in prison [Hn, TNTC].

QUESTION—Is 'prisoner' used metaphorically, and how is this noun related to 'Christ Jesus' in the genitive construction δέσμιος Χριστοῦ Ἰησοῦ 'a prisoner of Christ Jesus'?

1. Paul is a prisoner in the literal sense of the word.
   1.1 His relationship to Christ caused men to imprison him [Blm, ICC, Lg(H), MNTC, NCBC, NIC, TH, TNTC, WBC; TEV, TNT]: I am a prisoner because I have served and preached about Christ Jesus. He is a prisoner for the sake of Christ [Blm, NIC, WBC; TEV, TNT].
   1.2 Christ's providential rule determined that Paul would be imprisoned by men [El, MNTC, My]: I am a prisoner, made so by Christ Jesus. He is a prisoner because this is Christ Jesus' plan for him.
   1.3 He is a prisoner who belongs to Christ [Hn, Lns]: I am a prisoner, one who belongs to Christ Jesus.
2. Paul is referring to a figurative imprisonment in order to describe his relationship with Christ [CGTC, EGT, WPC]: I am like a prisoner in my subjection to Christ Jesus, who is like my jailer. This spiritual bondage is one in which every true Christian participates [EGT].

3. Paul includes both the literal and the figurative sense [CBC]: I am a prisoner because I am loyal to Christ Jesus and I am like a prisoner captured by Christ to serve him.

**and Timothy the brother**[a]
LEXICON—a. ἀδελφός (LN 11.23): 'brother' [BAGD, Herm, Hn, ICC, LN, Lns, WBC; all versions except NEB], 'colleague' [NEB], 'fellow believer' [LN]. The article in the phrase ὁ ἀδελφός 'the brother' is also translated 'our' [all versions].
QUESTION—In what way is Timothy connected with Paul in writing this letter?
 Paul alone is the source of and the authority for the letter [Herm, ICC, NIC, TH, WBC]. The use of the singular first person references in the body of the letter is a proof of this [Herm, NIC, WBC]. Timothy is mentioned to indicate that he is joining in the greeting [CBC, NIC, TH]. He is mentioned here, rather than at the close with other associates, because of his more permanent partnership with Paul [ICC, NIC], because of his past association with Philemon and the church [EGT, ICC, Lg, Lt, MNTC, WBC], and because he joins Paul in the appeal to Philemon [EBC, Lns]. Perhaps Paul consulted with Timothy before writing and included some of his suggestions in the letter [MNTC].

**to-Philemon the beloved**[a] **and fellow-worker**[b] **of-us**
LEXICON—a. ἀγαπητός (LN 25.45): 'beloved' [BAGD, Herm, ICC, LN, Lns], 'dearly beloved' [KJV]. Some include an implied noun with this adjective: 'beloved friend' [NAB], 'beloved brother' [Hn; NASB], 'dear friend' [WBC; NEB, NIV, TNT]. This adjective is also translated as a»noun: 'friend' [TEV]. Some omit the 'and' and treat it as descriptive of 'fellow worker': 'dear fellow worker' [NJB], 'beloved fellow worker' [RSV].
 b. συνεργός (LN 42.44): 'fellow worker' [BAGD, Herm, Hn, LN, Lns, WBC; NAB, NASB, NEB, NIV, NJB, RSV, TEV], 'fellow laborer' [ICC; KJV], 'colleague' [TNT], 'helper' [BAGD].
QUESTION—What is the function of the dative case for Φιλήμονι 'Philemon'?
 This indicates that he is the recipient of the letter [CBC, Herm, Hn, Lns, Lt, NCBC, WBC]: Paul writes to Philemon. The verb is normally omitted in the salutation of a letter [CBC].
QUESTION—By whom is Philemon beloved?
 He is loved by Paul and Timothy (vs. 1) [Hn, ICC, Lns, My], and other colleagues of Paul [Hn, WBC]: whom we love.
QUESTION—In what way was Philemon their fellow worker?
 1. Philemon had previously worked together with Paul and Timothy [Lt, MNTC, NCBC, WBC]: you worked alongside us. This could have taken place in Ephesus [Lt, MNTC].

2. Philemon does the same kind of work that Paul and Timothy do [Alf, Blm, CBC, EGT, El, Herm, Hn, Lg, Lns, My, TH, TNTC]: you work for the gospel, as we do.

## **2** and to-Apphia the sister[a]

TEXT—Instead of ἀδελφῇ 'sister', the Byzantine text reads ἀγαπητῇ 'beloved'. This variant is not given in GNT. Only Blm, Brt, Lg, and KJV read 'beloved'.

LEXICON—a. ἀδελφή (LN 11.24): 'sister' [BAGD, Herm, Hn, ICC, LN, Lns, WBC; all versions], 'fellow believer' [LN].

QUESTION—What is indicated by the dative case for 'Apphia', 'Archippus', and 'the church'?

1. Although these words are grammatically parallel with 'Philemon' in the Greek text, Apphia, Archippus, and the church are not co-recipients of the letter but are greeted by Paul as a matter of friendship and courtesy [NIC, TH, WBC]: I, Paul, am writing to Philemon, and I greet Apphia and Archippus as well. The second person singular is used in the body of the letter and refers to Philemon.
2. This letter is addressed to them as well as to Philemon. It is not merely a personal letter [CBC, Herm, Hn, IB, NCBC]: I, Paul, am writing to Philemon, Apphia, Archippus, and the church. Philemon is the main recipient [CBC], but all hear and share in deciding what is to be done about Onesimus [Herm, Hn].

QUESTION—Who was Apphia?

Many commentators think that she was Philemon's wife [Alf, BAGD, Bg, Blm, Brt, CBC, EBC, EGT, El, EPC, Herm, Hn, ICC, Lg, Lns, Lt (p. 304), MNTC, My, NCBC, NIC, TNTC, WBC]. Some argue that she must be his wife, since a wife had responsibilities concerning the slaves [Bg, EBC, Herm, ICC, My, NCBC]. However, some point out that there is no real evidence that she was his wife [IB, TH]. She might be included merely as a matter of courtesy [WBC].

QUESTION—Why is Apphia called 'sister'?

She is called a sister in that she is a part of the Christian fellowship [CBC, Hn, ICC, Lt (p. 306), MNTC, My, TH, WBC, WPC]. This is the female counterpart to 'brother', the term used for Timothy. One commentator thinks that 'sister' suggests that she was a person of influence in the church, especially since she is mentioned between the references to a 'fellow worker' and a 'fellow soldier' [EGT].

## and to-Archippus the fellow-soldier[a] of-us

LEXICON—a. συστρατιώτης (LN 34.19): 'fellow soldier' [BAGD, Herm, Hn, ICC, LN, Lns, WBC; all versions except NEB], 'comrade-in-arms' [BAGD; NEB].

QUESTION—Who was Archippus?

Some commentators think he was a member of Philemon's family, probably Philemon's son [Alf, Blm, CBC, El, EPC, Hn, ICC, Lns, Lt (p. 306), MNTC,

NIC, TNTC]. Others think he was a friend of Philemon [EBC, EGT, Herm, IB, Lg].

QUESTION—In what way was Archippus their fellow soldier?

This is a metaphor. It emphasizes that Archippus was opposed by enemies of the gospel and that he suffered in his work for the gospel [My, NCBC, TH]. He, like Paul and his companions, was actively serving Christ. Some consider this term to be equivalent to 'fellow worker' [EBC, Herm, Lns]. Some think that he was the head of the local church [EBC, EGT, MNTC] or had some other position in it [Blm, Brt, CBC, EBC, Herm, ICC, Lg, Lns, Lt (p. 307)], or that he had previously worked with Paul somewhere [Lt, NIC, TNTC, WBC], perhaps in Ephesus [Lt], or that he had a part in the common cause of the gospel [MNTC].

**and to-the church[a] in[b] your house:[c]**

LEXICON—a. ἐκκλησία (LN 11.32): 'church' [BAGD, Hn, ICC, LN, Lns, WBC; all versions except NEB], 'community' [Herm], 'congregation' [LN; NEB].

b. κατά (LN 89.4): 'in' [BAGD, Herm, Hn, Lns; all versions except NEB], 'at' [NEB], 'which assembles in' [ICC], 'that meets in' [WBC].

c. οἶκος (LN 7.2): 'house' [BAGD, Herm, Hn, ICC, LN, Lns, WBC; all versions except NIV], 'home' [NIV].

QUESTION—In the phrase οἶκόν σου 'your house', what is the significance of the singular pronoun σου 'your'?

1. The singular pronoun refers to Philemon, and by using it Paul is stating that it is Philemon's house in which the church meets [Bg, CBC, EBC, El, EPC, Herm, Hn, ICC, Lg, Lns, MNTC, My, NCBC, NIC, TH, WBC]: the church which meets at your (Philemon's) house. The use of the singular form is also mentioned as support for the conclusion that Philemon alone is the addressee of the letter [NIC, WBC].
2. Since 'Archippus' stands closest to 'your', two commentators mention that the pronoun might refer to Archippus rather than to Philemon, which would imply that the church met at the house of Archippus [EGT, IB] and even that the slave Onesimus belonged to Archippus rather than to Philemon [IB]: the church which meets at your (Archippus') house. Neither one argues that this is the correct interpretation.

QUESTION—Who are included in the church referred to here?

The church is not merely Philemon's family, but rather a group of Christians at Colossae [Alf, CBC, EBC, EGT, El, EPC, Herm, Hn, ICC, Lg, Lns, MNTC, My, NCBC, TH, WBC, WPC]: and to the Christians who gather at your house for worship.

**3 grace[a] to-you and peace[b]**

LEXICON—a. χάρις (LN 88.66): 'grace' [BAGD, Herm, Hn, ICC, LN, Lns, WBC; all versions], 'favor' [BAGD], 'kindness' [LN].

b. εἰρήνη (LN 22.42): 'peace' [Herm, Hn, ICC, LN, WBC; all versions], 'tranquility' [LN].

QUESTION—What is the significance of this greeting?

This is the common greeting of the Pauline letters, combining the Greek concept of 'grace' with the Hebrew concept of 'peace' [CBC, EGT, MNTC], grace referring to God's unmerited favor [Hn] and peace referring to maintaining a right relationship with God and one's fellow men [TH, WBC]. However, some commentators place more emphasis on peace as reconciliation and the obtaining of peace [CBC, Hn, IB] and peace of heart [TH]. The unexpressed verb would be in the optative mood, εἴη 'may there be', indicating Paul's prayer or desire that God would grant this favor [El, Lg, TH; TEV].

QUESTION—To whom does ὑμῖν 'you' refer?

This pronoun is plural and refers to all of those mentioned in verses 1 and 2 [Herm, NCBC, NIC, TH, WBC].

**from God Father of-us and Lord Jesus Christ.**

QUESTION—What is the significance of this phrase?

God and Christ together are the source from which Paul desires that the grace and peace may come [NIC, TH; TEV]: May God the Father and the Lord Jesus Christ give you grace and peace.

**DISCOURSE UNIT: 4–7** [Alf, CBC, CGTC, EBC, EPC, GNT, Herm, Hn, Lg, Lt, MNTC, My, NCBC, NIC, TH, TNTC, WBC, WPC; NAB, NIV, NJB, TEV]. The topic is Paul's thanksgiving for Philemon [CBC, CGTC, EPC, MNTC, NCBC, NIC, TNTC, WPC], thanksgiving and prayer for him [EBC, Herm, Hn, WBC; NIV, NJB], Philemon's character and usefulness [Alf], Philemon's faith and love [GNT; NAB, TEV].

**4** I thank[a] the God of-me always[b]

LEXICON—a. pres. act. indic. of εὐχαριστέω (LN 25.100, 33.349): 'to thank' [Herm, Hn, ICC, LN, Lns, WBC; all versions except TEV], 'to give thanks' [BAGD; TEV], 'to be thankful' [LN].

b. πάντοτε (LN **67.88**): 'always' [BAGD, Herm, Hn, ICC, LN, WBC; all versions except TEV], 'every time' [LN, Lns; TEV].

QUESTION—How are God and Paul related in the genitive construction τῷ θεῷ μου 'the God of me'?

The words 'my God' is not intended to imply a special or exclusive relationship by Paul, but rather grows out of his deep sense of a personal relationship with God and of God's love for him [El, Lg(H), TH, TNTC, WBC]: I thank God, with whom I have a personal relationship; or, I thank God, whom I worship.

QUESTION—What does πάντοτε 'always' qualify?

1. It qualifies the preceding main verb εὐχαριστῶ 'I thank' [Alf, Brt, CGTC, EGT, Herm, Hn, ICC, Lg, Lt, My, NIC, WBC; NAB, NASB, NEB, NIV, NJB, RSV]: I always thank my God, when I make mention of you in my prayers.

2. It qualifies the following participial phrase μνείαν ποιούμενος 'making mention' [El, TH; KJV, TNT]: I thank God, always making mention of you in my prayers.

QUESTION—For what is Paul thanking God?
Since God has brought about Philemon's love and faith, thanks are due to God [Herm]. See the comments on verses 5–6.

**mention/remembrance[a] of you making in[b] the prayers[c] of-me,**

LEXICON—a. μνεία (LN 29.18): 'mention' [BAGD, Hn, ICC, LN, Lns; KJV, NASB]. This noun is also conflated with ποιούμενος 'making': 'to mention' [CGTC, WBC; NEB, NJB, TEV], 'to commend' [NAB], or 'to remember' [Herm; NIV, RSV, TNT]. It is used in the NT only of mentioning in prayer [BAGD].

b. ἐπί (LN 67.136): 'in' [Herm, Hn, ICC, Lns, Lt, NIC, WBC; all versions except TEV], not explicit [TEV].

c. προσευχή (LN 33.178): 'prayers' [Herm, Hn, ICC, LN, Lns, WBC; all versions except TEV]. This noun is also translated as a verb: 'to pray' [TEV].

QUESTION—What relationship is indicated by the participial phrase μνείαν ποιούμενος 'making mention/remembrance'?
  1. It indicates the circumstance or time when Paul thanks God [BAGD, EBC, Herm, ICC, Lg, Lns, My, WBC]: I always thank God when I mention you in my prayers. This also explains and limits the use of the adverb πάντοτε 'always' [Brt, Herm, ICC, WBC].
  2. It indicates a restatement of the preceding verb to further amplify it [Alf]: I thank God; that is, I mention you to him in my prayers.

QUESTION—What is meant by μνείαν ποιούμενος making mention/remembrance'?
  1. This means 'to mention' to another person [CGTC, El, Herm, Hn, ICC, Lns, Lt, My, TH, WBC; KJV, NAB, NASB, NEB, NJB, TEV]: I mention you to God in my prayers.
  2. This means 'to remember' [Herm; NIV, RSV, TNT]: I think of you as I pray. However, this implies that the person who is remembered is also mentioned in the prayer [Herm, Lt].

QUESTION—To whom does σου 'you' refer?
The pronoun is singular and refers to Philemon alone [CBC, EBC, El, Herm, Lg, Lns, Lt, MNTC, My, NIC, TH, WBC]. This applies here and in every instance through verse 21.

QUESTION—What relationship is indicated by ἐπί 'in (my prayers)'?
It indicates the circumstance of the preceding participial phrase 'making mention' [EBC, El, Herm, ICC, Lg, Lns, MNTC, My, WBC]: I mention you as/when I pray.

**5 hearing[a]**

LEXICON—a. pres. act. participle of ἀκούω (LN 33.212): 'to hear' [Herm, Hn, ICC, LN, Lns, WBC; all versions], 'to learn of' [BAGD]. The present tense indicates repeated hearing [El, Lns, My, WBC; NAB]: from time to time I hear.

QUESTION—What relationship is indicated by the participle ἀκούων 'hearing'?

It indicates the reason for the main verb εὐχαριστῶ 'I thank' (vs. 4) [Alf, EBC, El, Herm, Hn, ICC, Lg(H), Lt, My, NCBC, TH, WBC; NAB]: I thank God because I have been hearing of your love and faith. This implies that Paul recognizes that God is responsible for these good qualities shown by Philemon [CBC, Herm]. Paul would have heard from Onesimus [Bg, Lg, My], or Epaphras (vs. 23) [EGT, Hn, Lg(H), Lt, NIC], or both [Lns, WBC].

**of-you the love[a] and the faith/faithfulness[b] which you have toward[c] the Lord Jesus and for[d] all the saints,[e]**

LEXICON—a. ἀγάπη (LN 25.43): 'love' [BAGD, Herm, Hn, ICC, LN, Lns, WBC; all versions except TNT]. This noun is also translated as a verb: 'to love' [TNT].

b. πίστις (LN 31.85): 'faith' [BAGD, Herm, Hn, ICC, LN, Lns, WBC; all versions except TNT], 'trust' [BAGD]. This noun is also translated as a verb: 'to trust' [TNT].

c. πρός (LN 90.58): 'in' [BAGD, Herm, WBC; NIV, TEV], 'toward' [Hn, Lns; KJV, NAB, NASB, RSV], 'towards' [ICC; NEB], 'for' [NJB]. The phrase πρὸς τὸν κύριον Ἰησοῦν is also translated as the object of the verbs: 'how you love and trust the Lord Jesus' [TNT].

d. εἰς (LN 90.59): 'for' [Herm, Hn, Lns, WBC; NIV, NJB, TEV], 'to' [ICC], 'toward' [KJV, NAB, NASB, RSV], 'towards' [NEB]. The phrase εἰς πάντας τοὺς ἁγίους 'for all the saints' is also translated as the object of verbs: 'how you love and trust all God's people' [TNT].

e. ἅγιος (LN 11.27): 'saints' [BAGD, Herm, Hn, ICC, Lns, WBC; KJV, NASB, NIV, RSV], 'God's people' [LN; NAB, NEB, TEV, TNT], 'God's holy people' [NJB].

QUESTION—To what is σου 'of you (sg.)' related?

Some commentators relate it grammatically to both 'love' and 'faith' [EBC, EGT, El, Herm, ICC, Lg, Lns, Lt, WBC, WPC; KJV, NAB, NEB, NIV, NJB, TNT]: your love and your faith; or, I hear that you love and that you have faith. Others relate it grammatically only to 'love' [Hn, My; NASB, RSV]: your love and the faith which you have. However, this still means: I hear that you love and you have faith.

QUESTION—To whom are the love and the faith directed and what is meant by πίστιν 'faith/faithfulness'?

1. Philemon's love is directed to the saints, and his faith is directed to the Lord Jesus [Bg, Brt, CGTC, EGT, Herm, Hn, Lg, Lns, Lt, TH, WBC, WPC; NIV, TEV]: your love for all the saints and your faith in the Lord Jesus. In this case, πίστιν means 'faith': he believes in Christ [CGTC, EGT, Herm, Hn, Lg, Lns, Lt, TH]. In support of this interpretation some

commentators point to the change in prepositions, love to (πρός) the Lord Jesus and faith to (εἰς) the saints [EGT, Lg, Lns, Lt, WBC]. Some regard this as a chiastic construction, (a) love and (b) faith to (b) the Lord Jesus and to (a) the saints [Bg, CGTC, EGT, Herm, Hn, Lg, Lt, TH, WBC]; others attribute the arrangement to the relative clause ἣν ἔχεις 'which you have' [Lns].
2. Both his love and faith are directed to both the Lord Jesus and to all the saints [Alf, NIC, WPC; NEB, NJB, TNT]: you have both love and faith for the Lord Jesus and all the saints. In this case, πίστιν means 'faithfulness': they are faithful to both the Lord and the saints [NIC].
3. Both his love and faith are directed to the Lord Jesus and his love is also directed to the saints [CBC, EBC]: your love and faith toward the Lord Jesus and your love for all the saints. In this case, πίστιν means 'faith': he believes in Christ.
4. The phrase 'your love' is one unit, and 'the faith which you have toward the Lord Jesus and for all the saints' is a separate unit [El, My; NASB, RSV]: I hear of your love and faith, which faith you show to the Lord Jesus and to all the saints. In this case πίστιν means 'faithfulness': they are faithful to both the Lord and the saints [My]. Or, the different prepositions can be accounted for by taking them to mean faith to (πρός) the Lord Jesus and faithfulness shown toward (εἰς) all the saints [El]. It is implied that their love is directed toward Christians [El, My].

## 6 that<sup>a</sup>

LEXICON—a. ὅπως (LN 89.59, but see also ἵνα 90.22): 'that' [BAGD, Hn, ICC, Lns, WBC; all versions], not explicit [Herm].
QUESTION—What relationship is indicated by this word?
1. It does not grammatically modify any preceding word. It picks up the reference to Paul's prayers for Philemon (vs. 4, 'making mention of you in my prayers') and states the contents of those prayers [BAGD, Blm, Brt, CBC, CGTC, EBC, EGT, El, Herm, Hn, ICC, Lns, MNTC, NCBC, NIC, TH, WBC; NAB, NASB, NEB, NIV, NJB, RSV, TEV, TNT]: I pray that the sharing of your faith may become effective, etc. Being the content of a prayer, it at the same time implies the purpose for the prayer [Alf, ICC, Lg, Lt]: I pray in order that the sharing of your faith may become effective, etc., and my purpose is that this may occur.
2. It introduces the purpose [Bg] (or the tendency [My]) of ἔχεις 'you have' in verse 5: you have love and faith in order that the sharing of your faith may become effective, etc.

## the sharing<sup>a</sup> of-the faith<sup>b</sup> of-you

LEXICON—a. κοινωνία (LN 34.5, 57.98): 'sharing' [BAGD, Herm, Hn, LN; NAB, RSV], 'participation' [BAGD], 'communication' [ICC; KJV], 'generosity' [WBC], or 'fellowship' [LN, Lns; NASB, NEB, NJB, TEV]. This noun is also translated as a verb: 'to share' [NIV, TNT].

b. πίστις (LN 31.85, 31.102, 31.104): 'faith' [BAGD, Herm, Hn, ICC, LN, Lns, WBC; all versions except TEV], 'Christian faith' [LN]. This is also translated as 'as believers' [TEV].

QUESTION—What area of meaning of κοινωνία 'sharing/fellowship' is intended and how are the two event words and the pronoun related in the double genitive construction ἡ κοινωνία τῆς πίστεώς σου 'the sharing of the faith of you'?

1. This means that Philemon shares (communicates) his faith with others by telling them about it [Alf; NAB]: you share what you believe with others.
2. This means that Philemon shares (participates) in the Christian faith with others by means of his own faith [EBC, Herm, Lg]: you share in the faith all Christians have by means of your believing in Christ.
3. This means that Philemon shares with others (gives to others) what belongs to him as a result of his faith [EPC, Hn, ICC, Lt, NIC, WBC]: you share your possessions with others because you believe in Christ.
4. This means that Philemon shares (fellowships) with all Christians.
4.1 This fellowship is a result of his faith [Lns, My, TNTC]: you fellowship with Christians, because you believe in Christ.
4.2 This fellowship is in respect to the Christian faith [CBC, EBC, EGT, Herm; NEB]: you fellowship with Christians in respect to the Christian faith you all hold.
5. This means that Philemon shares (fellowships) with Christ by means of his faith [MNTC]: you fellowship with Christ by having faith in him.

**may-become effective[a] in[b] true-knowledge[c] of every good-thing,[d] the (thing) in[e] us**

TEXT—Instead of ἡμῖν 'us', some manuscripts read ὑμῖν 'you (pl.)'. GNT chooses 'us' with a C rating, indicating a considerable degree of doubt. If 'you' is read here, it is the only use of the plural 'you' in the body of the epistle. Only Lns, KJV, and NASB read 'you'.

TEXT—Some manuscripts add Ἰησοῦν 'Jesus' after Χριστόν 'Christ'. GNT does not mention this variant. Only Lns, KJV, and NASB read 'you'.

LEXICON—a. ἐνεργής (LN **13.124**): 'effective' [BAGD, Herm, LN; NASB], 'effectual' [KJV], 'active' [BAGD; NIV], 'energetic' [Lns], 'energetically stimulated' [Hn], 'powerful' [BAGD]. The phrase ἐνεργὴς γένηται 'may become effective' is translated 'may prove itself' [ICC], 'may lead you effectively' [WBC], 'may enable' [NAB], '(we all) may be enabled' [TNT], 'may deepen' [NEB], 'may come to expression' [NJB], 'may promote' [RSV], 'will bring about' [TEV].

b. ἐν (LN 89.5, 89.48, 90.23): 'in' [Herm, ICC, Lns; NJB], 'through' [NASB], 'by' [Hn; KJV], 'into' [WBC], not explicit [NAB, NEB, NIV, RSV, TEV, TNT].

c. ἐπίγνωσις (LN **28.2**): 'true knowledge', 'knowledge' [BAGD, Herm; NASB, RSV], 'full knowledge' [ICC, Lns; NJB], 'acknowledging' [KJV], 'clear recognition' [Hn], 'understanding' [NEB], 'deeper understanding'

[WBC; TEV], 'full understanding' [NIV], 'recognition' [BAGD]. This noun is also translated as a verb: 'to know' [LN; NAB], 'to understand more and more fully' [TNT].
   d. ἀγαθός (LN 88.1): 'good' [LN]. The phrase παντὸς ἀγαθοῦ 'every good thing' is translated 'every good thing' [Lns; KJV, NASB, NIV], 'all the good' [Herm, Hn; NAB, NJB, RSV], 'every blessing' [WBC; TEV], 'every spiritual blessing' [ICC], 'all the blessings' [NEB]. The phrase παντὸς ἀγαθοῦ τοῦ ἐν ἡμῖν 'of every good thing which is in us' is combined by the following: 'how richly blessed we are' [TNT].
   e. ἐν (LN 83.9, 83.13): 'in' [Herm, Lns; KJV, NASB], 'among' [CBC], 'in the midst' [Lns]. The phrase τοῦ ἐν ἡμῖν 'which is in us' is translated 'that is ours' [Hn; RSV], 'which is ours' [NAB], 'which we as Christians possess' [ICC], 'which belongs to us' [WBC], 'we have' [NIV], 'we can do' [NJB], 'which we have in our life' [TEV]. The phrase τοῦ ἐν ἡμῖν εἰς Χριστόν 'which is in us for Christ' is translated 'that our union with Christ brings us' [NEB].
QUESTION—What relationship is indicated by ἐν 'in'?
   1. It indicates the result of Philemon's effectively sharing his faith [EPC, Lg, Lt, MNTC, NCBC, NIC, TNTC, WBC; NAB, NEB, NIV, NJB, RSV, TEV, TNT]: I pray that the sharing of your faith may result in your knowing every good thing in us.
   2. It indicates the means by which the sharing is made effective [Blm, EBC, Hn; KJV, NASB]: I pray that the sharing of your faith may be made effective by means of knowing every good thing in us.
   3. It indicates in what respect the sharing is to be made effective [Alf, EGT, Herm]: I pray that the sharing of your faith may be made effective in respect to knowing every good thing in us.
QUESTION—To what does παντὸς ἀγαθοῦ 'every good thing' refer?
   The good things are the blessings God gives us [Bg, CBC, Hn, ICC, My, NIC, TH, TNTC, WBC], his gifts and grace [Alf, EGT], salvation [Herm], or the Christian teachings [ICC]. Or, this refers to the good Philemon will do in releasing Onesimus [NCBC].

**for/in[a] Christ.**
LEXICON—a. εἰς (LN 90.23, 89.57): 'for' [Herm, Hn; NJB], 'for the sake of' [NASB], 'for the glory of' [ICC], 'regarding' [Lns], 'in' [WBC; KJV, NAB, NIV, RSV], 'in union with' [TEV], '(our) union with' [NEB], 'as (Christ's) followers' [TNT], 'as fellow members in (the body of Christ)' [WBC], 'as (Christ's) followers' [TNT].
QUESTION—What relationship is indicated by εἰς 'for/in'?
   1. It indicates the purpose of becoming effective: for Christ's glory [Alf, Blm, Herm, Hn, ICC, Lg(H)], for Christ's honor [Bg, CBC, El], for the advancement of Christ's cause [ICC, Lg, My]. Christ is honored because he is credited for the blessings [CBC].

2. It indicates close spiritual fellowship or union. This is equivalent to ἐν 'in' [EPC, NIC, WBC; TEV].
2.1 All the good that is ours because we are in fellowship with Christ [EPC, NIC].
2.2 All the good that is ours, we who are in union with Christ [WBC].
3. It means 'as regards to' [Lns]: every good thing as regards Christ.
4. It indicates the goal of becoming effective: leading to Christ as the goal [Lt, TH, TNTC, WPC], leading to a deeper trust in Christ and obedience to him [TNTC], bringing us unto a closer relationship with Christ [CGTC].

## 7 For[a]

LEXICON—a. γάρ (LN 89.23): 'for' [Herm, Hn, ICC, Lns, WBC; KJV, NASB, NEB, RSV], not explicit [NIC; NAB, NIV, NJB, TEV, TNT].
QUESTION—What relationship is indicated by this word?
1. It indicates a further reason for Paul's thanksgiving in verse 4 [Hn, ICC, Lg, Lt, My, TNTC, WBC]: I thank my God, because I hear about you (vs. 4) and because I have gotten much joy and encouragement from your love. Verse 6 is parenthetical [Lt]. The γάρ clause is related to both verse 6 and verse 4 [NIC], since both verse 7 and verse 5 state the reasons for Paul's thanksgiving [Hn]. Reason is also implied by translating this as 'when' [TNT].
2. It indicates the grounds for Paul's prayer in verse 6 [Alf, EBC, El, Lns]: it is appropriate for me to pray thus, since I have gotten much joy, etc. Verse 7 justifies Paul's references to 'full understanding' and 'every good thing' in verse 6 [CBC, EBC].

## much joy[a] I-have-gotten[b] and encouragement[c] on-account-of[d] your love,

TEXT: Instead of ἔσχον 'I have gotten', some manuscripts read ἔχομεν 'we have'. GNT does not include this variant, and only KJV reads 'we have'.
LEXICON—a. χαρά (LN 25.123): 'joy' [BAGD, Herm, Hn, ICC, LN, Lns, WBC; all versions except NEB, TNT], 'gladness' [LN]. This noun is also translated as a verb: 'to be delighted' [NEB], 'to be cheered' [TNT].
b. aorist act. indic. of ἔχω (LN 90.65): 'to have' [ICC, LN, Lns; KJV, NASB], 'to be given' [NIV], 'to receive' [NJB], 'to derive' [Herm, Hn, WBC; RSV], 'to find' [NAB], '(your love) has brought' [TEV], 'to experience' [LN]. The use of the aorist refers to the joy at the moment he heard [EGT, El, ICC, My, NIC], or it refers to the beginning of the action [Lns], or it is an epistolary aorist looking back to the time of the writing from the anticipated time the letter is read [CGTC].
c. παράκλησις (LN 25.150): 'encouragement' [LN, NIC; NIV, NJB, TEV], 'consolation' [BAGD; KJV], 'comfort' [BAGD, Herm, Hn, ICC, Lns, Lt, WBC; NAB, NASB, RSV]. This noun is also translated as a verb: 'to be encouraged' [NEB], 'to be comforted' [TNT].

d. ἐπί (LN 89.13, 89.27, 90.9): 'on account of' [ICC, WBC], 'in' [KJV, NAB, NASB], 'by' [NEB, NJB], 'from' [Herm, Hn, WBC; RSV], 'over' [Lns], 'to hear of' [Lt], 'at the news of' [NIC], not explicit [TNT].

QUESTION—What does πολλήν 'much' modify?

It modifies both nouns [El, Lg, My; TEV]: I had much joy and much encouragement.

QUESTION—Who are the implied participants of the event word ἀγάπῃ 'love'?

The pronoun σου 'your' is a subjective genitive; the implied actor is Philemon [Alf, CBC, EBC, EPC, Herm, Hn, IB, Lg, Lns, Lt, MNTC, NCBC, TH, WBC]: you have acted in love. Philemon's love is directed towards his fellow believers [Alf, CBC, Herm, Hn, IB, Lg, MNTC, TH, WBC], or his slaves [Lns].

**because<sup>a</sup> the hearts<sup>b</sup> of-the saints<sup>c</sup> have-been-refreshed<sup>d</sup> through<sup>e</sup> you, brother.**

LEXICON—a. ὅτι (LN 89.33, 90.21): 'because' [Herm, Hn, ICC, Lns, NIC, WBC; KJV, NAB, NASB, NIV, RSV], not explicit [NEB, NJB, TEV].

b. σπλάγχνον (LN 26.11): 'hearts' [Herm, Hn, ICC, LN, Lt, NIC, WBC; NAB, NASB, NIV, NJB, RSV, TEV, TNT], 'viscera' [Lns], 'entrails, inward parts' [BAGD], 'bowels' [KJV]. The phrase τὰ σπλάγχνα τῶν ἁγίων 'the hearts of the saints' is also conflated: 'God's people' [NEB].

c. ἅγιος (LN 11.27): 'holy'. The substantive is translated: 'the saints' [BAGD, Herm, Hn, ICC, Lns, NIC, WBC; KJV, NASB, NIV, RSV], 'God's people' [LN, Lt; NAB, NEB, TEV, TNT], 'God's holy people' [NJB].

d. perf. pass. indic. of ἀναπαύω (LN 23.80): 'to be refreshed' [BAGD, Herm, Hn, Lns, WBC; KJV, NAB, NASB, RSV], 'to be much refreshed' [NEB], 'to receive refreshment' [ICC], 'to be rested' [LN]. The verb is also translated in the active voice: 'you have refreshed the hearts of the saints' [NIV], 'you have set the hearts of God's holy people at rest' [NJB], 'you have cheered the hearts of all of God's people' [TEV]. The perfect tense implies that the effect of the refreshment still continues [Lns, WBC], perhaps from Philemon's regular acts or from one conspicuous act [WBC].

e. διά (LN 90.4)): 'by' [Herm, WBC; KJV], 'through' [Hn, Lns; NAB, NASB, NEB, RSV], 'from' [ICC].

QUESTION—What relationship is indicated by ὅτι 'because'?

1. It indicates the reason for Paul's joy and encouragement [Lns, NIC, TNTC]: I rejoiced and was encouraged because you refreshed the hearts of the saints.
2. It explains the specific aspect of Philemon's love which Paul has in mind [Alf, El, ICC, My, WBC]: your love, namely, that you refreshed the hearts of the saints.

PHILEMON 1:7 117

QUESTION—What is meant by τὰ σπλάγχνα 'the hearts'?
Literally, this word refers to the vital organs of the body (not the intestines, 'bowels'); here it is used figuratively to refer to the seat of the emotions, the inmost feelings [CGTC, EGT, El, Herm, Lg, Lt, TH, WBC, WPC], the deepest affection [NCBC]. One commentary notes that this refers to the person who has the emotions instead of referring specifically to the expression of the emotions [CGTC].

QUESTION—What is meant by ἀναπέπαυται 'have been refreshed'?
The ἀνα- compound form indicates temporary rest [EGT, EPC, Hn, ICC, Lt], implying encouragement [CBC, Herm, NCBC], comfort [Herm, NCBC], hospitality [Bg, CBC], gifts of money [CBC], or refreshing [TH].

QUESTION—What is the significance of the position of ἀδελφέ 'brother'?
This affectionate word [CBC, Hn, ICC, Lg, Lns, My] is placed last in the sentence, making it emphatic [EGT, El, Lt], the climax of the thought [Hn]. It effectively leads into the request which follows [Alf].

**DISCOURSE UNIT: 8–22** [EBC, GNT, Hn, TH, WPC; TEV]. The topic is Paul's request in behalf of Onesimus [EBC, GNT, Hn, TH, WPC; NJB, TEV], and Paul's request for lodging for himself [Hn].

**DISCOURSE UNIT: 8–21** [Alf, EPC, Lg, My, TNTC; NJB]. The topic is Paul's request in behalf of Onesimus [Alf, EPC, Lg, My, TNTC; NJB, TNT].

**DISCOURSE UNIT: 8–20** [CGTC, Herm, ICC, NCBC, WBC; NAB]. The topic is Paul's request in behalf of Onesimus [CGTC, Herm, My, NCBC, WBC; NAB].

**DISCOURSE UNIT: 8–14** [MNTC, NIC, TNTC]. The topic is Paul's request in behalf of Onesimus [MNTC, NIC], Paul's interest in Onesimus [TNTC].

**DISCOURSE UNIT: 8–10** [CBC]. The topic is the opening of Paul's appeal to Philemon [CBC].

**8 Therefore,**
LEXICON—διό (LN 89.47): 'therefore' [BAGD, Herm, NIC, WBC; NAB, NASB, NIV, NJB], 'wherefore' [ICC, Lns; KJV], 'accordingly' [Hn; NEB, RSV], 'for this reason' [BAGD; TEV], 'so' [TNTC].

QUESTION—To what verb is this word connected?
1. It is connected with παρακαλῶ 'I appeal' (vs. 9) [Alf, Bg, El, Herm, Hn, ICC, Lg(H), Lns, Lt, My, TH, WBC; all versions except TEV]: therefore…I appeal to you.
2. It is connected with παρρησίαν ἔχων 'having boldness' [Lg; TEV]: therefore I could have boldness to command you. It is not stated how the preceding verses give the grounds for Paul's boldness to command him.

QUESTION—What relationship is indicated by this word?
1. It indicates an exhortation grounded on Philemon's actions in the latter part of verse 7 [Alf, Blm, Brt, Hn]: since you are a person who refreshes the hearts of God's people, therefore I appeal to you (vs. 9).

118 PHILEMON 1:8

2. It indicates an exhortation grounded on Paul's joy and encouragement over Philemon's loving conduct [El, ICC, Lg, My]: since I have so much joy and encouragement over you, therefore I appeal to you.
3. It indicates an exhortation grounded on Paul's statements about the good things he has heard about Philemon in verses 4–7 [EGT, Lns, Lt, TH, TNTC, WBC]: since I have heard the good things about you which I have just mentioned, I appeal to you. The appeal is to live up to their reputation [EGT].

**having[a] much boldness/authority[b] in[c] Christ**

LEXICON—a. pres. act. participle of ἔχω (LN 90.65): 'to have' [LN]. The phrase πολλὴν παρρησίαν ἔχων 'having much boldness' is translated: 'though I might be much bold' [KJV], 'although I feel that I have every right' [NAB], 'although I might make bold' [NEB], 'although I could be bold' [NIV], 'although I have no hesitations' [NJB], 'although I am bold enough' [WBC; RSV], 'I could be bold enough' [TEV], 'although I am quite free' [Hn], 'although my relations to you would warrant me' [ICC].

b. παρρησία (LN 25.158): 'boldness' [BAGD, LN], 'courage' [BAGD, LN], 'confidence' [BAGD, Lg, Lt; NASB], 'freedom' [TNT], 'frankness' [Lns], 'liberty' [NIC], or 'authority' [Herm]. This noun is also translated as an adjective: 'bold' [WBC; RSV, TEV].

c. ἐν (LN 89.119): 'in' [Herm, Hn, Lns, WBC; all versions except NAB, TEV, TNT], 'as your brother in' [TEV], 'in the fellowship of' [TNT], not explicit [NAB].

QUESTION—What relationship is indicated by the participle ἔχων 'having'?

The participle is concessive [CGTC, El, Herm, Hn, ICC, Lg, Lns, My, TH, WBC; all versions except TEV]: although I have much boldness to command you, yet I appeal to you.

QUESTION—What is meant by παρρησία 'boldness/authority'?
1. It means 'boldness' or 'confidence' [Alf, IB, ICC, Lg, Lns, Lt, MNTC, My, NIC, TH, WBC]: having the boldness to command you. It implies that the boldness is the result of Paul's authority [IB, Lg, TH] and also their Christian relationship [ICC].
2. It means 'right' or 'authority' [Blm, EBC, El, Herm]: having the authority to command you.

QUESTION—What relationship is indicated by ἐν 'in'?
1. It refers to Paul's apostleship, which is the basis for his confidence or authority [Blm, CBC, Lt, MNTC, TNTC]: I have much boldness because of my authority as Christ's apostle.
2. It is the source on which his boldness rests [Alf, El, Lns]: I have much boldness, the source of which is Christ.
3. It indicates Paul's fellowship with Christ which is the basis of his confidence [Lg, My]: I have much boldness because of my fellowship with Christ as his apostle.

4. It refers to Paul's fellowship with Philemon in union with Christ [TH, WBC]: I have much boldness because of our mutual fellowship as Christians.

**to-command<sup>a</sup> you (to do) the fitting-(thing),<sup>b</sup>**

LEXICON—a. pres. act. inf. of ἐπιτάσσω (LN **33.325**): 'to command' [BAGD, Herm, WBC; NAB, RSV], 'to order' [BAGD, Hn, LN; NASB, TEV, TNT], 'to enjoin' [ICC; KJV], 'to point out' [NIC; NEB], 'to tell' [NJB], 'to direct' [Lns].

b. pres. act. participle of ἀνήκω (LN 66.1): 'to be fitting' [LN]. The participial phrase ἀνῆκον 'the to-be-fitting (thing)' is translated 'that which is convenient' [KJV], 'what ought to be done' [NAB], 'that which is proper' [NASB], 'your duty' [Hn; NEB], 'what you ought to do' [NIV], 'what your duty is' [NJB], 'what is required' [RSV], 'what should be done' [TEV], 'what is right' [TNT], 'what is fitting' [Herm, ICC, WBC], 'the fitting thing' [Lns], 'the path of duty' [NIC].

QUESTION—What relationship is indicated by the infinitive form ἐπιτάσσειν 'to command'?

It is an explanatory infinitive, giving the content of παρρησίαν ἔχων 'having boldness' [El, WPC]: my boldness is a boldness to command.

QUESTION—What is implied by ἐπιτάσσειν 'to command'?

It implies Paul's authority as an apostle [Bg, EGT, Herm, ICC, Lg, WBC], a superiority in rank [TH].

QUESTION—What is meant by τὸ ἀνῆκον 'the proper thing'?

The proper thing is what Paul is about to request, viz., that Philemon receive Onesimus [Alf, El, Herm, Lg, NCBC, TH, WBC,] which is the proper thing for Philemon to do as a Christian [Blm, Herm, MNTC, WBC], or as the fulfillment of a moral obligation [EGT, My].

**9 because-of<sup>a</sup> the love rather<sup>b</sup> I-appeal;<sup>c</sup>**

LEXICON—a. διά (LN 89.26) with accusative object: 'because of' [BAGD; NEB, TEV], 'in the name of' [NAB], 'on the basis of' [NIV], 'for the sake of' [BAGD, Herm, Hn, ICC, Lns, NIC, WBC; KJV, NASB, RSV, TNT], 'encouraged by' [Lt]. The whole phrase is also translated 'I am rather appealing to your love' [NJB].

b. μᾶλλον (LN 89.126): 'rather' [BAGD, Hn, Lns; KJV, NASB, NEB, NJB, TNT], 'instead' [TEV], not explicit [NIV]. This is also translated as a verb: 'I prefer' [Herm, ICC, Lt, NIC, WBC; NAB, RSV].

c. pres. act. indic. of παρακαλέω (LN 33.168): 'to appeal' [BAGD, Hn, LN, NIC, WBC; NAB, NASB, NEB, NIV, NJB, RSV, TNT], 'to beseech' [KJV], 'to request' [BAGD, LN], 'to make a request' [TEV], 'to ask as a favor' [ICC], 'to urge' [Lns], 'to entreat' [BAGD, Lt].

QUESTION—What relationship is indicated by διά 'because of'?

It indicates the reason for the following exhortation [Herm, Hn, ICC, Lg, Lns, MNTC, My, NCBC, NIC, TNTC, WBC; KJV]: because of love, I appeal to you.

QUESTION—Who are the implied actors in the event word τὴν ἀγάπην 'the love'?
1. Christian love in general is in view [Alf, El, Herm, Hn, ICC, Lg, Lt, My]: because of the love which should characterize Christians in their dealings. The presence of the article defines love as a characteristic attribute [Lg].
2. The mutual love of Paul and Philemon is in view [Blm]: because of our love for one another.
3. Both Paul's love for Philemon and Philemon's for Onesimus are in view [Bg]: because of my love for you and your love for Onesimus.
4. Philemon's love manifested toward others is in view (vss. 5, 7) [CBC, MNTC, WBC]: because of the love which you have manifested toward others.

QUESTION—What relationship is indicated by μᾶλλον 'rather'?
It indicates contrast with 'command' (vs. 8) [ICC, Lg, My]: I appeal rather than command.

QUESTION—To whom is the verb παρακαλῶ 'I appeal' directed?
1. The implied indirect object is Philemon [Hn, ICC, Lns, MNTC; KJV, NASB, NEB, NIV, NJB, RSV, TNT]: I appeal to you.
2. It is purposely without an indirect object, since Paul is focusing on the action itself [Lg; NAB, TEV]: what I am doing is appealing rather than commanding.

**being such-a-person as Paul an-old-man/ambassador,[a] and now also prisoner of-Christ Jesus,**

LEXICON—a. πρεσβύτης (LN 9.31): 'old man' [BAGD, Hn, ICC, LN, Lns; NIV, NJB], 'elderly man' [Herm], 'the aged' [KJV, NASB], or 'ambassador' [Lt, NIC, WBC; NAB, NEB, RSV, TEV, TNT].

QUESTION—How are the nouns Παῦλος 'Paul' and πρεσβύτης 'old man/ambassador' related?
1. 'Old man/ambassador' describes 'Paul' [Herm, IB, Lns, Lt, MNTC, My, NCBC, NIC, TNTC]: I am Paul, an old man/ambassador.
2. These words are two separate ideas [Bg, Blm]: I am Paul, (and) I am an old man/ambassador, and I am a prisoner. Paul bases his request on three claims: he is Paul the apostle, he is an old man, and he is a prisoner because of the gospel [Blm].

QUESTION—What is meant by πρεσβύτης 'old man/ambassador'?
1. Paul is referring to himself as an aged man [Alf, Bg, Blm, Brt, EBC, El, Herm, Hn, ICC, Lg, Lns, MNTC, My]: I am Paul, an aged man. Paul is not referring to his authority as an apostle here; he is referring to his age [Herm].
2. Paul is referring to himself as an ambassador [CBC, CGTC, EGT, EPC, IB, Lt, NCBC, NIC, TH, TNTC, WBC, WPC]: I am Paul, an ambassador. Paul refers to himself as a prisoner as a term of pride, and so he probably means πρεσβύτης as a term of pride also, therefore 'ambassador' [NIC].

PHILEMON 1:9

QUESTION—What relationship is indicated by the participial form ὤν 'being' and how much is included with this participle? (Also involved in the question are the referent for τοιοῦτος 'such a person' and meaning of πρεσβύτης 'old man/ambassador'.)

When 'being' is interpreted as cause or grounds, then the meaning 'old man' is to be taken so that 'old man' and 'prisoner' evoke pity as a motive for heeding the appeal [Bg, Lns]. When 'being' is interpreted to be concessive, then the meaning 'ambassador' is to be taken so that 'ambassador' and 'prisoner' imply the authority Paul has to back up a command [CGTC, TH; TEV].

1. This whole phrase is connected with the first part of the verse [Bg, CGTC, Lns, Lt, TH; KJV, NJB, TEV].
   1.1 'Being' indicates the reason or grounds for the preceding statement and 'such a person' is defined by the following phrases [Bg, Lns]: I appeal to you, because/since I am such a person as Paul, an old man and a prisoner.
   1.2 'Being' indicates a concession to the preceding statement [CGTC, TH; TEV]: I appeal to you, although I am such a person as Paul an ambassador and prisoner.
2. This phrase is divided so that 'Paul' begins a new sentence that continues into the next verse and 'such a person' refers backward [Alf]: I appeal to you because/since I am such a person who makes appeals. As Paul, an old man and now a prisoner also, I appeal to you concerning Onesimus.
3. Some enclose this whole phrase within dashes, to separate it from what precedes and follows [Hn; NASB, RSV]. Since the same verb precedes and follows, it can apply to either.
4. This whole phrase is connected with the following verse [Herm, ICC, Lg, Lg(H), MNTC, My, WBC; NAB, NEB, NIV, TNT].
   4.1 'Being' indicates the reason or grounds for the appeal [Herm, ICC, Lg, MNTC, My].
      4.1.1 'Such a person' is defined by the following phrases [Herm, ICC, Lg]: I appeal to you. Because/Since I am such a person as Paul, an old man and a prisoner, I appeal to you concerning Onesimus.
      4.1.2 'Such a person' refers back [Lg(H), My]: I appeal to you. Since I am such a person that makes appeals, I, as Paul, an old man and a prisoner, appeal to you concerning Onesimus.
   4.2 'Being' indicates a concession to the following statement [WBC]: although I am such a person as Paul, an ambassador and a prisoner, I appeal to you concerning Onesimus.

QUESTION—How are the nouns related in the genitive construction δέσμιος Χριστοῦ Ἰησοῦ 'prisoner of Christ Jesus'?

See verse 1 for this phrase.

## 10 I-appeal to-you concerning/on-behalf-of[a] my child,

LEXICON—a. περί with genitive object (LN 89.6, 90.39): 'concerning' [Bg, Lns], 'about' [NEB], or 'on behalf of' [EBC, ICC; TEV], 'for' [Herm, Lt, NIC, WBC; all versions except NEB, TEV], 'in the interest of' [Hn].

QUESTION—What is the relationship between παρακαλῶ 'I appeal' here and the same verb in verse 9?

It is repeated emphatically here after the parenthetical comments in verse 9 [Bg]. It is repeated as Paul begins to state his specific request with the object of the verb added [Herm, Lns, WBC]: I appeal…(Yes,) I appeal to you concerning Onesimus.

QUESTION—What is meant by περί 'concerning/on behalf of'?

1. It indicates the subject of the appeal [Bg, Lns; NEB]: I appeal to you concerning my child.
2. Instead of its usual meaning 'concerning', it is used here with the more specific meaning 'in behalf of' [BAGD, EBC, Herm, Hn, ICC, NCBC, TH, WBC; all versions except NEB]: I entreat you in behalf of my child. It is for Onesimus's benefit that he makes his appeal [TH].
3. It indicates the content of the request [IB, NIC]: I appeal to you for my child. This means that he wants Philemon to send Onesimus back to him.

QUESTION—What is the significance of ἐμοῦ 'my'?

It is emphatic [El, Lns, My, TH]: I am entreating you for my own child. The word is a possessive adjective, which is stronger than the possessive pronoun μου 'my' [Lns].

QUESTION—Why does Paul call Onesimus his child?

1. Onesimus became a Christian through Paul's ministry, and he is therefore Paul's spiritual child [El, EPC, Herm, IB, ICC, MNTC, My, NIC, TH, WBC]: he is my spiritual child. Paul frequently refers to his converts as his children [NIC].
2. Paul was expressing his affection [Bg, CBC, Hn, Lns]: I care for him as if he were my child. This affectionate term was used by Christians for other Christians for whom they had responsibility [CBC].

## whom I-have-begotten[a] in[b] the bonds,[c]

LEXICON—a. aorist act. indic. of γεννάω (LN 23.58): 'to beget' [BAGD, Herm, Hn, LN, Lns, WBC; KJV, NAB, NASB], 'to become a father of' [LN, Lt, NIC; NEB, NJB, RSV], 'to become a spiritual father of' [TEV]. The active voice is also translated passively: 'who became my son' [NIV, TNT], 'who has been converted through my instrumentality' [ICC].

b. ἐν (LN 13.8, 83.13) with dative object: 'in' [Hn, Lns, NIC; KJV, NASB, NEB, RSV], 'during' [ICC; NAB]. The phrase ἐν τοῖς δεσμοῖς 'in the bonds' is also translated 'while I was in chains' [NIV], 'while wearing these chains' [NJB], 'while in prison' [WBC; TEV], 'during my imprisonment' [ICC], 'after I was imprisoned' [TNT], 'amidst the sorrows of my bonds' [Lt].

c. δεσμός (LN 37.115): 'bonds' [BAGD, Hn, Lt; KJV], 'chains' [NIV, NJB], 'imprisonment' [BAGD, ICC, LN, Lns, NIC; NAB, NASB, RSV], 'prison' [BAGD, WBC; NEB, TEV].

QUESTION—What is meant by ἐγέννησα 'I have begotten'?

Paul was responsible for Onesimus's spiritual birth [Blm, Brt, CBC, CGTC, Herm, Hn, IB, ICC, Lg, NIC, WBC, WPC]: I was responsible for his spiritual birth. This is a common metaphor for bringing about a person's conversion both in the NT and in Jewish writings.

QUESTION—What relationship is indicated by ἐν 'in'?

1. It indicates time [ICC, WBC; NAB, NIV, NJB, TEV, TNT]: whom I have begotten while I was a prisoner.
2. It indicates location [CBC, Hn, MNTC, NCBC, NIC; NEB]: whom I have begotten here in prison.

**Onesimus,**

QUESTION—What does the name Ὀνήσιμος 'Onesimus' mean?

It means 'profitable' [CGTC, EBC, Hn, ICC, Lg, MNTC, NCBC, NIC, TH, WBC], 'useful' [BAGD, EBC, EPC, Hn, IB, Lg, My, NCBC, NIC, TNTC, WBC; NAB], 'helpful' [EPC], and 'beneficial' [TH].

QUESTION—What is this word connected with and why is it in the accusative case?

1. It is in apposition with and identifies τέκνου 'child', but it is in the accusative case instead of the genitive because of attraction to the case of the relative pronoun ὅν 'whom' [Alf, El, Herm, ICC, Lt, My, NCBC, NIC, WBC]: I entreat you for my own child, Onesimus.
2. It is intentionally related to the accusative pronoun ὅν 'whom'. It may mean that Onesimus was now true to his name [CGTC, EGT, IB, MNTC, WPC]: I have begotten him to be Profitable. From now on he will live up to his name and be profitable [EGT].
3. Paul may have given him the new name 'Onesimus' following his conversion [EPC, IB]: I have begotten him spiritually and have given him the name Onesimus.

QUESTION—Why is Onesimus's name placed after the preceding descriptions?

Paul wishes to create a favorable impression of the person he is speaking about before identifying him by name [Bg, Herm, Hn, Lg, Lns, Lt, MNTC, NIC, WBC]: I entreat you for my own child, whose spiritual father I have become here in prison, for Onesimus.

**DISCOURSE UNIT: 11–16** [CBC]. The topic is Paul's request for Onesimus.

**11 the (one) (who was) formerly[a] to-you useless[b] but now both to-you and to-me (is) very-useful,[c]**

TEXT—Some manuscripts omit the first καί 'both'. GNT encloses this word in brackets but does not discuss it. It is omitted by Lns, KJV, and RSV.

LEXICON—a. ποτέ (LN 67.9): 'formerly' [Herm, Hn; NAB, NASB, NIV, RSV], 'previously' [WBC], 'before' [NJB], 'once' [NEB, TNT], 'at one time' [Lns; TEV], 'in time past' [KJV].
  b. ἄχρηστος (LN **65.33**): 'useless' [BAGD, Herm, Hn, ICC, Lns, WBC; NAB, NASB, NIV, RSV, TNT], 'so little use' [NEB], 'of no use' [LN; NJB, TEV], 'far from useful' [Lt], 'unprofitable' [NIC; KJV].
  c. εὔχρηστος (LN **65.31**): 'very useful' [Herm], 'useful' [BAGD, Hn, LN, Lns, Lt, WBC; NASB, NIV, NJB, TEV], 'useful indeed' [NAB, NEB, RSV, TNT], 'profitable' [ICC, NIC; KJV].

QUESTION—What is the function of this phrase?
1. It is a further comment about Onesimus, with a play on the meaning of his name [Alf, BAGD, CBC, EGT, El, EPC, Hn, IB, ICC, Lg, Lt, MNTC, My, NCBC, NIC, TH, TNTC, WBC]: Onesimus/Profitable, who formerly was unprofitable but now is very profitable.
2. It is not a play on the name 'Onesimus', but it is a play on the words χρηστός 'profitable' and Χριστός 'Christ', since these two words were pronounced alike [Herm]. His change of character is attributed to his conversion to Christ.
3. It includes both of the above interpretations [EBC].
4. It is not a play on either 'Onesimus' or 'Christ' [Lns, WPC].

QUESTION—What is implied by the word ἄχρηστον 'useless'?
This is a litotes (a negative statement implying the emphatic opposite) [Bg, Blm, Lg]: he formerly wronged you. Onesimus was useless because he had run away and was no longer there to serve his master [Alf, Lns, TH], or because he had done something wrong, such as stealing from his master [Alf, El, TH] or because he was unreliable in his work [Blm, CBC, CGTC, Hn, NCBC, WBC, WPC].

QUESTION—What is implied by the phrase καὶ σοὶ καὶ ἐμοί 'both to you and to me'?
This is the third of three contrasts expressed in this verse: ποτέ 'formerly' and νυνί 'now', ἄχρηστον 'unprofitable' and εὔχρηστον 'very profitable', and σοί 'to you' and καὶ σοὶ καὶ ἐμοί 'both to you and to me'. The meaning must include both earthly and spiritual profit. Onesimus will be profitable to Philemon both by his better service at work [Alf, Hn, ICC, Lg, My, TH, TNTC] and as a Christian brother [Alf, ICC]. He was profitable to Paul as a source of satisfaction for having led him to Christ [Alf, El, ICC, Lg, My], or because of his service to Paul [ICC, TNTC]. He had helped Paul in prison [CBC], and Paul is making a sacrifice in parting with him [MNTC]. Since in normal Greek word order ἐμοί 'to me' would precede σοί 'to you', the phrase 'and to me' is an afterthought [Lt], or perhaps it means that Philemon will have to satisfy himself about the change in Onesimus [Herm, WBC]. It may be merely a matter of courtesy [Bg]. The usefulness of Onesimus to Philemon would be in sending Onesimus back to help Paul in Philemon's place [NIC].

**12** whom I-have-sent-back[a] to-you, him, that is, my heart;[b]

TEXT—Instead of ὃν ἀνέπεμψά σοι, αὐτόν 'whom I have sent back to you—him', one manuscript reads ὃν ἀνέπεμψα, σὺ δὲ αὐτόν 'whom I have sent back, and you him', which could read be read 'whom I have sent back (to you), and you (send) him (back to me again)'. Other manuscripts, in various ways, add the imperative προσλαβοῦ 'receive', so that it means 'whom I have sent back, and you receive (imperative) him'. GNT reads 'you–him' with a B rating, indicating some degree of doubt. Only El, My, and KJV accepts the addition of the verb.

LEXICON—a. aorist act. indic. of ἀναπέμπω (LN **15.70**): 'to send back' [BAGD, Herm, Hn, ICC, LN, Lns, Lt, NIC, WBC; NASB, NEB, NIV, NJB, RSV, TEV, TNT], 'to send' [NAB], 'to send again' [KJV].

b. σπλάγχνον (LN **25.50**): 'heart' [BAGD, Herm, Hn, Lns, Lt, NIC, WBC; NAB, NASB, NIV, NJB, RSV, TEV], 'bowels' [KJV]. The phrase τὰ ἐμὰ σπλάγχνα is also translated: 'a part of myself' [NEB, TNT], 'dear though he is to me' [ICC], 'my beloved' [BAGD], 'this one for whom I have such deep affection' [LN]. See this word at verse 7.

QUESTION—What is this clause connected with?

It carries on the reference to Onesimus and this relative clause gets to the heart of the epistle. However, none of the commentaries discuss these items.

QUESTION—What is indicated by the aorist tense of the verb ἀνέπεμψά 'I have sent'?

It is an epistolary aorist, meaning that the action will have occurred by the time Philemon reads the letter [CGTC, EGT, El, Herm, Hn, IB, ICC, Lg, Lns, Lt, TH, WBC]: I am sending him with this letter and he will be present with you when you read it. Onesimus himself is the bearer of this letter [EGT, Lg, Lt, WBC].

QUESTION—What is the function of the word αὐτόν 'him'?

It repeats the meaning of ὅν 'whom' [Herm, Hn, Lns, WBC]: whom I am sending…yes, him. It adds emphasis to the reference [EGT, Hn, ICC]. It emphasizes ὅν 'whom' [ICC]: whom I am sending in his own person. It is also in apposition with the following phrase τὰ ἐμὰ σπλάγχνα 'my very heart' [Hn, Lns, TH]. Some discuss the possibility that it may be a Semitic construction, repeating 'whom' redundantly [CGTC, Herm, Hn, WBC], but none accept this interpretation. For those who follow a different text, αὐτόν 'him' is the object of the expressed or understood verb προσλαβοῦ 'receive' (from vs. 17) [Alf, Blm, El, Lg, My]: whom I have sent back; and you receive (impera.) him.

QUESTION—What does Paul mean by calling Onesimus 'my very heart'?

Paul means that Onesimus was very dear to him [Alf, Bg, Blm, CBC, CGTC, EBC, El, EPC, Herm, Hn, IB, ICC, Lg, Lns, Lt, MNTC, My, NCBC, NIC, TH, TNTC, WBC]: it is as if I were sending my own heart, a part of myself. Some say that τὰ ἐμὰ σπλάγχνα (literally, 'my vital organs') implies 'my son' [Blm] (i.e., 'he is from my vital organs'), but others deny this [Alf,

CGTC, El, Herm, ICC, Lg, Lt, My, NIC]. The possessive adjective ἐμά 'my' is emphatic [EGT, My].

**13 whom I could-have-wished<sup>a</sup> to-keep<sup>b</sup> with myself,**

LEXICON—a. imperf. mid. (deponent = act.) indic. of βούλομαι (LN 25.3): 'to wish' [BAGD, Hn, Lns; NASB], 'to want' [BAGD, LN; NAB], 'to desire' [LN], 'to like' [Herm, NIC, WBC; NEB, NIV, NJB, TEV, TNT], 'to be glad' [BAGD; RSV], 'to have a mind' [ICC]. The phrase ἐγὼ ἐβουλόμην 'I was wishing to keep' is translated 'I would have retained' [KJV], 'I would gladly have detained' [Lt]. The verb is stronger than ἠθέλησα 'I wished' in verse 14 [Alf], implying purpose rather than mere willingness [EGT, Lt].

  b. pres. act. infin. of κατέχω (LN 13.150): 'to keep' [BAGD, Herm, Hn, ICC, LN, WBC; all versions except KJV], 'to detain' [EGT], 'to retain' [KJV].

QUESTION—What is the function of this clause?

  It shows that Paul is confident that Onesimus was now trustworthy [Bg, Blm].

QUESTION—Why is the emphatic word ἐγώ 'I' used?

  Paul is contrasting his own wishes with his recognition of Philemon's rights [Alf, El, My]: I in my own interest.

QUESTION—What is indicated by the imperfect tense of the verb ἐβουλόμην 'I was wishing'?

  1. The imperfect tense refers to a desire over a period of time [Alf, IB, ICC, My]: for a while I was wishing to keep him, (but finally I came to the decision not to keep him).
  2. The imperfect tense implies a tentative process that was not fulfilled [EGT, El, Herm], or a wish that for some reason the writer feels he cannot fulfill [Hn, Lg(H), Lns, Lt, NIC, TH, TNTC, WBC]: I could have wished to keep him, (but I decided not to keep him).

**in-order-that<sup>a</sup> in-behalf-of<sup>b</sup> you me he-might-serve<sup>c</sup>**

LEXICON—a. ἵνα (LN 89.59): 'in order that' [Hn, ICC; RSV], 'so that' [Herm, WBC; NIV, TEV], 'that' [Lns; KJV, NAB, NASB], 'to' [NEB, NJB, TNT], not explicit [NJB].

  b. ὑπέρ (LN 90.36) with genitive object: 'in behalf of' [Hn, Lt, NIC; NASB, RSV], 'in one's stead' [BAGD, Lg, Lns; KJV], 'in one's place' [BAGD, Herm, WBC; NAB, NIV, TEV, TNT], 'as you would wish' [NEB], 'as you yourself would gladly have done' [ICC]. The phrase is also translated 'so that he could take your place in helping me' [NIV, WBC], 'he could have been a substitute for you, to help me' [NJB].

  c. pres. act. subj. of διακονέω (LN 35.19): 'to serve' [BAGD, Herm, LN, NIC; NAB, RSV], 'to render service' [Hn, LN], 'to minister' [ICC, Lns, Lt; KJV, NASB], 'to look after', [NEB], 'to help' [LN, WBC; NIV, NJB, TEV, TNT].

QUESTION—What relationship is indicated by ἵνα 'in order that'?

It indicates Paul's purpose for wishing to keep Onesimus with him [El, ICC, My]: my desire to retain Onesimus was in order that he could serve me in your behalf. Paul presents the matter almost as if Philemon had sent Onesimus to help Paul [EPC].

QUESTION—What is implied by the word order within this clause?

Both ὑπὲρ σοῦ 'in behalf of you' and μοι 'me' are emphatic by forefronting; however, none of the commentators discuss this point.

QUESTION—What kind of service had Onesimus rendered to Paul?

He had cared for his needs [CBC, EGT, Lg, MNTC, My, NIC]: in order that he might care for my needs.

QUESTION—In what way had Onesimus's service been in behalf of Philemon?

Onesimus helped Paul as Philemon would have helped Paul if he had been there [Alf, Bg, Blm, Brt, EBC, EGT, Herm, Hn, Lt, My, TH, WBC]: he has helped me as you would have helped me. Onesimus helped Paul as a representative of Philemon [El, Herm, ICC, Lg, Lns, MNTC, NCBC]. Thus Paul implies that Philemon is obligated to Onesimus, since Onesimus has served in Philemon's place [EGT].

**in the bonds[a] of-the gospel,**

LEXICON—a. δεσμός (LN **37.115**): 'bonds' [Hn, Lt; KJV], 'imprisonment' [ICC, Lns, WBC; NASB, RSV], 'chains' [NIC; NIV, NJB]. The phrase ἐν τοῖς δεσμοῖς 'in the bonds' is also translated 'while I am in prison' [LN; NAB, TEV], 'while I am in chains' [NIV, NJB], 'here in prison' [NEB], 'while I am a prisoner' [TNT], 'during my imprisonment' [Herm, WBC; RSV], 'in my imprisonment' [Hn, ICC; NASB].

QUESTION—How are the two nouns related in the genitive construction ἐν τοῖς δεσμοῖς τοῦ εὐαγγελίου 'the bonds of the gospel'?

The gospel is the reason for his imprisonment [Alf, CGTC, EGT, El, EPC, ICC, Lg, Lt, My, TH; NJB]: I am in prison because I have preached the gospel.

**14 but[a]**

LEXICON—a. δέ (LN 89.124): 'but' [Herm, Hn, ICC, Lns, WBC; all versions except NJB, TEV], 'however' [NJB, TEV].

QUESTION—What relationship is indicated by this word?

It indicates contrast. Paul has given his reasons for wanting Onesimus to remain with him; now he looks to Philemon for his decision [EBC, ICC, WBC]: I wanted to keep him; however, you must decide what to do about him.

**without[a] your consent[b] nothing I-wished[c] to-do,**

LEXICON—a. χωρίς (LN 89.120) with genitive object: 'without' [BAGD, Herm, Hn, ICC, Lns, Lt, NIC, WBC; KJV, NAB, NASB, NEB, NIV, NJB, RSV, TNT], 'unless (you agree)' [TEV].

b. γνώμη (LN **31.14, 31.3**): 'consent' [BAGD, Herm, Hn, Lt, NIC, WBC; all versions except KJV, TEV], 'agreement' [LN], 'concurrence' [ICC], 'decision' [Lns], 'opinion' [LN], 'mind' [KJV]. This noun is also translated as a verb: '(unless) you agree' [TEV].

c. aorist act. indic. of θέλω (LN 25.1): 'to will' [Herm, WBC; KJV, NEB], 'to want' [LN; NAB, NASB, NIV, NJB, TEV], 'to desire' [LN], 'to prefer' [RSV], 'to wish' [Hn, LN, Lt; TNT], 'to resolve' [Lns]. The phrase οὐδὲν ἠθέλησα ποιῆσαι 'nothing I wished to do' is translated 'I was unwilling to do anything' [ICC], 'I refused to do anything' [NIC].

QUESTION—What is indicated by the use of the possessive adjective σῆς 'your'?

It is emphatic [El], in contrast with the emphatic ἐγώ 'I' (vs. 13): without your own decision.

QUESTION—What is indicated by the aorist tense of ἠθέλησα 'I wished', following the imperfect tense 'I was wishing' (vs. 13)?

It indicates a decision after deliberation [Alf, EGT, Hn, ICC, Lg, My]: I decided. He gave up his former wish [Lns].

**in-order-that[a] not as according-to[b] necessity[c] the good-(thing)[d] of-you might-be but according-to[b] voluntary (choice).[e]**

LEXICON—a. ἵνα (LN 89.59): 'in order that' [Lns; RSV], 'so that' [Herm, WBC; NEB, NIV], 'that' [Hn; KJV, NAB, NASB], not explicit [NJB, TEV, TNT].

b. κατά (LN 89.4, 89.8) with accusative object: 'according to . . . according to', 'by . . . of' [Lt; NASB, RSV], 'of...of' [NEB], 'by way of...by way of' [Lns], 'because of' [BAGD]. The following combine one or both instances of κατά with its object: κατὰ ἀνάγκην...κατὰ ἑκούσιον 'according to necessity...according to voluntary (choice)': 'of...willingly' [KJV], 'compulsory...voluntary' [Hn], 'voluntary...of necessity' [ICC], 'compulsorily...on your willing initiative' [NIC], 'forced...spontaneous' [WBC]. The following recast the entire clause: 'that kindness might not be forced on you but might be freely bestowed' [NAB], 'so that any favor you do will be spontaneous and not forced' [NIV], 'it would have been forcing your act of kindness, which should be spontaneous' [NJB], 'I do not want to force you to help me; rather, I would like for you to do it of your own free will' [TEV], 'you must not be compelled to be kind, you must be quite free' [TNT].

c. ἀνάγκη (LN **71.30**): 'necessity' [ICC; KJV], 'compulsion' [Herm, Lns, Lt; NASB, NEB, RSV], 'obligation' [LN].

d. ἀγαθός (LN 65.20): 'good' [LN], 'good deed' [Herm, NIC], 'kindness' [NAB, NEB], 'service to me' [ICC], 'favor' [Lns, WBC; NIV], 'kindly offices' [Lt], 'benefit' [KJV].

e. ἑκούσιος (LN **25.65**): 'free will' [Herm, LN, Lt; NASB, NEB, RSV], 'free volition' [Lns].

PHILEMON 1:14

QUESTION—What relationship is indicated by ἵνα 'in order that'?

It indicates the purpose of the preceding clause [WBC]: I did not wish to do anything without your consent, in order that your goodness might be voluntary.

QUESTION—What relationship is indicated by ὡς 'as'?

1. It implies the appearance of his motives [Alf, EGT, El, Herm, IB, ICC, Lg, Lt, My]: in order that your good thing might not seem to be by necessity. Paul does not say that it would really be by necessity, but that it should not even have that appearance [EGT]. Philemon would probably have been willing for Paul to keep Onesimus, but his good service to Paul would have had the appearance of necessity rather than free choice [El, ICC].
2. It does not imply mere appearance, but rather actual necessity [Bg, CBC, Hn, TH, TNTC, WBC]: in order that your good thing might not be by necessity. 'As' simply lessens the force of 'by necessity' [Bg, Lg].

QUESTION—What is implied by the phrase τὸ ἀγαθόν σου 'your good thing'?

1. This is a general expression; it does not limit Philemon to a specific action [Alf, Herm, My]: the good thing which you decide to do. The specific application is indicated in verse 13 [My].
2. It specifically refers to the favor of permitting Paul to keep Onesimus with him [ICC], or to the benefit Paul would receive by keeping Onesimus with him [Lg, Lns, Lt]: the favor of allowing me to keep Onesimus with me.
3. It specifically refers to the good act of forgiving and accepting Onesimus [Hn]. Paul expects that he himself will be released and will be able to visit Philemon in the future, so he does not need Onesimus's service later on [Hn, MNTC].

QUESTION—How are the noun and pronoun related in the genitive construction τὸ ἀγαθόν σου 'the good thing of you'?

The pronoun indicates the source of the good thing [El, Herm, Lns]: the good thing you do.

QUESTION—What relationship is indicated by ἀλλά 'but'?

It introduces the mutually exclusive contrast between the two possible motivations [Herm, NCBC, WBC]: not by necessity, but on the contrary, by your free choice.

**DISCOURSE UNIT: 15–21** [TNTC]. The topic is Paul's appeal in behalf of Onesimus.

**DISCOURSE UNIT: 15–20** [MNTC, NIC]. The topic is Paul's request that Philemon forgive Onesimus [MNTC], or the reinforcement of Paul's request [NIC].

**15** For[a]

LEXICON—a. γάρ (LN 89.23): 'for' [Herm, Lns; KJV, NASB, NEB], not explicit [ICC, WBC; NAB, NIV, NJB, RSV, TEV, TNT].

130        PHILEMON 1:15

QUESTION—What relationship is indicated by this word?

It indicates a reason why Paul decided not to keep Onesimus with him [Alf, El, ICC, Lg, Lt, My, WBC]: I wished to do nothing about keeping him here, because, etc.

**perhaps[a] on-account-of[b] this he-was-separated[c] for an-hour,[d]**

LEXICON—a. τάχα (LN 71.12): 'perhaps' [BAGD, Herm, Hn, Lns, NIC, WBC; all versions except NJB, TEV], 'I suppose' [NJB], 'it may be that' [TEV], 'it may have been' [Lt], 'it occurred to me that' [ICC].
- b. διά (LN 90.44): 'on account of'. The phrase διὰ τοῦτο 'on account of this' is translated 'for this reason' [BAGD, Lns, WBC; NAB, NASB], 'the reason was/is' [Herm, NIC; NIV], 'the reason why was this' [Hn], 'this is why' [NEB, RSV], 'therefore' [KJV], not explicit [ICC, Lt; NJB, TEV, TNT].
- c. aorist pass. indic. of χωρίζω (LN **85.41**): 'to be separated' [Herm, ICC, LN, Lns, NIC, WBC; NAB, NIV], 'to be parted' [Hn, Lt; NASB, RSV], 'to be taken away' [BAGD; TNT], 'to depart' [KJV], 'to go away' [BAGD], 'to be away' [TEV]. The verb is also translated with 'you' as the subject: 'you lost (him)' [NEB], 'you have been deprived of (Onesimus)' [NJB].
- d. ὥρα (LN 67.148): 'an hour' [Lt], 'a season' [Lt; KJV], 'a while' [BAGD, Herm, LN; NAB, NASB, RSV, TNT], 'a little while' [WBC; NIV], 'a time' [ICC, Lns, NIC; NEB, NJB], 'a short time' [TEV], 'a short period' [Hn].

QUESTION—What is implied by the word τάχα 'perhaps'?

1. It implies that Paul does not claim to know absolutely [Bg, EPC, Herm, IB, ICC, Lns, TH, WBC]: perhaps it was for this reason.
2. It is used in a polite sense, to soften the force of the verb [Alf, El, Lg(H), My, TNTC]: I might suggest that he was separated. One commentary states that Paul's use of this word implies no doubt at all of God's providence in the matter [TNTC].
3. It includes both of the above interpretations [Lg].
4. It implies that Philemon might keep Onesimus instead of sending him back to Paul [CGTC, Hn, NIC]: perhaps to be yours, unless you send him back to me.

QUESTION—To what does τοῦτο 'this' refer?

It refers forward to the following clause [Herm, Lg, Lns, NIC, WBC]: he was separated because of this, namely in order that....

QUESTION—Why was the verb ἐχωρίσθη 'he was separated' used and what is the significance of its passive form?

It is an intentionally mild word, used instead of stating that Onesimus had run away [Alf, Bg, Blm, EBC, EGT, El, Herm, ICC, Lg, Lt, MNTC, My, TH, TNTC]. Many commentators understand the passive voice to imply that God's providence has been at work to bring about eternal fellowship [Blm, EBC, EPC, Herm, Hn, IB, ICC, Lns, Lt, MNTC, NCBC, NIC, TH, TNTC,

WBC]. Another commentator thinks that the passive voice of the verb has the force of the middle voice and merely means 'he departed' [Lg(H)].

QUESTION—Since it has been some time since Onesimus ran away, traveled to where Paul was in prison, and began helping Paul, what does Paul mean by the phrase πρὸς ὥραν 'for an hour'?

It is in contrast with αἰώνιον 'forever' in the following clause, indicating that the separation had been brief by comparison [Alf, Bg, El, Herm, ICC, Lg, Lns, Lt, My, TH, TNTC, WBC]: he was separated from you for a short time. His absence had been brief in comparison with the anticipated eternal fellowship [Bg], or in comparison with what was accomplished during that time [Lt].

**in-order-that[a] forever[b] him you-might-have-back,[c]**

LEXICON—a. ἵνα (LN 89.59): 'in order that' [BAGD, ICC], 'so that' [WBC; NJB, TEV], 'that' [BAGD, Herm, Hn, Lns; all versions except NJB, TEV].
- b. αἰώνιος (LN 67.96): 'forever' [BAGD, Herm, Hn, Lns, Lt, NIC, WBC; KJV, NAB, NASB, NJB, RSV, TNT], 'for good' [NEB, NIV], 'for all time' [TEV], 'eternal' [LN], not explicit [ICC].
- c. pres. act. subj. of ἀπέχω (LN 57.137): 'to have back' [Herm, Hn, Lns, WBC; all versions except KJV, NAB], 'to regain' [Lt], 'to possess' [NAB], 'to receive' [KJV], 'to receive in full' [LN], 'to have to yourself' [NIC], 'to keep' [BAGD]. The words αὐτὸν ἀπέχῃς 'him you might have back' is translated 'he might come back to you' [ICC].

QUESTION—What relationship is indicated by ἵνα 'in order that'?

It indicates God's purpose in what had happened [Hn, ICC, Lg, Lns, My, WBC]: God's purpose in all this was that you should have him back forever. This clause gives the meaning of τοῦτο 'this' in the preceding clause [Lns, WBC].

QUESTION—What is the meaning of αἰώνιον 'forever'?
1. It implies a new relationship through Christ, which is to be eternal [Alf, Bg, Blm, Brt, EGT, El, Herm, Hn, ICC, Lg, MNTC, NIC, TNTC, WBC, WPC]: you will have him back to be a Christian brother forever.
2. It means a permanent lifetime relationship [CBC, CGTC, TH]: you will have him back as a slave permanently. The deeper spiritual relationship is dealt with in the following verse [CGTC].

QUESTION—What is the meaning of ἀπέχῃς 'have him back'?
1. It means to have him completely [Alf, Bg, El, Herm, IB, ICC, Lg, My]: that you might have him back in full possession.
2. It means to have him back after his absence [Lt, TH, WBC]: that you might have him back again.

**16 no-longer[a] as a-slave[b] but more-than[c] a-slave,[b] a-brother beloved,[d]**

LEXICON—a. οὐκέτι (LN 67.130): 'no longer' [BAGD, Herm, Hn, LN, Lns, WBC; all versions except KJV, TEV], 'not now' [KJV, TEV].

b. δοῦλος (LN 87.76): 'slave' [BAGD, Herm, Hn, LN, Lns, WBC; all versions except KJV], 'servant' [ICC; KJV].

c. ὑπέρ (LN 87.30) with accusative object: 'more than' [NIC; NAB, NASB, NEB, RSV], 'much more than' [Herm, WBC; TEV, TNT], 'better than' [BAGD, Hn; NIV], 'something much better than' [NJB], 'above' [KJV], 'beyond' [Lns]. The whole phrase is also translated 'a better servant and a Christian brother besides' [ICC], 'he left thee as a slave, only that he might return to thee a beloved brother' [Lt].

d. ἀγαπητός (LN 25.45): 'beloved' [Herm, Hn, LN, Lns, WBC; KJV, NAB, NASB, RSV, TNT], 'dear' [LN; NEB, NIV, NJB, TEV]. See this word at verse 1.

QUESTION—What relationship is indicated by οὐκέτι 'no longer'?

This form is used with the indicative mood (cf. μηκέτι 'no longer' with other moods), which shows that it is not governed by the preceding purpose clause (with the subjunctive mood). Instead of meaning 'in order that you might have him back . . . no longer as a slave', it states the actual fact of Onesimus's status: 'in order that you might have him back forever, no longer a slave' [Lt, WBC].

QUESTION—What relationship is indicated by ὡς 'as'?

1. While still remaining a slave, he will no longer be treated 'only' as a slave [Alf, EGT, Herm, Hn, ICC, Lg, Lns, MNTC, My, NCBC, NIC, TH, TNTC, WPC]: in order that you might have him back, no longer merely according to his legal status as a slave. Some commentators understand the word 'as' to show that Paul is not suggesting that Onesimus be emancipated [Alf, El, Hn, Lg].

2. It indicates how Onesimus is to be treated, without implying whether or not he is to continue to be a slave [Herm, ICC, Lt, WBC]: in order that you might have him back, but no longer to be considered as a slave.

3. It indicates that Onesimus will no longer be a slave [IB, NIC; probably EBC]: in order that you might have him back, no longer to be a slave.

QUESTION—What does ὡς 'as' govern?

1. It governs only 'slave' [Alf, Bg, EBC, Hn, IB, Lg, Lns, Lt, TNTC, WBC; all versions except NAB, NEB]: no longer as a slave; he will be more than a slave, he will be a brother beloved. Paul does not say 'as more than a slave, as a brother beloved'; he wants the relationship actually to be that of a Christian brother [Bg]. The parallel to 'as' is 'more than' [My]. Paul may be suggesting emancipation for Onesimus [EBC, IB].

2. It governs both 'slave' and 'more than a slave, a brother beloved' [EGT, Herm, ICC; NAB, NEB]: no longer to be considered as a slave, but to be considered as more than a slave; that is, as a brother beloved. However, some who render it in this way (e.g., Herm, IB, ICC) may be using 'as' to mean 'actually so' and not merely 'considered so'.

QUESTION—What relationship is indicated by ἀλλά 'but'?

Its primary connection is with the following phrase 'a brother beloved' [Bg]: no longer should you treat him as a slave but (what is more than a slave) make him a brother beloved. The word 'but' introduces the antithesis to 'slave': no longer as a slave; on the contrary, he is a brother beloved [WBC].

QUESTION—How is the phrase 'more than a slave' related to the phrase 'a brother beloved'?

The two phrases are in apposition; 'brother beloved' defines what Paul means by 'more than a slave' [Herm, ICC, Lns, My, WBC]: more than a slave; I mean he is to be a brother beloved. This relationship is based on their mutual union with Christ [Herm].

**especially[a] to-me, but[b] by-how-much[c] more to-you**

LEXICON—a. μάλιστα (LN 78.7): 'especially' [BAGD, Herm, Hn, LN, Lns, WBC; KJV, NAB, NASB, NJB, RSV, TNT], 'very much' [LN], 'very (dear)' [NEB, NIV], 'how much!' [TEV], 'above all' [BAGD].

b. δέ (LN 89.94, 89.124): 'but' [Herm, Hn, Lns, WBC; KJV, NASB, NIV, NJB, RSV], 'and' [NAB, NEB, TEV], not explicit [TNT].

c. πόσος (LN 59.17): 'how much more' [Herm, Hn, Lns, WBC; all versions except NEB, NIV], 'how much (dearer)' [NEB], 'even (dearer)' [NIV].

QUESTION—What relationship is indicated by the two dative pronouns ἐμοί 'to me' and σοί 'to you'?

They both relate to the phrase ἀδελφὸν ἀγαπητόν 'a brother beloved' [Bg, EGT, El, EPC, Herm, Hn, Lns, My, WBC]: a beloved brother to me and to you.

QUESTION—What is meant by μάλιστα ἐμοί 'especially to me'?

1. It means that Onesimus is a brother loved by Paul more than by any other person outside of Philemon's household [Alf, Bg, El, Hn, My, NIC, WBC]: loved by me more than by anyone else outside your household. Onesimus was a beloved brother to Paul because he was Paul's convert and because he had helped Paul [Lg]. The word μάλιστα 'especially' is literally a superlative, 'most of all', but the following phrase 'but by how much more to you' makes it clear that here it has the meaning of 'especially' rather than the literal sense 'most of all' [CGTC, Herm, Hn].

2. The word μάλιστα is used as a true superlative here, 'most of all' [EGT, TNTC]: a beloved brother, most of all to me.

QUESTION—What is meant by πόσῳ μᾶλλον σοί 'by how much more to you'?

The meaning is that Onesimus should be a brother who is loved by Philemon even more than he is by Paul [Alf, Bg, CGTC, EGT, El, EPC, Herm, Hn, ICC, Lg, Lns, Lt, My, NIC, TNTC, WBC]: he will be a brother loved by you even more than he is by me. The reason for such love is the twofold relationship described in the following clause [Lg]. For those who take the second interpretation of the preceding question, the meaning will be a degree higher than superlative here [EGT, TNTC]: he is a brother loved by me most of all, but even more than most of all by you.

**both in<sup>a</sup> (the) flesh<sup>b</sup> and in<sup>a</sup> (the) Lord.**

LEXICON—a. ἐν...ἐν (LN 13.8, 89.119): 'in...in' [Herm, Hn, Lns, WBC; KJV, NASB, RSV], 'as (a man)...as (a Christian/fellow-Christian/brother-in-the-Lord)' [NEB, NIV, TEV, TNT], '(you will know him both) as...in' [IB; NAB], 'on (the natural plane) ...in' [NJB].
  b. σάρξ (LN 26.7): 'flesh' [BAGD, Herm, Hn, Lns, WBC; KJV, NASB, RSV], 'man' [BAGD; NAB, NEB, NIV, TNT], 'human aspects' [LN], 'slave' [TEV], 'natural plane' [NJB].

QUESTION—What is the meaning of these two ἐν 'in' phrases?

The sense is 'in human relationships' and 'in our union with the Lord Jesus' [CGTC, El, EPC, Herm, Hn, IB, ICC, Lg, Lt, MNTC, My, NIC, TNTC, WBC]. Both phrases explain the previous phrase 'by how much more' [ICC]. In human affairs Philemon's spiritual brother will serve better as his slave; from the spiritual point of view Philemon's slave will be his brother [ICC, Lg, My].

QUESTION—What is the function of καί...καί 'both...and'?

An equal emphasis on both elements is indicated [El, EPC, Lt, My]: both in the flesh and in the Lord.

**DISCOURSE UNIT: 17–22:** [CBC]. The topic is Paul's appeal.

**17 Therefore<sup>a</sup>**

LEXICON—a. οὖν (LN 89.50): 'therefore' [KJV], 'then' [NAB, NASB, NEB, TNT], 'so' [NIV, NJB, RSV, TEV].

QUESTION—What relationship is indicated by this word?

1. It indicates a return to Paul's main point after the preceding parenthetical comments [El, Herm, ICC, My, WBC]: now, to return to my main point.
2. It indicates an exhortation based on the preceding circumstances [Lg]: since Onesimus is returning to you under these circumstances, receive him as you would receive me.

**if you-consider/have<sup>a</sup> me a-partner,<sup>b</sup>**

LEXICON—a. pres. act. indic. of ἔχω (LN 31.1): 'to consider' [Hn, LN, WBC; NIV, RSV], 'to count' [KJV, NEB], 'to regard' [LN, Lt, NIC; NAB, NASB, TNT], 'to think of' [TEV], 'to have' [Lns], 'to grant' [NJB], not explicit [ICC].
  b. κοινωνός (LN 34.6): 'partner' [Hn, LN, NIC, WBC; all versions except NJB], 'one in fellowship' [Lns], 'fellowship with (yourself)' [NJB], 'mutual fellowship' [ICC], 'friend and companion' [Lt].

QUESTION—What relationship is indicated by this condition-of-fact clause?

This clause, which Paul believes Philemon accepts as true, states the condition for the fulfillment of the following clause [Lg, Lns]: If you regard me as your partner (as I am confident you do), receive him. The implication is that for Philemon to reject Onesimus would be to imply that Paul was not his partner [Lg, My].

PHILEMON 1:17

QUESTION—What is meant by ἔχεις 'you consider', (literally) 'you have'?
1. It means 'to consider' or 'to regard' [Hn, LN, Lt, MNTC, NIC, WBC; KJV, NAB, NASB, NEB, NIV, RSV, TEV, TNT]: if you regard me as your partner.
2. It means 'to have' [Bg, My]: if you have me as a partner.

QUESTION—Why does Paul refer to himself as Philemon's partner?
1. They are partners in the Lord's service [Alf, CBC, EBC, Herm, Hn, ICC, Lns, My, NCBC, NIC, TH, TNTC, WBC]: if you and I are partners in the Lord's service, grant this request. The partnership goes beyond their mutual love for Onesimus and includes the totality of their Christian fellowship [Alf]. They are partners in their faith in Jesus and their service for him [CBC, El].
2. They are partners in the Christian faith and Christian principles [El, WPC]: if you and I are partners in the Christian faith, grant my request.
3. They are partners in the sense that, because of their mutual faith, what belongs to one of them—specifically, Onesimus—belongs to the other [Bg, EPC, IB]: since we share with one another, you should receive Onesimus as you would receive me.
4. They are partners due to their personal friendship [Lt]: if you consider me as a friend, grant this request.

**receive[a] him as me.**
LEXICON—a. aorist act. impera. of προσλαμβάνω (LN 34.53): 'to receive' [ICC, LN, Lns, NIC; KJV, RSV], 'to welcome' [WBC; NAB, NEB, NIV, NJB, TEV, TNT], 'to accept' [Hn, LN; NASB], 'to take to oneself' [Lt], 'to welcome' [LN].

QUESTION—What is implied by προσλαβοῦ 'receive him'?
It implies that he should be received in a kind and joyful manner [Lg, TH]: receive him joyfully and kindly. Philemon should receive Onesimus into personal fellowship [Lns]: receive him to yourself.

QUESTION—What is meant by the phrase ὡς ἐμέ 'as me'?
It means that Philemon should receive Onesimus in the same manner as he would receive Paul [EBC, El, Hn, ICC, Lns, MNTC, NCBC, NIC, TNTC, WBC; all versions except KJV]: receive him as you would receive me. It includes acceptance into the Christian fellowship [ICC] in addition to receiving him with kindness [El, MNTC]. Paul is asking that Onesimus be received as a fellow worker in the gospel [NIC]. Paul will consider Philemon's love for Onesimus as given to himself [Herm].

**18 But[a]**
LEXICON—a. δέ (LN 89.94, 89.124): 'but' [NASB], 'and' [NEB], not explicit [all versions except NASB, NEB].

QUESTION—What relationship is indicated by this word?
It introduces a contrast with the favorable comments preceding it [Alf, El]: on the other hand.

**if anything[a] he-has-wronged[b] you or owes[c] (you),**

LEXICON—a. τι (LN 92.12): 'anything' [NAB, RSV, TEV, TNT], 'aught' [KJV], 'in any way' [NASB, NJB], 'any (wrong)' [NEB, NIV].

b. aorist act. indic. of ἀδικέω (LN 88.22): 'to wrong' [ICC, NIC, WBC; KJV, NASB, NJB, RSV], 'to do a wrong' [LN, Lns; NEB, NIV, TEV, TNT], 'to do an injury' [Lt; NAB], 'to cause loss' [Hn].

c. pres. act. indic. of ὀφείλω (LN 57.219): 'to owe' [Herm, Hn, ICC, LN, Lns, WBC; all versions except NEB], 'to be in one's debt' [NEB].

QUESTION—What relationship is indicated by this conditional clause with εἰ 'if'?

1. Paul does not know whether Onesimus had wronged Philemon [Hn]: if he has (although I don't know whether he has). Paul was not certain, but knew that it was possible [Hn].

2. Paul knows that Onesimus had wronged Philemon, even though he states the matter hypothetically.

   2.1 Paul knows that Onesimus had wronged Philemon by running away and depriving Philemon of his service [Blm, Herm, Lns], or possibly by being lazy previously [Blm]: if he has wronged you by depriving you of his services (as I know he has). Paul would not be stating the matter so lightly if he knew Onesimus had stolen money from Philemon; it would have required confession by Onesimus and forgiveness by Philemon. The wrong was that Onesimus deprived his master of his services by fleeing [Lns].

   2.2 Paul knows that Onesimus had stolen money from Philemon [Alf, Bg, EGT, EPC, IB, ICC, Lg, Lt, MNTC, My, TH]: if he has wronged you by stealing money from you (as I believe he has). Paul's way of stating this matter illustrates his tact [ICC]. If Paul were referring merely to Philemon's loss of his slave's service he would not have stated it by a conditional clause [My], since there was no doubt about that. Onesimus had probably stolen from Philemon and run away to avoid punishment [Lt], which enabled him to travel to Rome [MNTC].

QUESTION—What is the relationship of the two verbs ἠδίκησέν 'wronged' and ὀφείλει 'owes'?

1. They refer to the same thing [Alf, Bg, Brt, CBC, EBC, El, Lg, Lns, Lt, My]: if he has wronged you, or in other words, owes you anything. The word 'owes' specifies what is meant by 'wronged' [Alf, Lg, Lt]. It is a milder word than 'wronged' [Bg, El].

2. They refer to different things [Blm, TH]: if he has wronged you, or if he owes you anything.

QUESTION—In what way had Onesimus wronged Philemon?

1. Onesimus had deprived Philemon of his services by running away [Herm, Lns], or perhaps by being lazy before running away [Blm], or by committing some misdeed [TH]: if he has wrongfully deprived you of his proper services or owes you anything.

2. Onesimus had stolen money from his master, and as a result he owes him [Lt, MNTC, My, TNTC]: if he has wronged you and as a result owes you money. If Paul were referring merely to the wrong of running away from his master, he would hardly have used a conditional ('if') clause, since it was obviously true [My].

**this to-me charge;**[a]
LEXICON—a. pres. act. impera. of ἐλλογέω (LN **57.226**): 'to charge' [Hn, Lns, WBC; NAB, NIV, RSV], 'to charge to one's account' [LN; NASB, TEV], 'to put on one's account' [ICC; KJV], 'to put down to one's account' [NIC; NEB, NJB, TNT], 'to set down to one's account' [Lt].
QUESTION—Why does Paul say this?
Paul is accepting the responsibility for any indebtedness of Onesimus to Philemon [Bg, Blm, CBC, EBC, EGT, El, EPC, Herm, Hn, IB, ICC, Lg, Lns, Lt, MNTC, My, NCBC, NIC, TH, TNTC, WBC], since he wishes to avoid any hindrance to Philemon's accepting Onesimus [My, WBC]: if he owes you any money, charge it to me. Paul may be thinking of any punishment which Onesimus deserves as well as his debt of money [Lg]. Paul is truly offering to pay Onesimus's debts to Philemon [Hn], although he may suspect that Philemon will not ask for payment [IB, MNTC]. Some commentators think that he probably intends that Philemon cancel any such financial debt rather than actually charge it to Paul [Alf, Herm].

**19 I Paul have-written with-the my hand, I will-repay;**[a]
LEXICON—a. fut. act. indic. of ἀποτίνω (LN **57.156**): 'to repay' [Hn, ICC, Lt, NIC; KJV, NASB, NEB, RSV, TNT], 'to pay back' [NIV, NJB, TEV], 'to remunerate' [LN], 'to pay' [Lns, WBC; NAB].
QUESTION—Why does Paul use the emphatic ἐγώ 'I' twice, the emphatic ἐμῇ 'my', and insert his own name?
He is emphasizing his acceptance of the responsibility of paying Onesimus's debt to Philemon [Blm, IB, Lg, WBC]: I (emphatic) Paul have written with my (emphatic) hand, I (emphatic) will repay. The insertion of his name gives the effect of a formal signature [EGT, Lt]. The statement 'I, Paul, write it with my own hand' is Paul's promissory note [ICC, WBC].
QUESTION—How much did Paul personally write?
1. Paul is indicating that he wrote the letter himself [Alf, EGT, Lns, Lt]: I have written this, as well as the rest of the letter, personally. It is very unlikely that Paul would take the pen from his amanuensis to write this sentence [Alf]. The mention of his own handwriting at this point in the letter indicates that he wrote the entire letter himself [Lt]. The personal nature of this letter would account for Paul's writing it personally [EGT]. The epistolary aorist implies that Paul wrote at least the preceding verse, and probably the entire letter, himself; the present tense would normally have been used here if Paul had taken the pen just at this point [El].

2. Paul is indicating that at this point he takes the pen from his amanuensis [CBC, EPC, IB, MNTC, NIC, TH]: I am now writing this with my own hand. He continues to write the rest of the epistle personally [CBC].

QUESTION—Why does Paul say, 'I will repay'?

Paul is emphasizing his earnestness in accepting Onesimus's debt to Philemon [Bg, EPC, Herm, ICC, MNTC, NCBC]. Paul binds himself by these words [IB, NCBC]. This phrase repeats the meaning of 'charge this to me' [Lg]. Paul does not really expect that Philemon will require the payment from him [El, Lg]. The verb used here, ἀποτίσω 'I will make compensation' [Herm, Lg], is stronger than ἀποδώσω 'I will give back', which is the more common term for paying back [EGT, WBC].

**in-order-that not I-may-say**[a] **to-you that even yourself to-me you-owe.**[b]

LEXICON—a. pres. act. indic. of λέγω (LN 33.69): 'to say' [LN]. The phrase ἵνα μὴ λέγω 'in order that I may not say' is translated 'albeit I do not say how' [KJV], 'not to mention that' [CGTC, Hn, MNTC; NAB, NEB, NIV], 'lest I should mention that' [NASB], 'I make no mention that' [NJB], 'to say nothing of' [RSV], 'I should not have to remind you that' [TEV], 'I need not mention that' [NIC; TNT], 'though I might intimate that' [ICC], 'for I will not insist that' [Lt], 'surely it is not necessary for me to mention to you (that)' [TH].

b. pres. act. indic. of προσοφείλω (LN **57.220**): 'to owe' [NIC; NAB, NIV, RSV, TEV, TNT], 'to owe besides' [Hn, WBC; KJV], 'to owe as well' [NASB, NEB], 'to owe (as) a further debt' [NJB], 'to owe in addition' [Lns], 'to owe in return' [LN], 'to be indebted' [Lt]. The phrase μοι προσοφείλεις 'to me you owe to' is translated 'it is you who are my debtor' [ICC].

QUESTION—What relationship is indicated by ἵνα 'in order that'?

1. It indicates Paul's purpose for saying, 'I will repay' [El, ICC, Lt, MNTC, My, NIC]: I say, 'I will repay', in order that I may not say to you that you owe me your very self. It is almost as if Paul were speaking to himself with these words [EGT], or saying that he did not wish to press the matter of Philemon's debt to him [El]. It is like the English idiom, 'not to mention that', in which the speaker does mention what he says he will not mention [Hn, Lg, WBC].
2. It gives the purpose of an understood thought [Alf, EBC]: (grant me this request) in order that I may not (have to) say [Alf], (I am silent) in order that I may not say [EBC].
3. It gives Paul's purpose in saying 'charge it to me', and the following phrase 'to you' gives the alternative [Lns]: I say, 'Charge it to me', in order that I may not say, 'I will charge much more to you', because you owe me your very self.

QUESTION—What is the meaning of σεαυτόν μοι προσοφείλεις 'you owe me yourself'?

It refers to the fact that Philemon had been converted through the ministry of Paul, either directly or indirectly [Alf, Bg, Brt, CBC, CGTC, EGT, El, EPC, Herm, Hn, ICC, Lg, Lns, Lt, MNTC, My, NCBC, NIC, TH, TNTC, WBC]: you are indebted to me for your salvation. One commentator thinks it likely that Philemon's conversion came about directly through Epaphras and thus indirectly through Paul [MNTC]. But it is more likely that it was through Paul's direct influence [CBC, EPC, Herm, Lg, Lns, Lt, My, NIC]. The expression seems too strong to refer merely to indirect influence [WBC].

QUESTION—What is the meaning of the προσ- compound προσοφείλεις 'you owe to'?

1. It does not refer to an additional obligation, but rather an offsetting and greater obligation; it means that Philemon is a debtor to Paul not merely for as much as Paul offers to repay for Onesimus, but for far more, namely, for his salvation [CBC, El, EPC, Herm, Hn, ICC, Lg, My, WBC]: you owe me as much as I might pay to you for Onesimus and far more—you are obligated to me for your salvation.
2. It means that Philemon has an obligation to forgive Onesimus, and in addition has an obligation to Paul for his own salvation [Bg, Brt]: you are obligated to forgive Onesimus and in addition you are obligated to me for your salvation.
3. It means that Philemon is indebted to Paul both for his salvation and for the return of Onesimus [Lns]: you owe to me your salvation and the return of Onesimus.

**20 Yes, brother,**

QUESTION—What is the function of this phrase?

The word ναί 'yes' adds emphasis to Paul's appeal [Alf, El, Herm, ICC, Lg, My, WBC], and ἀδελφέ 'brother' reinforces the affectionate relationship between Paul and Philemon [EGT, Hn, Lt, WBC]: I repeat, dear Christian brother. These words form a warm appeal involving three brothers—Paul, Philemon, and Onesimus [Lt, WBC].

**I from-you would-like-to-benefit[a] in[b] (the) Lord;**

LEXICON—a. aorist opt. of ὀνίνημι (LN **35.4**): 'to benefit'. All versions combine ἐγώ σου ὀναίμην 'may I benefit from you': 'let me benefit from you' [NASB], 'let me have some benefit from you' [Hn], 'I want some benefit from you' [RSV], 'let me experience a favor from you' [LN], 'I do wish that I may have some benefit from you' [WBC; NIV], 'I want to make you useful to me' [NAB], 'may I for my part have this profit from you' [NIC], 'be generous with me' [NEB], 'I would like to be paid back' [TNT], 'I would like to make a profit off thee' [Lns], 'let me receive a return from you' [Lt], 'let me have some return from you' [MNTC], 'I am counting on you' [NJB], 'please do me this favor' [TEV], 'render me a personal favor' [ICC], 'let me have joy of thee' [KJV].

b. ἐν (LN 89.119): 'in' [KJV, NAB, NASB, NIV, NJB, RSV]. The phrase ἐν κυρίῳ 'in the Lord' is also translated 'as a Christian' [NEB], 'in a Christian way' [TNT], 'for the Lord's sake' [TEV].

QUESTION—What is the significance of the verb ὀνίνημι 'to benefit'?

1. It is an intentional word play [Alf, Bg, Brt, CGTC, EGT, El, Hn, IB, ICC, Lg, Lt, My, NIC, WPC], since the name Onesimus ('Profitable') is from the same root as this verb [EBC]: I would like for you to 'Onesimus' me. A word-play is likely, since this is the only occurrence of this verb in the NT It is common to make word-plays on names in Hebrew [Lt]. Some consider this as a possibility rather than as a certainty [Brt, CGTC, EBC, Hn, Lt, WPC].

2. It is not a word play on the name of Onesimus [Herm, Lns, NCB, NCBC, WBC]. A word-play is doubtful, since the expression occurs frequently in secular Greek literature [Herm, NCBC, WBC]. Moreover, it is from Philemon that Paul desires this profit, not from Onesimus. Reference to Onesimus occurs too far back to make a word play likely [Lns].

QUESTION—What does the optative mood of the verb ὀναίμην 'to benefit' indicate?

It expresses a wish that is possible of fulfillment [CGTC, EBC, EPC, Lns, My, WBC]: may I have this benefit from you. Since Onesimus will now benefit Philemon, Philemon should now benefit Paul [Bg].

QUESTION—What is implied by Paul's request for 'benefit' from Philemon?

1. Paul has become deeply involved with Onesimus; he will consider Philemon's favorable treatment of Onesimus as a benefit to himself [El, Hn, ICC, Lg, Lns, Lt, My, WBC]: may I benefit from you by your favorable treatment of Onesimus. ἐγώ 'I' is emphatic [EGT, El, ICC, Lns, Lt, My, WBC], as is also σου 'you' by forefronting [Alf, Lns]. The emphatic ἐγώ 'I' indicates that Paul is identifying himself with the cause of Onesimus [EGT, Lt, WBC].

2. Paul's benefit will be in seeing that Philemon understands and acts in accordance with the gospel [MNTC]: let me have the benefit of seeing that you act in accordance with the gospel message.

3. Paul is suggesting that Onesimus be sent back to him [IB, NIC, WPC]: may I have Profit—that is, Onesimus—from you.

QUESTION—What is meant by ἐν κυρίῳ 'in the Lord'?

This phrase here seems to have the general and rather broad meaning of 'as is appropriate in our relationship of union with the Lord (Jesus)'. It has numerous parallels in this sense in Paul's epistles. Compare this phrase, for example, in Gal. 5:10, Eph. 4:17, 5:8, 6:1, 21, Phl. 2:24, 29. This sense seems to be in harmony with most of the references to it by the commentators.

**refresh<sup>a</sup> my vital-organs<sup>b</sup> in<sup>c</sup> Christ.**

TEXT—Instead of Χριστῷ 'Christ', some manuscripts read κυρίῳ 'Lord'. GNT does not deal with this variant. Only Blm, TNTC, and KJV read 'Lord'.

LEXICON—a. aorist act. impera. of ἀναπαύω (LN 23.84): 'to refresh' [KJV, NAB, NASB, NIV, RSV], 'to set at rest' [NJB], 'to cause to rest' [LN], 'to relieve anxiety' [NEB], 'to cheer up' [TEV, TNT]. See this word at verse 7.

b. σπλάγχνον (LN 8.58): 'vital organs', 'intestines' [LN], 'bowels' [KJV], 'heart' [Hn, Lns, NIC, WBC; NAB, NASB, NIV, NJB, RSV], 'spirits' [Lt]. The phrase ἀνάπαυσόν μου τὰ σπλάγχνα 'refresh my vital organs' is translated 'relieve my anxiety' [NEB], 'cheer me up' [TEV, TNT], 'affording me joy and refreshment' [ICC], See this word at verses 1 and 12.

c. ἐν (LN 13.8, 89.119): 'in' [all versions except TEV, TNT]. The phrase 'in Christ' is also translated 'as a fellow Christian' [TNT], 'as a brother in Christ' [TEV].

QUESTION—What is meant by Paul's request to refresh his vital organs?

Paul's heart (τὰ σπλάγχνα, the vital organs as the seat of the affections [CGTC, El]) will be refreshed if Philemon grants Paul's request [Alf, Bg, Herm, IB, Lg, My, WBC]: refresh my heart by granting my request. Paul asks to be included with the others whose σπλάγχνα 'hearts' Philemon has refreshed [Hn, IB, NCBC, NIC]. μου 'my' is emphatic by its word order [WBC].

QUESTION—What relationship is indicated by ἐν 'in'?

See the preceding clause.

**DISCOURSE UNIT: 21–25** [CGTC, Herm, MNTC, NCBC, WBC]. The topic is the close of the letter and personal matters.

**DISCOURSE UNIT: 21–22** [NIC]. The topic is Paul's promise to visit Philemon.

**21 Being-confident<sup>a</sup> of-the obedience<sup>b</sup> of-you**

LEXICON—a. perf. pass. participle of πείθω (LN 31.82, 33.301): 'to be confident' [Hn, Lns, WBC; NAB, NEB, NIV, RSV], 'to have confidence' [LN, NIC; KJV, NASB], 'to have full confidence' [Lt], 'to be sure' [TEV, TNT], 'to be assured' [ICC], 'with complete confidence' [NJB]. The perfect tense implies a present state [Lns].

b. ὑπακοή (LN 36.15): 'obedience' [Hn, LN, Lns, NIC, WBC; KJV, NASB, NIV, RSV], 'compliance' [Lt; NAB, NJB], 'obedient spirit' [ICC]. The noun is also translated as a verb: 'to do what one asks' [TEV, TNT], 'to meet one's wishes' [NEB].

QUESTION—What relationship is indicated by the participial form πεποιθώς 'trusting'?

It may be a participle of manner, although no commentator discusses this point: confidently, in full confidence of your obedience, I have written to you. It implies Paul's full confidence in Philemon's response [Herm, Hn, Lns]. Or it could indicate Paul's reason for writing: I have written to you because I am confident of your obedience.

QUESTION—To whom is Philemon to be obedient?

1. He is to be obedient to God's will or to the requirements of the gospel [Hn, ICC, MNTC, WBC]: I am confident that you will obey God's will. It is more than obeying Paul's counsel [Hn]. It is a matter of his duty as a Christian [ICC]. Paul has already said that he would not use his own apostolic authority to command him [MNTC].
2. He is to be obedient to Paul's apostolic authority [Alf, EGT, El, Herm, IB, Lns, My, NCBC, NIC, WPC], or to Paul's request [NIC, TH, TNTC]: I am confident that you will do what I have requested. It does not mean obedience to a command, but rather heeding what Paul has said [Lns, NIC]. Obedience to God is implied, although Paul is the one who is expressing God's commands [NCBC].

**I-have-written to-you,**

QUESTION—What is indicated by the aorist tense ἔγραψα 'I have written'?

This is an epistolary aorist; Paul is writing at the moment, but it will be past time when Philemon reads the letter [EGT, El, ICC, Lg, Lns, Lt, NIC]: I have written. The epistolary aorist refers to what precedes this verb, not merely to what follows [El]. See the same form of this verb at verse 19.

**knowing[a] that even/also[b] above[c] what I-say you-will-do.**

LEXICON—a. perf. act. participle of οἶδα (LN 28.1): 'to know' [LN; all versions except NJB, TNT], 'to be sure' [NJB, TNT].

b. καί (LN 89.93, 91.12): 'even' [NASB, NIV, NJB, RSV, TEV, TNT], 'in fact' [NEB], or 'also' [KJV], not explicit [NAB].

c. ὑπέρ (LN 78.29) with accusative object: 'above', 'more than' [ICC, Lt, NIC, WBC; KJV, NAB, NASB, NIV, NJB, RSV], 'better than' [Hn; NEB], 'more' [TEV, TNT], 'beyond' [Lns].

QUESTION—What relationship is indicated by the participle εἰδώς 'knowing'?

This participle gives the reason for πεποιθώς 'being confident' [My; NASB]: I am confident of your obedience, because I know that you will do even more.

QUESTION—What is the implied object of ποιήσεις 'you will do'?

The object is what Philemon will do concerning Onesimus [Bg]: knowing that you will do more than I say regarding Onesimus.

QUESTION—What is implied by καὶ ὑπὲρ ἃ λέγω 'even above what I say'?

1. It implies treating Onesimus better than the bare minimum of Christian requirements [CBC, El, Herm, Hn, ICC, Lns, MNTC, My, NCBC]: more than the minimum of what you ought to do. Paul leaves it to Philemon to

decide what additional things he will do [Herm, MNTC, My]. Nothing is implied about granting freedom to Onesimus [Herm, Hn, NCBC]. It is possible that Paul hopes that Onesimus will be set free [ICC, NCBC].
2. It implies granting freedom to Onesimus [Alf, Brt, EBC, EGT, Lt, TH, TNTC, WPC]: more than I say, by granting freedom to Onesimus. Paul has already suggested that he would like Philemon to send Onesimus back to him; anything 'above' that could hardly be less than granting freedom for Onesimus [EBC, WPC]. The idea of freedom for Onesimus seems to be in Paul's mind throughout this letter, although he never states it openly [EGT, Lt]. He does no more than hint at freedom for Onesimus [TNTC].
3. It implies that Paul would like Onesimus to be returned to him to assist him in the gospel ministry [IB, WBC]: more than I have stated, by sending Onesimus back to minister with me.

QUESTION—What does ἃ λέγω 'what I say' refer to?
It refers to what Paul has stated in this letter [My]: what I have stated here.

QUESTION—What is implied by καί 'even/also'?
It implies doing what Paul has requested, and more besides [Alf, Lg, My]: knowing that you will do what I have requested, and more than that as well.

**DISCOURSE UNIT: 22–25** [Alf, EPC, Lg, TNTC]. The topic is the request for lodging for Paul, personal greetings, and conclusion.

**DISCOURSE UNIT: 22** [My, TNTC]. The topic is the request for lodging.

**22** And<sup>a</sup> at-the-same-time<sup>b</sup> also<sup>c</sup> prepare<sup>d</sup> for-me a-lodging;<sup>e</sup>

LEXICON—a. δέ (LN 89.94): 'and' [NAB, NASB, NEB, NIV], 'but' [KJV], not explicit [RSV, TEV, TNT].
  b. ἅμα (LN 67.34): 'at the same time' [Hn, Lns, Lt, NIC, WBC; NASB, RSV, TEV, TNT], 'withal' [KJV], 'one thing more' [NEB, NIV], 'there is another thing' [NJB], 'while you thus receive Onesimus' [ICC], not explicit [MNTC; NAB].
  c. καί (LN 89.93): 'also' [KJV, NASB]. Probably this has been conflated with the preceding word by many.
  d. pres. act. impera. of ἑτοιμάζω (LN 77.3): 'to prepare' [Hn, ICC, LN, Lt, NIC, WBC; KJV, NASB, NIV, RSV, TNT], 'to get ready' [NAB, NJB, TEV], 'to have ready' [NEB], 'to make ready' [LN, Lns].
  e. ξενία (LN **7.31, 34.57**): 'a lodging' [ICC; KJV, NASB], 'lodging' [Lns], 'a room' [LN; NAB, NEB, TEV, TNT], 'a guest room' [Hn, NIC, WBC; NIV, RSV], 'a place to stay in' [NJB], 'hospitality' [LN]. The phrase μοι ξενίαν 'for me a lodging' is also translated 'to receive me on a visit' [Lt], 'a room/place for me to stay in' [LN].

QUESTION—What is the purpose of this request?
It would give added reason for Philemon to receive Onesimus as Paul had previously requested, since Paul himself expected to visit him soon and could see what Philemon had done about the request [Alf, EBC, Herm, Hn, Lg, Lt, My, NCBC, TNTC, WBC]. It also reveals Paul's hope to be released

from prison soon [Bg, Brt, CBC, Herm, ICC, My, TH, WBC]. Some commentators think that Paul had been planning for some time to make another journey to Asia Minor, and that this request is in the nature of his latest travel arrangements [EGT, El].

QUESTION—What is implied by the phrase ἅμα δὲ καί 'and at the same time also'?

1. It means that at the same time when Philemon is receiving Onesimus he should prepare to receive Paul [Alf, EGT, ICC, Lg, Lns, My, WBC; NASB]: at the same time that you are receiving Onesimus, prepare a guest room for me. It is an additional request to Philemon [El].
2. It means that Paul is making a second request at the same time that he makes the first request [Herm, TH; NEB, NIV, NJB]: at the same time that I am requesting you to receive Onesimus I request you to prepare to receive me.

QUESTION—Why does Paul request a ξενίαν 'lodging'?

Paul makes his request in advance because he would doubtless be accompanied by others [Lns]. The word ξενία means both 'guest room' and 'hospitality'. Most understand it to be a place for Paul to stay, but the quality of hospitality could also be included [EBC, ICC]. The request does not necessarily mean a room in Philemon's own house [Lt, NIC].

**for**[a]

LEXICON—a. γάρ (LN 89.23): 'for' [KJV, NASB, NEB, RSV, TNT], 'because' [NIV, TEV], not explicit [NAB, NJB].

QUESTION—What relationship is indicated by this word?

It introduces the reason for Paul's request that a guest room be prepared for him [WBC]: prepare a lodging for me because I hope to be released and come to see you.

**I-hope**[a] **that through**[b] **the prayers**[c] **of-you I-shall-be-granted**[d] **to-you.**

LEXICON—a. pres. act. indic. of ἐλπίζω (LN 25.59): 'to hope' [Hn, ICC, LN, Lns, Lt, NIC, WBC; all versions except KJV], 'to trust' [KJV].

b. διά (LN 89.76) with genitive object: 'through' [Hn, Lns, Lt; KJV, NAB, NASB, NJB, RSV], 'in answer to' [ICC, WBC; NEB, NIV, TNT], 'thanks to' [NIC]. The phrase διὰ τῶν προσευχῶν ὑμῶν 'through your prayers' is translated 'God will answer the prayers of all of you' [TEV].

c. προσευχή (LN 33.178): 'prayers' [LN; all versions]. See this word at verse 4.

d. fut. pass. indic. of χαρίζομαι (LN **57.102**): 'to be given' [Lt; KJV, NASB], 'to be restored' [WBC; NAB, NIV, NJB], 'to be granted' [Hn, Lns, NIC; RSV], 'to be given' [LN], 'to be permitted' [ICC]. The passive form is also translated actively: 'God will grant me to you' [NEB], 'God will give me back to you' [TEV], 'God will help me to visit you' [TNT].

QUESTION—What is implied by the verb ἐλπίζω 'I hope'?

It implies that Paul is confidently expecting a favorable outcome [Lns, TH, WBC]: I confidently expect that I will be freed. It must mean that Paul has

PHILEMON 1:22                                                                 145

learned that his case will soon be dealt with [Lns]. One commentator thinks that Paul is not really confident that he will be restored to them [MNTC].

QUESTION—To whom do the plural pronouns ὑμῶν 'your' and ὑμῖν 'you' refer?

1. They refer to Philemon, Apphia, Archippus, and the church that meets in their house (vss. 1–2) [Alf, El, Herm, Hn, Lg, Lns, My, NCBC, NIC, TH]: I hope that through the prayers of all of you I shall be able to visit you all.
2. The first of these pronouns, ὑμῶν 'your', refers to Philemon and his household; the second, ὑμῖν 'you', refers to the Christian community [WBC]: I hope that through the prayers of you and your household I shall be able to visit you all.

QUESTION—What is implied by the verb χαρισθήσομα 'I shall be granted'?

It implies that Paul believes that it will be only by God's operation that he will be freed [Herm, ICC, MNTC, NCBC, NIC, TH, WBC]: I hope that through your prayers God will enable me to be freed and to visit you. The verb indicates that the Christians are asking a favor from God [TH].

**DISCOURSE UNIT: 23–25**: [Bg, CBC, EBC, GNT, Hn, ICC, Lt, My, TH, TNTC]. The topic is closing greetings and benediction.

**DISCOURSE UNIT: 23–24**: [NIC]. The topic is greetings from those who are with Paul.

**23** **Greets**[a] **you Epaphras the fellow-prisoner**[b] **of-me in**[c] **Christ Jesus,**

LEXICON—a. pres. mid. (deponent = act.) indic. of ἀσπάζομαι (LN 33.20): 'to greet' [Hn, LN; NAB, NASB], 'to salute' [Lns, Lt; KJV], 'to send greetings' [LN, NIC, WBC; NEB, NIV, NJB, RSV, TEV], 'greetings' [TNT].

b. συναιχμάλωτος (LN 37.118): 'fellow prisoner' [Hn, LN, NIC, WBC; KJV, NAB, NASB, NIV, RSV, TNT], 'prisoner with me' [NJB], 'fellow captive' [Lt], 'captive like myself' [NEB], 'fellow war captive' [Lns]. The phrase ὁ συναιχμάλωτός μου 'my fellow prisoner' is translated 'who is in prison with me' [TEV].

c. ἐν (LN 89.119): 'in' [KJV, NAB, NASB, NIV, NJB, RSV], 'for the sake of' [TEV, TNT], not explicit [NEB].

QUESTION—To whom does σε 'you' refer?

It is a singular pronoun, referring to Philemon alone [Herm, Lg, Lns, NIC, TH, WBC]: (these persons) greet you, Philemon.

QUESTION—Why is prominence given Epaphras by placing his name first in the list?

Some suggestions are that Epaphras is mentioned first because he was in prison along with Paul [Bg, Lg], he was a prominent church leader in the area [Lns], he was from Colossae and was an evangelist in that region, and was probably well known to Philemon [Lt, NIC, WBC], whereas the others named were probably not personally known to Philemon [NIC].

QUESTION—What is meant by the phrase ὁ συναιχμάλωτός μου 'my fellow prisoner'?
1. It means that Epaphras was also a prisoner along with Paul [Bg, Brt, CBC, Lg, NCBC, WBC]: Epaphras, who is in prison along with me.
2. It probably means that Epaphras is with Paul as a companion [Herm, MNTC]: Epaphras, who is staying with me here in prison as a companion. Paul's friends may have taken turns in voluntarily sharing his imprisonment; Aristarchus is called his fellow prisoner in Colossians [MNTC].

QUESTION—What relationship is indicated by ἐν 'in'?
1. It relates to the verb ἀσπάζεταί 'greets' and means that the greetings are being sent to a fellow Christian [NIC]: they greet you as a fellow Christian.
2. It relates to ὁ συναιχμάλωτός μου 'my fellow prisoner' [El, Lg, My] and means that Epaphras is a prisoner because of his Christian ministry [TH]: Epaphras, who is a prisoner with me because of his Christian ministry, greets you.
3. A conjectural emendation is that only the words 'in Christ' relate to 'my fellow prisoner', and that Ἰησοῦ 'Jesus' (dative case) was originally written Ἰησοῦς 'Jesus' (nominative case) but lost the final ς. According to this interpretation, Jesus is parallel to the other names and refers to Jesus who is called Justus in Col. 4:11 [Herm]: Epaphras, my fellow prisoner in Christ, (and) Jesus. There is no manuscript evidence whatever to support this conjecture (of all the commentaries only WBC points out this fact). Other commentators specifically state that Jesus Justus is not included in this list [Alf, El, ICC, Lg, Lns, Lt, MNTC, My, NIC, TH, WBC].

**24** **Mark, Aristarchus, Demas, Luke, the co-workers[a] of-me.**
LEXICON—a. συνεργός (LN 42.44): 'co-workers' [WBC], 'fellow workers' [Hn, LN, Lns, NIC; NAB, NASB, NEB, NIV, NJB, RSV, TEV, TNT], 'fellow laborers' [Lt; KJV]. See this word at verse 1.

QUESTION—What relationship is indicated by the phrase οἱ συνεργοί μου 'co-workers of me'?
These men are working with Paul [Herm, TH, WBC]: they are working with me. They are not imprisoned with Paul [Lns], but are at liberty for more active service [MNTC].

**DISCOURSE UNIT: 25** [NIC]. The topic is the final benediction.

**25** **The grace[a] of-the Lord Jesus Christ (be) with[b] the spirit[c] of-you.**
TEXT—Some manuscripts add ἡμῶν 'of us' after κυρίου 'Lord'. GNT omits this word with a C rating, indicating a considerable degree of doubt. ἡμῶν 'of us' is read by Lns, Lt, Lg, KJV, NAB, NJB, and TNT.

## PHILEMON 1:25

TEXT—Some manuscripts add ἀμήν 'amen' at the end of this verse. GNT omits this word with a B rating, indicating some degree of doubt. Only Lns and KJV include 'Amen'.

LEXICON—a. χάρις 'grace' [BAGD, Herm, Hn, ICC, LN, Lns, WBC; all versions]. See this word at verse 3.

    b. μετά (LN 89.108) with genitive object: 'with' [Hn, Lns, Lt, NIC, WBC; all versions].

    c. πνεῦμα (LN 26.9): 'spirit' [Hn, LN, Lns, Lt, NIC, WBC; all versions except TEV, TNT]. The phrase τοῦ πνεύματος ὑμῶν 'your spirit' is translated 'you all' [TEV, TNT].

QUESTION—How are the event word 'grace' and 'the Lord Jesus Christ' related in the genitive construction ἡ χάρις τοῦ κυρίου Ἰησοῦ Χριστοῦ 'the grace of the Lord Jesus Christ'?

Paul prays that the Lord Jesus Christ will extend his grace to the recipients of the letter [MNTC, TH, TNTC]. Other commentators take it to mean that God will extend his grace to them through the Lord Jesus Christ [CBC, Lns]. Of the various meanings of 'grace', central here is that of God's free unmerited gift of forgiveness and renewal [IB].

QUESTION—What is meant by μετὰ τοῦ πνεύματος ὑμῶν 'with your spirit'?

1. 'Spirit' refers to the whole person [CBC, Herm, NCBC, NIC, TH, WBC]: may God's grace be with you.
2. 'Spirit' refers to the highest of the three parts of a man's being [El, Hn]: may God's grace be with your inner spirit. The spirit is the inner point of contact with God [Hn]. It is through the spirit that we perceive and receive God's grace [IB].
3. Since 'spirit' is in the singular, it refers to the spiritual unity of those to whom Paul refers [MNTC]: may Christ bestow God's grace on you in your spiritual unity.

QUESTION—What relationship is indicated by ὑμῶν 'you (plural)'?

'You' refers to all those mentioned in verses 1–2 [EGT, EPC, Herm, Lg, Lns, Lt, NCBC, NIC, TNTC, WBC]: with you all. It includes the entire Christian community to whom the letter will be read [Herm, Hn, NCBC].

www.ingramcontent.com/pod-product-compliance
Lightning Source LLC
Chambersburg PA
CBHW070302230426
**43664CB00014B/2611**